Prelude to Literacy

A Preschool Child's Encounter with Picture and Story

Maureen and Hugh Crago

Southern Illinois University Press
Carbondale and Edwardsville

Copyright © 1983 by the Board of Trustees,
Southern Illinois University
Printed in the United States of America
Designed by Kathleen Giencke
Production supervised by John DeBacher

Library of Congress Cataloging in Publication Data

Crago, Maureen, 1939–
   Prelude to literacy.

   Bibliography: p.
   1. Children—Books and reading. 2. Picture books for
children. 3. Storytelling. 4. Language arts (Preschool)
I. Crago, Hugh, 1946–. II. Title.
Z1037.C918 1982 [PN1009.A1] 155.4′13   82-19235
ISBN 0-8093-1077-5

For Anna

Contents

Illustrations

Preface

This book is an account of the ways in which one child experienced and responded to the picture books and stories she met between the ages of twelve months and five years. It is a tale that has, in fact, been heard before—but rarely, and never in the breadth and depth of detail which we have been able to accord it. Nor have the one or two earlier published records of preschool children's interactions with books offered much in the way of analysis of the material they presented. This, too, we have supplied, in a manner which is both sensitive to the idiosyncrasies of our data (one child in one particular environment) and suggestive of more general patterns and hypotheses.

From the inception of the research to the final revision, the manuscript has taken ten years of our working lives; it is with both pride and humility that we see it published now, a record not only of our daughter's learning the world of fiction but of our own learning to become precise observers, our own gradually growing ability to see order and pattern in the mass of data we had collected. The road that we undertook, in 1972, was not an easy one, and we encountered reactions ranging from polite skepticism about the point of such an exercise to bitter allegations that we had wronged our own child by "experimenting on her." It is with especial gratitude, then, that we recall here the people who in the early stages of our work encouraged us by their faith in its validity: Val Watson, Mary Spickernell, Sheila Apted, and Wayne Hooper.

As we began to write up our findings, we faced problems of a different kind. Our chosen subject did not readily fit into any of the established categories: it was not "children's literature" (though it was obviously relevant to those concerned with fiction for children); it was not exactly "developmental psychology"; it was not "education" or one of its subspecies, like "language arts"; it was not "psycholinguistics" or "folklore"--to those editors, then, who were sympathetic to an unconventional area and an interdisciplinary approach, we also owe a debt.

Southern Illinois University Press's readers offered some useful suggestions, and for reading parts of the manuscript and commenting at the draft stage we thank Ann McMillan, Nancy Chambers, Rosemary Milne, Peter Lucich, Nicholas Tucker, Celia Berridge, Doug Hill, Virginia Lowe, Jill Le Messurier, Hugh Craig, Barbara Kamler, and Kay Johns. Don Boadle was a meticulous and inventive proofreader.

Portions of the manuscript drafts were typed by Nerina Hirst, Pauline McGilvray, Wendy Bellany, and Bernadette Post, and we acknowledge their efficiency with gratitude. Riverina College subsidized part of the cost of typing for one draft with a grant from its Regional Research Fund. M. F. C. typed the final revised draft herself.

As explained in the Prologue, M. F. C. was responsible for undertaking and maintaining the records on which this study has been based. In the completed manuscript, she is primarily responsible for chapters 8, 10, 11, and 14, and for the Selected Bibliography. H. C. is primarily responsible for the introductory and concluding chapters and for chapters 7, 9, 12, 13, and 15. Chapters 1 to 6 were expanded by H. C. from diary material originally written by M. F. C.

Acknowledgments

Grateful acknowledgment is made for permission to reproduce the following text excerpts and illustrations:

Text excerpt from Trude Alberti, The Animals' Lullaby. Bodley Head, 1967. By permission of Atlantis Verlag.

Text excerpts and two illustrations from Tove Jansson, Finn Family Moomintroll. Ernest Benn, 1950. By permission of Ernest Benn.

Text excerpt from Michael Dugan, Stuff and Nonsense. Collins, 1974. By permission of Michael Dugan.

Text excerpts and illustration from A Lion in the Meadow by Margaret Mahy, illustration by Jenny Williams. Copyright © 1969 text and illustrations by Franklin Watts, Inc. Used by permission of Franklin Watts, Inc.

Illustration from King Midas and the Golden Touch by Carol Barker. Copyright © 1972 by Franklin Watts, Ltd. Used by permission of Franklin Watts, Ltd.

Text excerpts and illustrations from The Little Red Lighthouse and the Great Gray Bridge by Hildegarde H. Swift and Lynd Ward. Copyright 1942 by Harcourt Brace Jovanovich, Inc.; copyright 1970 by Hildegarde Hoyt Swift and Lynd Ward. Reproduced by permission of the publisher.

Text excerpt from Bread and Jam for Frances by Russell Hoban.
Courtesy of Harper & Row, Publishers, Inc.

Illustration from Zeralda's Ogre, written and illustrated by
Tomi Ungerer. Copyright © 1967 by Tomi Ungerer. By permission
of Harper & Row, Publishers, Inc.

Text excerpt from pages 14-15 of Johnny Lion's Rubber Boots by
Edith Thacher Hurd. An I CAN READ Book. Text copyright © 1972
by Edith Thacher Hurd. By permission of Harper & Row, Publishers, Inc.

Text excerpts from An Anteater Named Arthur by Bernard Waber.
Copyright © 1967 by Bernard Waber. Reprinted by permission of
Houghton Mifflin Company.

Text excerpts and illustration from Rapunzel by Felix Hoffmann. English translation copyright 1960 by Oxford University
Press. Reproduced by permission of Oxford University Press.

Illustration from King Tree by Fiona French. Copyright 1973
by Oxford University Press. Reproduced by permission of Oxford
University Press.

Text excerpt from The Bears' Picnic by Stan and Jan Berenstain.
Copyright © 1966 by Collins & Harvill. Reprinted by permission
of Random House, Inc.

Text excerpt from The Story of Doctor Dolittle by Hugh Lofting.
Blassinghame, McCauley & Wood.

We would also like to thank the following journals, in which
versions of material contained in this volume originally
appeared, for their permission to reproduce it or revise it
here.

Agathon Press, Inc., publishers of Children's Literature in
Education, where portions of chapter 4 appeared as "The
Untrained Eye?" in no. 22 and portions of chapter 10 appeared
as "Incompletely Shown Objects in Picture Books" in no. 34,
both copyright Agathon Press, 1976 and 1979, respectively.

The Thimble Press, Lockwood, Station Road, South Woodchester,
Stroud Glos. GL5 5EQ, England, publishers of Signal: Approaches
to Children's Books, where extracts from chapters 8 and 14
appeared as "Snow White: One Child's Response in a Natural
Setting" in no. 31, © Signal 1980.

The World Education Fellowship, publishers of the New Era, where part of chapter 11 was printed as "The Genesis of Taste" in vol. 68, no. 3, © 1982.

Orana, where an extract from the Epilogue appeared in "Missing Home, Missing Mother" in vol. 14, no. 3, © 1978.

Prologue

When our daughter Anna was born on 7 July 1972, she entered an
environment where books were important, and children's books
especially so; it was an entirely natural and predictable part
of her growing up that we should introduce her to books early
and read to her frequently: after she was six months old we
began showing her through picture books at irregular intervals, and shared them with her daily from eleven months. It
was at this time, too, that we began keeping a diary of her
responses to these books. The project had been in our minds
for some time, and we had something of a model in a New
Zealand librarian, Dorothy White, whose <u>Books before Five</u>
(1954) preserves a record of her daughter Carol's reactions to
the books she encountered in her preschool years. From the
beginning, we had determined that our diary would be as comprehensive as possible but at that early stage our aims in
keeping it were not clearly defined. By the time Anna turned
three, we had realized that it could be useful to have a verbatim record of everything she said in every reading session,
as well as to set down as much as possible of what she said
and did outside reading sessions, whenever her behavior could
clearly be seen to be inspired by book experiences. The volume
of data we were collecting was growing vastly; originally we
had envisaged a cutoff point at Anna's fifth birthday; now it
seemed that the interest of the material we had gathered was
such that we should continue, if only selectively, beyond that
date. We have kept to our initial intention as far as publication is concerned however, and this book is based largely on
records from 1973-76, thus dealing entirely with the period
before Anna learned to read.

In preparing this study we were able to draw on some 1000 manuscript pages of notes, covering four years of Anna's life and over 400 individual book titles. We have detailed accounts of her observed reactions--verbal, nonverbal, direct, oblique-- to the pictures and texts of the great majority of these titles.

In the remainder of this chapter, we will describe the questions we sought to explore and the relationship between our own work and other studies of young children. Before we can look at any of these things, however, we will need to give a more detailed account of the principles that governed our collection of data and of the way our methods changed over time, as this influenced both the quality and the quantity of the information available to us.

SELECTION AND RECORDING OF DATA

The keeping of the record was undertaken by Anna's mother, Maureen, and she continued to be primarily responsible for what later became a daily task throughout the years of our inquiry. As the parent constantly at home, Maureen was the principal reader and had the readiest access to Anna's speech and actions during the day. Though Hugh frequently read to Anna, the total number of diary entries written by him is small in proportion to the whole.

As we mentioned earlier, our regular recording of Anna's responses to picture books began about the end of her first year, and coverage of the period between eleven and eighteen months was sketchy (about six manuscript pages of the exercise book in which the diary was kept then). Anna's first consistently used words did not emerge until around fifteen months, so that the amount of verbal response to be observed was not great; but we now regret our ignorance of the potential significance of nonverbal behavior--smiles, gestures, evidence of attention or inattention--much of which must have been apparent and of which our diary makes no mention at this time.

During this period, our "reading" sessions (we use the term for convenience even when, as here, it is not strictly accurate) consisted largely of our identifying objects in pictures, and Anna's gradual mastering of some of these verbal labels. We then regarded this activity as routine, repetitious, and necessarily uninteresting to any future reader of our data. Accordingly we have no record of exactly which objects

or features in an illustration we consistently identified, or
what additional commentary we provided, or whether this input
altered from week to week (we may presume that it did), or of
how Anna's response to it changed. [1]

There are, of course, entries that describe what we considered
to be highlights, thus:

> October 1973 (1.3) She was also given at the end of Septem-
> ber, a Little Golden Book, My Teddy Bear which she adored,
> apparently because of the little girl who owned the bear.
> From it she learnt the word "bear", which I did not know she
> had acquired until we visited the doctor at 15½ months for
> her booster injection. She emerged from the surgery, and
> rushed up to a boy who had on his T-shirt a brown bear deal-
> ing with a honey-pot. "Bear, bear," she announced. Anna's
> own Ursula (a toy bear) is a blue and white check, and
> rather remote in appearance from the bear family, but the
> teddy of the book is brown and more bear-like.

The focus of this entry is on the acquisition of a new word
and on Anna's ability to perceive the similarity between two
different pictorial representations of a bear. We also noted
what seemed to be Anna's preference for My Teddy Bear over
other books. We were beginning to realize that we could gain
insights into how Anna built up mental images of what individual creatures or objects ought to look like; in the period
between eighteen months and two years, the diary became increasingly full of detail of this kind, and Maureen redrew
portions of book illustrations to exemplify Anna's perceptual
skills and difficulties.

Entries as a whole grew in length and specificity during the
period 29-35 months, in which the record occupied a second
exercise book of 187 manuscript pages (compare the 150 pages
of the first exercise book, which covered the much longer
period 11-29 months). In one respect, however, entries retained the selective quality of those in the earlier volume:
they regularly omitted Anna's countless "what is that?" and
"what is he doing?" questions, which would be asked time after
time about the same detail at each successive reading. At this
stage we still did not realize the value in a quantitatively
exact report of all responses to a picture over time. Apart
from this, however, the accuracy of entries in this period
was good. Though the diary was normally written up some
hours after an actual reading session had occurred, Maureen
trained herself to rehearse in her mind the form of words Anna

employed so that there was little danger of subtly altering
Anna's meaning by recasting her syntax in a form more acceptable to the adult ear. Whenever our memory seemed to have
weakened, our rule was "when in doubt, leave out." Though most
of the entries of this period do not permit statistical analysis, they do faithfully preserve Anna's content preoccupations
and the shifts of focus that accompanied increasing acquaintance with a book. We quote as an example an entry dated 24
April 1975 (Anna 2.9 [i.e., 2 years 9 months; Anna's age will
be thus abbreviated throughout]):

> I borrowed The Flying Shoes by Cynthia Jameson, pictures
> by Lawrence Di Fiori . . . a week ago today, partly for
> Anna. She has been asking for it each day, and so I didn't
> return it [i.e., to the library] today. She is entirely con-
> fused about whether the boy hero owns the flying shoes or
> not and expressed it as "he doesn't wear those shoes" (which
> are on him), and we've been repeating "they don't belong to
> him." Now she has taken to fussing about the trousers above
> the shoes. For a child engrossed already by questions like
> "Is it mine?" and "Is it yours?" it is hard to see beyond
> the complexities of ownership in this story.
>
> The last three nights she has repeated a protest "I don't
> want shouting in this book"--it is full of loud voices
> (which I read dramatically)--and I've had to read it more
> evenly. There is a little girl who waves a soup ladle, and
> Anna and I argued about which was her mother--Anna has
> awarded her a mother and a grandmother. It is a little
> "girl" (as far as I can see, it could be a boy) who attracts
> Anna in a busy page where the tax-collector's gold rains
> down upon poor people. "Why is that little girl holding her
> mother?" (Behaving like Anna, in fact!) Before that, the key
> figure for her was a boy climbing a tree (Anna is venturing
> on the rudiments of treeclimbing since she has seen her
> idols from the playground, Phillip and Michelle, climbing
> an ash-tree).
>
> In the last two scenes that concern the tax-collector, Anna
> is very interested in why he can't go into his house, and in
> the last scene of all, Anna is of course fussing again about
> whether this is the old man who owns the shoes. For rather
> a difficult book, this is having a lot of impact.

This entry is essentially a summary of readings over a week,
and its contents suggest that the amount of comment by Anna in
any single reading was quite manageable. Not long after that

entry, however, Anna's input in each session began placing a
considerable strain on the parent writing up the diary. We had
already used a portable cassette tape recorder on several
occasions since Anna's second birthday. At 3.1 we determined
to tape every reading session, thus eliminating for good the
chance of misremembering or slightly editing Anna's utterances,
and in addition making it possible to note exactly when Anna
broke into the reading to contribute her remark.

While there were a few occasions when taping was omitted and
some holiday weeks when no record of book responses was kept
at all, we can say that for the years between Anna's third and
fifth birthdays, the record (now arranged in loose-leaf folders
by book title, indexed chronologically) was substantially a
complete one--every statement she made about almost every book
she encountered during formal reading sessions. To this we
added all allusions to books outside the reading sessions.
In the same period, we began taping and transcribing her now-
frequent monologues (spontaneous improvised narratives) as
often as we could afford the time to do so. We could not have
hoped to transcribe them all, but we have a substantial sample, spread over several years. Similarly, we expanded our
coverage of portions of Anna's behavior which, while not
directly relevant to books, could supply a context for her
book responses. We began paying greater attention to her play,
to her conversations with us, and to her drawing. Much of this
went into the record, along with transcripts of her attempts
to retell for our benefit stories she had seen on a neighbor's
television, or which had been read to her by her grandmother
during holidays. Increasingly, we were building up a picture
of Anna in her entire cultural context, but we were omitting
its most significant determinants--ourselves.

We had been aware previous to Anna's third year of the potential influence of our input into the reading sessions. An
amusing case in point was recorded when Anna was 2.11: after
hearing Maureen read Charles Keeping's Black Dolly three times,
Anna listened to Hugh read it, asking him the questions that
still puzzled her. She wanted to know what "brass" meant, and
Hugh was bewildered to see her pinch the bridge of her nose
between her fingers as he explained. She repeated this unchar-
acteristic gesture, as if it were meaningful. When Hugh reported this to Maureen, she recognized the gesture as one she
herself used when wrestling with a difficult problem. Clearly
she must have used the gesture when searching for ways in
which to explain "brass" to Anna, and Anna had accepted it as
an integral part of the explanation! However, it was not until

regular taping that we realized the full extent of our power
to determine Anna's response, and we began to add notes if
it was clear that her comments had been provoked purely and
simply by our own reactions to the material we read, reactions
which showed through in our pace, intonation, or volume.
Sharing a book with a young child is a supremely interactive
process in which it is almost impossible to see any of the
child's behavior as "purely" spontaneous; that was brought
home to us again and again as we grew more sensitive to
nonverbal components in both her behavior and ours.

Initially, we had had a vague idea of building up from our
record a picture of those features of Anna's response which
were wholly her own: now we can only say that in the absence
of any adequate record of our own behavior during the whole of
Anna's life, certain statements and types of behavior do appear
to be altogether hers. When we write, as we will very often in
this book, of Anna's picture of the fictional world, of Anna's
patterns of thought and feeling, we want to be understood as
using such phrases in this qualified sense.

Now may be the time to consider in more detail the condition-
ing effect of the environment we provided for Anna and specifically to examine our behavior during shared readings, since
this in itself has affected our methods of data collection and
the type of data we could count on recording.

ANNA'S ENVIRONMENT

We will begin with one of the most obvious of all our influences upon Anna's attitude to stories and pictures. We are by
our own admission and by the consistent labeling of others
preeminently bookish people--our house and our talk are full
of them. Buying or borrowing books, reading them and discussing them are daily activities, and our care for books as
physical objects, in addition to our readiness to converse
about them and quote them, proclaims our sense of their value.
Anna could not help but absorb some of this. As well as
reading, we do a lot of talking--lengthy, wrangling, enthusi-
astic talking. Both of us learned in childhood that words were
comfortable and comforting, that words would assuage hurt
feelings, would bring adult approbation and academic success,
would give delight in and for themselves. That we have consistently valued language over touch, over meditative silence,
and over physical activity is not necessarily a matter for
praise, but it is a fact of our life and a part of the value
system in which Anna has grown up. She is by anyone's standards

a talkative child, fluent when confident of her surroundings, overloquacious when needing to prove herself: her linguistic habits mirror our own, and for the purpose of our study this has been a great asset.

By and large, Anna <u>articulated</u> the contents of her mind, and it is only because of the uncensored flow of questions, comments, and allusions to her fictional experience that we have been able to enter into that experience without having to interrogate her. In fact, in relation to books we asked Anna very few direct questions: her own remarks were almost always unprompted (if they were not, this has been noted). This is in marked contrast to some other children so studied.[2] Whether our policy actually made Anna resistant to questions during reading is impossible to say for sure, but she was normally unwilling to give more than perfunctory responses to direct queries. Even the refined questioning techniques developed by Piaget for his early work[3] did not prove particularly productive with Anna: this is changing as she grows older. Much more productive was our habit of quoting or chanting a line or two from some well-known story or poem in the course of ordinary conversation. While Anna did not necessarily imitate our choice of quotations, our practice seemed to give her license to allude widely and spontaneously to her books outside the context of readings, and her habit of doing so supplied us with more information on what she found memorable in her literary experience.

That Anna's joint engagement with books and with us has been so intense compared with most children's has been partly due to the relative depopulation of her environment. Until the advent of her sister Morwenna, born when Anna was 4.2, Anna was an only child. We have no car by choice, so she has traveled far less than many of her peers and come into contact with fewer people. She had contact with other adults and children in our street but, apart from one weekly play session with a slightly younger neighbor (Anna 2.4-3.10), spent little time in regular interaction with other children her own age.

Anna seemed reasonably content with this situation until about her fourth year, when she began actively searching for company in the neighborhood. From 4.7 she attended a small community school, which partly satisfied her need for contact with other children, though once again most of her schoolmates were older than she was.

That the preceding period did not stultify her social development is clear from the relative maturity of her behavior with other children now and her delight in being with them. Similarly her lack of experience with television viewing does not seem to have generated difficulty in following the visual conventions of moving pictures. On visits to other homes, she is an absorbed viewer of "Sesame Street," but she returns to a world of "stills" without complaint. While her upbringing has undoubtedly made her atypical in some ways, she has retained enthusiasm for many pastimes more generally accepted than listening to stories. She is no stereotyped bookworm.

THE READING SESSIONS

We come now to the reading sessions themselves. We have always enjoyed reading aloud and regularly do so for each other as well as for our children. There have undeniably been times when reading to Anna seemed a chore, a necessary silencer for an overwrought child, or a ritual on which she insisted for reasons unrelated to enjoyment, but most of the time the activity was pleasurable for us as well as for her. Unless the book in question happens to be particularly uninspiring, we normally read expressively, trying to allow the spirit of the text to come to life in our tone. We often use individualized "voices" for characters, and Anna has been accustomed to a reading style in which dialogue is distinguished by pace or intonation, as well as by accents or vocal idiosyncrasies, from the surrounding narrative. When the text cues us to do so, we shout, whisper, cough, hiccup, yawn, and snort.

We read to Anna at the same pace we would employ for an adult audience; the expectation is that Anna will interject if she wishes to ask a question or to comment on text or picture. In the early period (12-24 months) Maureen regularly simplified texts or talked about pictures in language better suited to Anna than the author's; there is no clear cutoff for this practice, since its persistence depended on the degree of difficulty of a given text as perceived by us, but it would be safe to say that by the time Anna was three, she was hearing most texts as they were originally written. We have always glossed an occasional word or phrase which we knew Anna would not be able to understand, but our general practice was to let a book speak for itself and to explain when Anna required it, not when we judged it necessary.

When Anna asked a question, our behavior depended on whether her question seemed genuine or ritual. In the latter case, where Anna seemed to be asking solely in order to display her own knowledge of the "right answer," or to test us, or as a

joke, we would normally answer her questions with "what do
you think?" Sometimes this would result in Anna's rephrasing
the question so that it was more obviously a genuine request
for information; sometimes it was clear that we had been
correct in diagnosing a ritual question. Not every repeated
question was necessarily a ritual one of course; there were
many occasions on which Anna showed by such repetition that
the answers we had originally given, and were continuing to
give, were out of touch with her real concern.

Most of Anna's genuine questions we simply answered directly
and as best we could. The following extract from the record
for Richard Scarry's What Do People Do All Day? is an extreme
case in the sense that the subject matter of the book (consist-
ing largely of simplified pictorial diagrams of various types
of machinery) demanded more frequent parental explanations
than most story books would have done, but the length and complexity of the individual answers given by Maureen are in no
way atypical (21 Sept. '75; Anna 3.2; p. 89):

A: What's that oven for?
M: That one's Able Baker Charlie's oven.
   But oh dear, it's bursting now!
A: Able Baker Charlie will have to use that one (pointing
   to a small oven to the left).
M: Yes, he will. [Reads text:] "The bakers play card
   games while waiting for the bread to bake. Oh my!
   Look at what's happening! Take out the tiny loaves
   of bread! Too late! I think you DID put too much
   yeast in your dough, Able Baker Charlie!
   Mmmmmmm! But it DOES taste good!"
A: Mm--why do you have to take out your bread out of
   ovens? When they burst?
M: Oh look darling, this doesn't happen ordinarily. I think
   it only happens in Richard Scarry books. People just
   wouldn't waste their dough like that. But, er, Able
   Baker Charlie's just put too much yeast in. Have you
   seen Father blow his oven up doing that?

To repeat: explanation normally formed a much smaller proportion of the total parental input than is exemplified in this
selection. The location, subject, and extent of adult explanations were largely controlled by Anna herself, who often
manifested impatience if one of our lectures went on too long.

Similarly, Anna exerted a fair measure of control over what
was read to her. Though her early books were selected by us on
the basis of their suitability, interest and difficulty, Anna

even at that point raided our shelves and came away with
choices of her own. About 1.10 we were sporadically borrowing
library books for her, and she was given her own borrowing card
at 2.0, in response to her eager demand for "more books." From
that time until she commenced school, Anna always had the
chance to select her own books except when ill; the choice had
to be guided by us in the early stages, since Anna would want
to take home piles of attractive-looking volumes and would
regularly exceed the library's borrowing limits if not checked.
On our return from the library newly borrowed books were nearly
always requested for immediate reading; after that, the frequency with which a book was read depended largely on Anna. We
made suggestions as to what might be read (usually with the aim
of calling attention to neglected titles) but these Anna was
free to reject. In the case of her own shelf of books, which
grew steadily over the years, we exercised greater influence;
titles from this source were often read at Maureen's suggestion. Anna's right to refuse was not illusory, but it should
be seen in the light of the fact that she would comply with
our suggestions unless she had a particularly strong objection.
(Her tendency to say "yes" when asked if she agreed was another
factor that prompted us to avoid direct questioning during the
reading sessions.)

How frequently did we read to Anna? There can be no simple
answer, since frequency of reading varied with (among other
things) the fullness of our own schedules, Anna's state of
health and the length of individual books. Bedtime reading was
a daily feature throughout the period covered by the study,
and as the average length of Anna's books increased, the number of picture book titles per bedtime session decreased from
approximately five to two in Anna's fifth year, or the equivalent length in chapters from a novel or story collection.
Similarly, the number of regular times for daytime reading
(dressing, toilet sitting, etc.) decreased as Anna grew older,
and her books less amenable to being fitted into brief reading
spaces. At a guess, Anna would have had at least thirty
minutes' reading time from us each day, and on many occasions
considerably more. Once again, such a background makes Anna
atypical and we might expect certain features of her understanding of artistic and literary experience to be advanced,
simply as a result of a great deal of exposure to books: few
parents expect their children to be ready for books (except as
toys) as early as we did, though it is of course possible to
begin even earlier.[4]

We have often been asked whether Anna knew she was being taped
or (less politely) told that such a practice must be unfair to

the child. In fact, Anna was aware of our use of the tape
recorder from 3.1 (when we began employing it regularly). She
rarely complained of its use during reading sessions, though
she did object (strenuously sometimes) to hearing her own voice
played back while we transcribed, and she objected to her spontaneous monologues being taped, so that we were often compelled
to smuggle the machine into her presence. Later in the period
studied she also objected to our noting fragments of her conversation. In general, then, self-consciousness seemed to grow
as she got older. We persisted in our recording despite her
objections, thinking that no real harm was involved. We also
explained our purpose in so doing. We believe that Anna was
not significantly influenced by her knowledge that we were
recording her: on the occasions when the tape recorder was out
of action, her volume of comment did not differ from the norm.
Only in some of the very latest monologues (4.5, 4.6, 4.7) was
it clear that she was consciously "performing," and in a few
cases she actually asked for the machine to be brought "so
that it can listen to me."

Gathering information under constantly fluctuating conditions,
learning what to look for and how to record it as we went
along, conscious of the atypical environment Anna shared with
us, we have come to realize that for all the messiness of our
procedures and for all the vagueness of our guiding principles,
our material has real strengths: our environment facilitated
the spontaneity of Anna's responses; the sheer volume of our
observations compensates for some of our methodological inconsistencies; despite the record's early selectivity, there is
much of value that can be deduced at each stage. First, we can
present full and accurate samples of what one child said in
response to certain books over a period of time. Published
reports of this kind have to date been few and insubstantial,
and the lengthiest--Dorothy White's diary mentioned earlier--
suffers from its fragmentary and selective nature. Mrs. White
wrote up her diary every few days, or even every few weeks;
she does not consistently cover everything her child said in
any one reading; in fact much of her space is given to personal evaluative comments on the books she read with Carol.
Our record can supply much more detailed evidence of the
child's own responses. Second, we can investigate the extent
to which Anna's response was determined by the intrinsic
qualities of content and style in a given book, or whether her
response embodied previously acquired and unchanging preoccupations which were expressed regardless of the characteristics
of that book.

From this it will be clear that our own interest, as people
originally trained in language and literature, is in what we
call the "experience of fiction" in a very young child. We can
investigate the extent to which fiction (and we use this term
throughout to cover both stories and narrative sequences of
pictures) is perceived by Anna as separate from "life"; we can
trace the processes by which she learned the rules of response
to fiction; we can look at evidence for developing response to
literary and artistic conventions and stereotypes. In this
matter our data is sufficient for us to see most of the links
in the associative chains by which Anna built up mental pictures of a "bad man" or a "princess," for example. Most important of all, we can compare Anna's comments in her role as
listener with her behavior as storyteller, creator of her own
narratives, thus forming a concept of how Anna herself perceived the structure, content, and style not of one particular
story but of story in general.

At this point it might be wise for us to state clearly what we
are not aiming to do in the pages that follow. First and most
obviously, we do not intend a rigorous work by the standards
of quantitative research in the social sciences; neither our
training nor our inclinations would fit us for such a thing.
Within the confines dictated by the nature of our material,
we have attempted to be as precise and objective as we could,
making clear at all times the multiple factors that might
conspire to undermine that objectivity. We have found patterns
that we suspect would be true of other children, given broadly
similar environments, and we have on occasion compared our
findings with the published material available, to test our
guesses. But we would emphasize for the benefit of parents
and children's librarians that our study does not constitute
a sort of annotated book list designed to show what picture
books are "suitable" or "will work" for a two-year old, or a
three-year old, or whatever. Our aim is to describe, not to
prescribe. In any case, Anna's selection of books, and ours,
followed no very clear pattern of age-related criteria. In
gross terms, Anna experienced at every stage books which would
normally be considered "too hard" for her whether textually or
pictorially; as she grew older she also experienced books
which were "too easy." While we do not reject the idea that it
is possible to find the right book for a particular child at
any stage of development, we feel that the criteria concerned
are likely to be so specific as to defy mass application. The
attempts of many books on children's literature to set up
general criteria of suitability for various age groups are for
us weakened by the failure of their authors to observe more

than the surface behavior of individual children in relation
to books. If our own inquiry provides an example of what may
be gained from close observation of individuals over time,
then we shall have achieved something of value.

RELATED STUDIES

A number of case studies of young children's responses to
books have originated from within the children's librarianship
field.[5] Most of these, published in article form in special-
ist but nonacademic journals, present somewhat unsystematic
data within interpretative frameworks that are either nonexistent or heavily value laden: a writer like Margaret Graetz
(1976) is primarily concerned to encourage other parents to
choose "quality" books for their preschoolers so that they
may learn to "work hard at their books" in order to achieve
satisfaction. The one writer who has gathered material
comparable with our own in quality and quantity is Virginia
Lowe, much of whose diary is as yet unpublished, and she has
generously given us access to it for our footnotes.

Most of these studies share with published criticism of
children's books in general an assumption that it is
appropriate to consider both purely aesthetic and educational
criteria in evaluating adult writing intended for children,
and their authors tend to examine children's reactions to
books primarily to see whether or not they support such
adult-formulated criteria.

Psychoanalytic students of early childhood offer us some
material of direct relevance to our concern with the interaction of child and book. In their focus on emotions and their
willingness to read behavior in terms of underlying affective
dynamics, the Freudians have given us valuable insights which,
as our conclusions will indicate, we have come to accept with
less skepticism than we originally brought to their work. However, we remain dubious about studies like Bruno Bettelheim's
(1976) The Uses of Enchantment, a recent example of the
astonishing willingness of some analytic scholars to generalize about the functions served by fiction on the basis of
slender or even nonexistent evidence of actual reader responses. In its respect for such evidence Norman Holland's
5 Readers Reading (1975), though devoted wholly to adult
readers, is a much more solid contribution. In the final
analysis, we have found it more profitable to apply the
hypotheses of psychoanalytic developmental psychologists like

Margaret Mahler (1976) directly to our material than to use
the work of psychoanalytic students of literature and literary
response.

If we turn to academic behavioral psychology, we find a very
different situation. Here, students have been only too willing
to gather evidence and to avoid anything that looks like a
generalization until a process of rigorous testing under controlled conditions has been accomplished. Unfortunately, a
picture book is a stimulus far too complex to be investigated
under such conditions. Behavioral psychology traditionally
studies one or two variables in relation to a group of subjects: a picture book contains multiple variables. Moreover,
the method normally used tests subjects at a single point in
time or at several points over a longer period; to such a
procedure the environmentally determined experiential background of each individual subject becomes irrelevant. Thus,
though there are many studies of individual variables which
would form part of the book response of a child[6]--studies of
form and color preferences, for example--the mold in which
they are cast has made it very difficult for us to use their
evidence. This is true even of the one major attempt to synthesize the findings of individual developmental studies,
Vurpillot's The Visual World of the Child (1976). Moreover,
the period of a child's life before school years has been
relatively neglected in many of these investigations--perhaps
because of the difficulty in obtaining from a child so young
cooperation and uninhibited verbal response in a test situation. Most studies of the aesthetic development of children,
for example, use six- or seven-year olds as their youngest
group of subjects.[7]

Arthur Applebee's 1978 study, The Child's Concept of Story,
is in the same tradition in many respects. Though he draws on
existing case studies of preschool children (White, 1954;
Weir, 1962) his major focus is on school-age respondents, and
his own research is survey/questionnaire based to a large extent. As Vurpillot does for the visual data, Applebee attempts
a synthesis of existing evidence and theoretical models, and
he thus provides a useful correlative to work like ours, which
documents the minutiae of a single child's changing pattern of
response over time.

Since the original draft of our book was completed, the
scholarly study of children's responses to literature and
art has suddenly gathered momentum. Though some of the recent

papers have a strong pedagogical focus, seeking, for example, "better ways of teaching literature" in a classroom, naturalistic observation is increasingly being employed to supplement adult-devised questionnaires, and contextual evidence is being taken into account, so that the methodology of, for example, Janet Hickman (1980) converges with our own. Concurrently, the first attempts are being made to synthesize already published diary material (Whalen-Levett, 1980); and Brian Sutton-Smith has published (1980) a monograph on preschool children's spontaneous narratives--a subject covered in our chapter 9-- on which nothing had previously appeared since Weir's psycholinguistic study Language in the Crib (1962).

THE ORGANIZATION AND SELECTION OF MATERIAL IN THIS VOLUME

We have planned this book so as to combine some of the advantages of diary-style presentation with the very different viewpoint provided by analysis of individual topics, for example, humor and emotional impact. Instead of trying to cover in summary, with appropriate illustration, all the major developments in Anna's response over the four years, we have decided simply to select and print in full, with interpretative notes, the diary record for approximately one book every six-month period. This constitutes the bulk of part 1.

While Anna's reading covered big books, little books, old books, new books, "quality" books and "pulp" books, it seemed expedient to restrict our selection for this portion of the study to titles that have some claim to classic status, not only because they are more likely to be familiar to our readers, but also because they stand a reasonable chance of continuing to be reprinted. We felt that the more widely-ranging references in the later chapters would balance this somewhat conservative selection as well as giving a truer indication of her acquaintance with mass audience books like those by Scarry and Seuss. Part 1, then, contains a series of case studies of Anna's response to particular books either in a short time span such as typified most library borrowings, or over longer periods (the record for Where the Wild Things Are, for example, covers six months).

This is the kind of data that has been virtually unobtainable up to now. In setting it out, we will also be providing concrete examples of how Anna's pattern of comment and question, her content preoccupations, and her emotional concerns changed through the years of our inquiry. Such issues are taken up in chapter 7, "The Shape of Anna's Response," and returned to in the Epilogue.

Part 2 supplements part 1 by providing detailed evidence of Anna's processing and use of literary input outside the context of adult-mediated reading sessions. We examine her games, dramas, and spontaneous monologues not simply for the light they shed on their fictional sources but as creations in their own right with distinctive structures and motifs.

Readers whose initial interest is not so much in the specifics of reaction to picture books over time as in a more general overview of Anna's response in relation to the traditional aesthetic categories—"picture preferences," "plot," "humor"—will find this in part 3. It begins with two chapters devoted to the purely visual aspects of Anna's picture book experience. With Anna, as with most children similarly educated, words were learned in relation to pictures, and illustrations continued to be of primary importance through the first half of the period we studied, only gradually yielding place to a response that was cued mainly to the text. Anna's aesthetic preferences thus evolved in relation to art rather than to literature, which is why this book includes a chapter on her pictorial preferences but no corresponding treatment of her evaluations of actual stories, which tended to be expressed in the form of statements of like or dislike for characters or situations rather than entire narratives. Needless to say, there have been many occasions on which it has been impossible to make a neat separation between textual and pictorial cues to response, and much of the material in the later chapters, which in title at least appear purely literary, is in fact related to pictorial as well as verbal narrative.

Chapter 12 covers Anna's evolving response to fictional humor; chapter 13 explores the extent to which she was aware of fantastic conventions, her understanding of animism, anthropomorphism and magic. Data on identification, gender-role stereotyping, and response to threatening characters are to be found in chapter 14. Chapter 15 covers her notions of plot and incident and her grasp of conventions of beginning, ending, and narrative voice. Our conclusions are set out in the Epilogue where we have utilized the data of part 3 to produce a tentative map of the ways Anna's overall pattern of response to picture and story can be seen to reflect the themes of her growth toward selfhood. Insofar as a case study can offer a model of developmental aesthetics, this chapter contains it in the form of findings that can be tested against evidence of future studies. We consider the "conservatism" of Anna's encounters with fiction, the difficulty of separating cognitive from affective concerns, and the degree to which her response differed from that of an adult reader. We consider that in essentials it did not: for us, one of the greatest rewards of our work has been the increased respect it has given us for the intellect and the sensitivity of a young child. The child in question happens to be our own, but it is unlikely either of us will ever underestimate any preschool child in future. We hope that our readers will be able to share some of this respect and wonder through the pages that follow.

Part 1
The Listener

Introduction

The chapters in part 1 are the core of this study. Here, in detail as complete as our records can muster, is evidence of what one child said and did in response to six books. That sounds little enough to represent reactions to hundreds of books spread over almost four years of mental and physical maturation. Yet in terms of sheer volume, it is a great deal. The briefest chapters are so by virtue of the summary nature of the diary at that point (A Lion in the Meadow) or the shortness of Anna's acquaintance with the book in question (The Little Red Lighthouse, borrowed from the library for a month only). The longer chapters cover periods of up to six months of readings, rereadings, and later memories.

Because of these factors, we have had to edit the diary records differentially. For A Lion in the Meadow we were able simply to reproduce our original manuscript entries, with minor changes of wording here and there in the interests of greater lucidity or precision. For A Lion in the Meadow and for The Little Red Lighthouse we could refer to Anna's later experiences of the books, where they shed light on the earlier entries chosen for reproduction here. Though we continued to read several of the books to Anna for years, we do not reproduce the later evidence in full, to avoid overlap.

In the case of Where the Wild Things Are, many of the original entries needed to be supplemented by a good deal of explanation, and this we have included without its later date of origin; in cases where an earlier interpretation of ours can plainly be seen to be wrong in the light of what we now know, we have deleted it silently unless it has provided an object lesson in adult obtuseness.

When Anna, from about 3.6, shifts her allegiance from picture books to "chapter books," a different set of problems is posed. Now the record, though full and accurate, may contain only one comment from Anna per several pages of text; reproduced as they stand, the entries for Finn Family Moomintroll and The Story of Doctor Dolittle would be nearly meaningless to a reader who was not prepared to read the book continuously with the diary. Accordingly we have "built up" these entries so that the narrative context of Anna's remarks is clear. The skeletal plot summaries that preface the record for each separate book are not intended to take the place of detailed acquaintance with the books, but we would be unrealistic if we expected all of our readers to remember everything. We were strongly tempted to recast the diary entries completely, so that they would read more coherently and compellingly, highlighting what we considered important developments and omitting or compressing what seemed trivial. But we decided that it was vital to give our readers access to a full picture of the sort of data we gathered, even if it meant a less smooth result in journalistic terms. Our own considered views have been largely confined, then, to the analysis sections.

And so to the choice itself. Two of the criteria we have already stated in our introduction: that the books should where possible be of established reputation, and that their primary impact should have come in the six-month period they were selected to represent. We did seek titles that evoked an interesting, rich response; in this sense the chosen six, though accurately representative of the type of response in their chronological period, could be claimed to be somewhat atypical in the amount of comment they generated, or its range of reference. We did not select the books for consistent content preoccupations or similarities of theme, though as we worked on them it became obvious that some strong thematic continuities are present. It is questions like this to which we address ourselves in the concluding chapter of this part, where we look at the developing pattern of Anna's responses in relation to the full range of experience offered by the individual books.

In reproducing and editing our diary record, we have followed these conventions:

1. In the original record "I" refers to whichever parent wrote the entry. This has been allowed to stand unless clarification was needed.

2. Entries have normally been reproduced in full. Occasionally here, and more frequently in part 2, entries have been edited of irrelevant material and cleaned up grammatically and syntactically. Details have been added to the entries where necessary for fuller comprehension.

3. Our original record often attempted to indicate some of Anna's characteristic pronunciations ("Thriday" for "Friday"), but we did not consistently use phonetic script; for this book we have regularized pronunciation for the sake of easier comprehension; Anna's characteristic grammatical forms (e.g., "goed" for "went") and word order have always been retained. "?" has been used whenever a transcribed word or phrase is unclear and hence doubtful.

4. Anna's speech has been punctuated by us in accordance with what seemed her own intent: where her pauses correspond with normal commas or periods, these have been used; but where she paused between words without a clear idea of where she was going next, or where she revised as she was going along, dashes have been employed. Some readers may feel surprised at times that Anna produced such smooth examples of relatively complex syntax--the volume of her literary experience may partly account for this.

5. Few picture books are paginated. Accordingly, we have referred wherever appropriate to "openings," numbering these ourselves (usually from the first page that contains actual text), e.g., "Op. 1."

6. Editions cited are those which Anna actually encountered, often a small format paperback reprint rather than the original hardcover edition. The list of books cited gives full details where U.K. and U.S. editions vary (e.g., in title).

7. Anna's age, in years and months, has been abbreviated thus: "2.1" (= 2 years 1 month).

1

A Lion in the Meadow

The text of A Lion in the Meadow, by Margaret Mahy and Jenny
Williams (1969), is in Mahy's consciously zany style. The
unnamed small-boy hero tells his mother about the lion in
their meadow. She gives him a matchbox which she says contains
a tiny dragon; she promises him that the dragon will grow and
chase away the lion. The dragon duly frightens both lion and
boy, who become playmates. "The dragon stayed where he was,
and nobody minded. The mother never made up a story again."

Jenny Williams has painted expansive, glowing scenes against a
white background. The illustrations combine the static effect
of clearly outlined trees, grasses, figures, and interiors
with dramatic confrontations and speedy movement on the part
of the characters themselves. The copy Anna possessed was a
paperback (U.K., Picture Puffin), much reduced version of the
hardback original, and measures 19.5 by 15 cm.

THE RECORD (ANNA 1.8-1.11)

Entry 1 (29 March '74) Anna 1.8
Anna was given A Lion in the Meadow in early February (1.6),
but it has not made a great hit with her. She turns fairly
quickly through it, stops at p. [13] where the lion is racing
into the house, and announces "broom" because of the shape of
his tail! When told it is a tail, she insists on her own identification. She is puzzled about the lion eating apples on p.
[19], but I can't say why. By the end of March, she is still

6

insisting the tail is a broom, but has forgotten her earlier puzzlement over apples.

Entry 2 (8 May '74) Anna 1.10

Yesterday I read Anna A Lion in the Meadow twice, finding that mostly Anna allows me time to read the text in this book now. Today she picked it unbidden from the shelf, saying "lion, boy!" Hugh says she has chosen this book on her own initiative before while he has been around, but I think I've not seen her do it. She flipped through the book, starting with p. [24] which she brought to me, then pp. [22-23] with its "baby rabbits." We had once more our argument about the lion's tail, in the scene where the lion is racing into the house: "broom" she announced, and when I said it was a tail she pointed to the corner where our brooms are kept. She subsided at last, but I think she is still sure that the lion has a broom affixed. Anna also turned to pp. [8]-9 where the mother is leading the unwilling boy into the meadow and said "naughty boy." I have explained that the boy can see the lion, but the lion is hiding so the boy's mother can't see it, so the boy's mother thinks the boy is being naughty. After a few minutes we left the room and the book had been put aside. Anna said spontaneously "naughty boy," and I wonder if Anna's sudden interest in the book was due to her understanding of the boy's naughtiness. Like the child in The Magic Circle who is in fact being good although her father (who is not in possession of the facts) scolds her for naughtiness, the boy in A Lion in the Meadow is shown to be telling the truth and has been unfairly accused.

Entry 3 (21 May '74) Anna 1.10

Yesterday evening we were at the table and Anna was sitting on the floor with her books. I looked around after a while, wondering why she was staying so quiet, and saw her looking intently at pp. 18-[19] of A Lion in the Meadow. I don't know exactly how long she gazed at the pictures, but it seemed a surprisingly long time--maybe a minute. Her eyes were moving round the page, but she said nothing. This is the first time I can remember for ages that she has not chattered about and "named" aspects of a picture, but just looked intently. The p. 18 illustration is the one showing lion and boy in the broom cupboard; p. [19] shows the lion eating apples thrown to him by the boy, and it was this side of the opening that claimed Anna's attention.

Entry 4 (27 May '74) Anna 1.10

Today Anna sat three of her dolls on her seat (a hassock) and announced "read book." Accordingly I placed in front of them A Lion in the Meadow open at pp. 2-3. Anna squatted down, adjusted the book so that she could more easily see it (although it was still right in front of the dolls) and said "where lion?" thus reproducing the question I ask her. The lion is screened by grass and flowers and is not seen by the boy's mother until late in the story, and this makes the question of looking for the lion much more important than a simple case of recognition. This is the first time she has asked the dolls a question about the book they were "reading," and the first time we have heard her say "where," although later in the day when hiding she called out "where Anna?"

Entry 5 (9 June '74) Anna 1.11

When I was away over last weekend (1-2 June) Anna asked Hugh to read A Lion in the Meadow, which she has lately been calling "lion meadow." But she asked for it as "nonsense boy." And this she has kept up. Why should Anna memorize this exclamation rather than, e.g., "I eat only apples" or "hide me! a dragon is after me!"? Probably because it is the only such statement to be repeated (on successive openings) and on both openings has the prominence that comes from being the final phrase in the passage of text. On 6 June, Anna was looking at the book and stopped at the lion eating apples. "Anna eat apple?" I gave her one.

ANALYSIS

The record for A Lion in the Meadow covers a period when Anna's verbal responses to books were largely confined to one- or two-word utterances. Inevitably, we had to interpret these cryptic reactions in the light of Anna's speech and her previous patterns of behavior while looking at books; inevitably much of this interpretation must be speculative. But despite the small amount of hard information available to us, some things are immediately clear. First, that Anna has already built up a range of types of response to the pictorial and verbal stimulus offered by a book: she identifies a pictured object or creature; she asks for clarification of what she fails to understand (the "puzzlement" referred to in the record is unspecific but almost certainly means a questioning look, or grunt, or both); she memorizes and quotes text phrases; she states her own interpretation of a character

or incident ("naughty boy"); she indicates intense interest
in a particular picture, by silent concentration; she reen-
acts in play part of an adult's behavior when reading to her;
she requests real food after seeing it referred to in the book
and thus evinces a concept of the book as a stimulus to
real action performed by herself. Questioning is as yet
rudimentary, and there is no clear verbal indication of a
purely affective or evaluative response, but with these
exceptions, Anna displays, in embryo, most of the types of
reaction that she will use consistently over the next three
years.

Second, some pictures in A Lion in the Meadow engaged Anna's
attention more than others: if we count the final page and
omit the title page the book contains twelve openings, but
Anna is recorded as having commented verbally or nonverbally
on only five. Her response is neither comprehensive nor
random, but selective. Apart from the question "where lion?"
which is a straight reproduction of Maureen's question, none
of her comments is a simple imitation of adult input, whether
textual or explanatory. Instead, she indicates by her focus
what features of the book are important to her. Her identification of "baby rabbits" (pp. 22-23) and her statement "naughty
boy" seem best described as brief flashes of articulated
contact between her own stock of concepts and those of the
book; neither is recorded as being repeated. In strong
contrast, two openings provoked recurrent response over a
period. In the case of pp. [12-13] what she saw (a broom) was
contradicted by Maureen's statement that it was the lion's
tail; this set up a powerful conflict between two different
sources of information, and Anna clung to her own identification for some time. Close examination of the "broom" tail
reveals some similarity to the real mop which the lion wields
in the cupboard illustration on p. 18. The mop also projects
to the left of the picture as the tail does on p. [13]. In the
light of our evidence it seems possible that Anna's "misidenti-
fication" was an early example of a visual gestalt (see chap.
10) and less illogical than it initially appears. Exactly what
was involved in the response to pp. 18-[19] cannot be settled.
So far as we know, Anna had no previous knowledge of a lion's
diet such as would enable her to see an apple-eating lion as
incongruous; perhaps, rather, Anna was puzzled that a fictional character should share our food preference? More
likely, Anna's bewilderment has its root in the fact that the
picture on p. [19] represents an event which not only fails to
follow that depicted on p. 18 in chronological order, but

which is outside the strict chronological sequence of the narrative altogether, since it shows a timeless state referred to in the lion's declaration "I eat only apples."

Now look again at pp. [12-13] and 18-[19], the two high points of Anna's response to A Lion in the Meadow. Both feature lion and boy (no wonder her private name for the book was "lion, boy"); the mother seems to be peripheral as far as Anna is concerned. Both embody color combinations for which she was later to exhibit a marked preference: pp. [12-13] contain an evening scene, with pink-purple trees, grass and flowers ranging from luminous blue-green to mauve, and a bright pink dragon. Page [19] is in much warmer colors against a white ground, but the lion and boy embattled in the broom cupboard stand out in light blue, gold and orange against luminous purple-black darkness. Could it be that Anna's interest in these pages is as much aesthetic as problem solving? There is, naturally, no way of establishing whether one or the other came first; but it is surely significant that later records show that these two openings went on drawing comment from Anna long after her original problems with them had dissipated.

2

Where the Wild Things Are

Where the Wild Things Are, by Maurice Sendak (1963), perhaps
the most celebrated picture book of the postwar period, needs
little introduction here. Less multidimensional than some of
Sendak's later books, Wild Things nevertheless possesses a
controlled lyricism of language and near-perfect integration
of text and picture that the artist has never surpassed. Max
is confined to his room for mischief committed while wearing
his wolf suit, but the bedroom transforms itself, page by
page, into a forest and Max steps into a convenient boat and
sails to where the Wild Things are. The fierce creatures,
ambiguously half-beast, half-human, are tamed by Max and they
make him their king. After three textless pages of Wild
Rumpus, the Wild Things sleep and Max, lonely, wishes to be
back home. The Wild Things are annoyed at his departure, but
he sails back across the sea and time and into his own room,
where his supper awaits him.

From the muted colors of the sparsely furnished, restrictive
domestic interiors with which it begins to the widening vistas
of romantic exotica that fill its central pages with pastel
palms and great textured monsters, there is a consistent economy of both color and form, with no wasted detail, so that the
entire design carries the viewer's eye (as it carried Anna's)
in the direction Sendak intends. Again, this book was owned by
Anna rather than borrowed from the library; her Puffin reprint
was equal in size to the hardcover version.

THE RECORD (ANNA 2.1-2.6)

The record for Wild Things differs considerably from that
for A Lion in the Meadow. It is much longer, for though many
of the entries are brief, it covers nearly six months; the
first entry, where Anna responded to the pictures alone before
hearing the text, bulks large here mainly because we have
added to the original diary a considerable amount of speculation and interpretation of Anna's somewhat cryptic responses.

Entry 1 (11 August '74) Anna 2.1

Puffin Wild Things on table along with other picture books
normally not seen by Anna, which I had been working with last
night. I "told" her Sir Orfeo and In the Night Kitchen (rapt
attention, but no obvious signs of excitement), then we
started on Wild Things. We had been going to keep this until
she was older, but thought it could do no harm. I opened the
title page and she was visibly excited. We decided to let her
make her own comments without prompting. This is what she said
(I told her the title):

Title opening: Frightened--been naughty--(looking at Max).
To the adult eye, Max certainly looks anything but frightened!
Is Anna simply insufficiently sure in her grasp of conventionalized facial expressions? We cannot be certain.[1] What we
can say with confidence is that Anna's comments do not identify the characters, as we might have expected at a first
viewing, but interpret their behavior and feelings (cf.
"naughty boy" in A Lion in the Meadow). Maybe the fact that
the figures stand alone against a plain white background is an
influence on this, since there is no pictorial context from
which the trio need to be differentiated?

Op. 1: Hurt book--hurt book soon. This comment is easily
explained by our knowledge of Anna's own experience. She is
not permitted to walk on her books (or ours) and "you'll hurt
the book" has been our consistent warning if she does step on
one. Hence Anna applies our stricture to Max (she has never
nailed "ropes" to walls, so this part of his mischief is alien
to her).

Op. 2: Oooh! The only purely exclamatory response in this
session, and by its very nature impossible to interpret mean-
ingfully. We have no dog, so it seems unlikely that jumping at
one would ring any bell for Anna. Max's dramatic leap is what
strikes us in the picture--but that's no guarantee of its
interest for her.

Op. 3: Then he gets in bed. This picture does not, of course, show Max getting into bed. That she casts her comment in this form is an indication that the first two frames have established for her a pattern of "actions by Max." In many picture books, movement happens between one frame and the next. Anna here embarks on a narrative syntax ("then he . . .") and will continue to be governed by it for two more frames.

Op. 4: Then he gets in bed. We notice first that Anna repeats her comment for Op. 3; next, that she says nothing about the growth of the trees. (In fact, Anna is not recorded as having made any comment on the transformation of the bedroom for the next four months.) "Then he gets in bed" is perhaps more fitting for this picture than the preceding, since Max has his eyelids lowered and is stepping toward the side of the room where the bed is.

Op. 5: Then he goes outside. The transformation has now proceeded far enough for "outside" to be a valid description. While we might conclude that Anna has interpreted Max's raised foot as implying motion ("he goes outside") it seems much more likely in view of Op. 3, where Max is absolutely stationary, that Anna is simply being governed by a syntactic pattern she has set up, and does not modify the pattern in order to incorporate new visual data of a minor kind.

Op. 6: Football. Anna herself plays football; one of Max's feet is raised as if to kick. Is she seeing the moon as a football? She is normally adept at spotting "moons," this being one of her earliest vocabulary acquisitions. But Anna's comments have focused up to this point solely on the protagonist: background features are seen only in relation to his actions. It would be entirely consistent with this pattern for a moon to be pressed into service as a football kicked by Max.

Op. 7: Gets in boat. Again, the syntax does not match the image precisely: Max is not shown entering the boat. The syntactic pattern continues to dictate rather than the subject matter.

Op. 8: Clothes off (pointing to sea monster). The monster, a new and exotic animal on the scene, has here supplanted Max as the focus of Anna's attention though the context of her remark is homely enough, seeing the horned and bearded beast in terms of her own experience of being dressed and undressed (very important to her at this period of her life, and frequently commented on in her responses to fictional characters). It seems possible that the creature's wing has been interpreted by her as an item of clothing shrugged from its shoulders and now lying in heavily wrinkled folds. It may also be that this is an injunction, which we could expand thus: "He's in the water. He should take his clothes off or he'll get them wet."

Op. 9 (no verbal comment, stares intently). This is the only time Anna made no comment on turning a page. Her silence seems to us to correspond neatly with what is after all the climax of the first half of the book--the first opening on which the picture stretches across the whole, the first to show the Wild Things en masse.

Op. 10: More clothes on--sharp teeth--sharp hands--two sharp hands--two old hands--two hands--. "More clothes on," by which Anna referred to the Wild Thing third from the right, shows the continuation of the preoccupation noted in Op. 9. The remaining statements, gratifyingly close to Sendak's own text of the preceding pages, are best interpreted not as separate comments on individual sets of claws but as Anna's attempts to find a satisfactory descriptive label for them all. We speculate that "old" (most often in Anna's early experience applied to dilapidated objects or people clearly different from her physically) is for her synonymous with "unlike me"--and clawed hands are certainly unlike hers.

Op. 11: Go sleep--oh dear! At this point I told Anna what Max's name was. The comment "go sleep" refers not to Max but to the foremost Wild Thing, who is bowing. At this stage, shut eyes are automatically interpreted by Anna as indicating sleep. It is impossible to tell what tone "oh dear" was uttered in, or what it represented.

Op. 12: Max crying--Max crying--but pirates not crying. Here Anna reads Max's open, blacked-in mouth and shut eyes as indicating crying. Shouting or singing are not yet in her repertoire of possible meanings for this conventionalized facial expression.

The "pirates" are of course the Wild Things, and fortunately we know exactly which pirates are the source of this identification: those Jill MacDonald drew for The Pirates' Tale (owned by Anna since 11 months). Though these violently hued buccaneers seem at first glance quite different from Sendak's pastel monsters, both have oval-shaped heads, goggle-eyes, frizzy hair, and "sweaters" in stripes--quite sufficient grist for Anna's gestalt-forming mill (see chap. 10, "Order from Chaos").

Op. 13: <u>Mak</u> [sic] <u>doing</u> <u>swinging--climbing</u> <u>tree</u>. Openings
13 and 14 embody a new development, in that Anna is now
commenting on two separate focal points. Max has returned to
prominence (maybe because he now occupies the center of these
openings rather than the extreme left, as in 10 and 11), but
Anna also continues to notice one or more of his huge companions. In "climbing tree" she was pointing to the bull-like
Wild Thing second from the right, whose right claw is round
the tree <u>trunk</u>--the rest are simply hanging from branches.
Probably Anna needs openings 9, 10, 11, to sort out the monsters, who are several, and larger than Max; once she has
assimilated them individually, she can push them into the
subsidiary role appropriate to them and reinstate Max as the
focus of her attention.

Op. 14: <u>Mak</u> <u>not</u> <u>here</u>--<u>there's</u> <u>Max</u>--<u>oh</u> <u>football</u>--<u>walking</u>
<u>stick</u>--<u>broom</u>. Here we are privileged to have access to the
way Anna processes her incoming sense impressions. In other
circumstances, she might well have said triumphantly "there's
Max" but suppressed any acknowledgment of her previous failure
to find him. (Did she search for him first at ground level in
this picture?) Similarly, in the course of a normal adult-
mediated reading, she would have asked us to identify Max's
scepter rather than supplying three guesses of her own. Now
look closely at these guesses: the first, "football," indicates that Anna has regarded as significant only the circular
head of the scepter (remember that she has already used the
word "football" to refer to a circular object associated with
Max in Op. 6). "Walking stick" and "broom" both take into
account the handle of the scepter. It seems almost as if Anna
is running through her stock of words for "long sticks with
blobs on the end," rather as she experimented with "two sharp
hands--two old hands" in Op. 11.

Op. 15: <u>Max</u> <u>sitting</u> <u>chair</u>--<u>wearing</u> <u>hat</u>. Max is once again
the sole focus of attention. Anna has seen crowns but never
one of this shape (hence "hat"); but why has she not commented
on its presence before? After all, Max has been wearing one
for several pages. Can we see a glimpse of a visual precedence
rule of Anna's here? Do objects held in the hand (e.g., the
scepter) rate interest before those attached to the head? Or
is it that there is a visual tension set up between the tent
and the crown, which is a sort of inverted tent? The tent's
downward diagonally-flowing yellow stripes echo palely the
peaks on the crown, and the tent is topped with an inverse
crown, to boot. The tent thus gives Max's crown greater prominence than it has had before.

Op. 16: <u>There</u> <u>Max</u>--<u>that</u> <u>one</u> <u>soon</u>--<u>that</u> <u>one</u> <u>soon</u>.

Op. 17: <u>Reading</u> <u>Max</u>. Anna's attention is beginning to flag,
and having identified Max, she puts in a request ahead of time
for another book from the pile she can see on the table, "that
one soon." Is it coincidental that her mind begins to wander
from the immediate stimulus on an opening which so closely
resembles a previous one (Op. 10)? Anna has now moved out of
the fictional frame; her self-conscious description of her own
behavior ("reading Max") seems to excuse the abrupt dropping
of the illusion, mediating between a state of totally absorbed
story making and a state of normal conversational interaction.
(See chap. 9, "Fiction Re-created," for examples of similar
behavior.)

Op. 18: <u>Max</u> <u>clothes</u> <u>off</u>--<u>clothes</u>--<u>jumper</u> <u>on</u> <u>now</u>. <u>Max</u> <u>go</u> <u>bed</u>--
<u>milk</u>--<u>cereal</u>. The "clothes" to which Anna refers are actually
the headpiece of Max's wolf suit; as we have already seen, the
putting on and taking off of clothing is consistently important to Anna, and it is significant that "jumper [i.e.,
sweater] on now"--the sole utterance in the entire monologue
which really elaborates well beyond the evidence of the pictures themselves--is also concerned with clothes. She means
"he will put his jumper on now"; similarly "Max go bed" is
most likely to mean "he will go to bed now" or "he should go
to bed" rather than "he is going to bed" (the use of the form
with "go" suggests that this is intended, not a description of
present action).

With these final remarks, Anna registers the presence of food
on the table, assuming that it would be food of the kind she
herself is familiar with (a nice parallel to Sendak's own
words "he found his supper waiting for him. And it was still
hot").

COMMENTARY ON ENTRY 1
Anna's responses give clear evidence of her ability to interpret successive frames of a pictorial narrative sequence in a
way which is not substantially at variance with an adult interpretation of the same frames. Only in her interest in clothes,
and arguably then, do Anna's choices of details on which to
comment reflect her own preoccupations more than those of the
book. Her focus shifts from Max to the Wild Things and back
again in a manner supported by the content and composition of
the pictures themselves. In no sense could it be said that
Anna is imposing a content grid derived from her own concerns
upon the book. We shall see these concerns begin to emerge in

subsequent readings, however, since this first response to
Where the Wild Things Are is atypical in a number of ways;
it seems that the freshness of the experience of the book, in
combination with the absence of adult comment or text reading,
enabled her to verbalize much of her primary reaction to the
book. Her secondary reaction, or processing, is what we must
now examine.

Entry 2 (11 August '74)

Yesterday when reading Where the Wild Things Are she identified the sea monster as "giraffe" and one of the Wild Things
(far right of Op. 12) as a "dinosaur." (See discussion of her
early preoccupation with Dinosaurs and All That Rubbish,
chap. 12, "Funny Ha-Ha and Funny Peculiar.")

Entry 3 (14 August '74)

Anna opened Please and Thank You Book and stood on it. I
said "Oh Anna, that's bad." She said "No, not bad," as she
got off the book. I wonder if she was being Max? (q.v. Op. 1).

Entry 4 (21 August '74)

After its early impact, Max seems to have fallen away. I
think that at first it was the large size, novel color scheme,
and huge creatures that struck her--but in spite of her apparent perception of some of what was going on when she first saw
the book, it would seem now that she doesn't get enough from
it without a full explanatory commentary from us to keep her
interest up very long. The text is beyond her, seemingly, and
I for one am loath to paraphrase it because it seems so good
as it is.

Entry 5 (22 August '74)

She worried again about Max's shut door. She is distressed
that he is shut in and so I spent some time explaining that we
do not close her door because she is naughty, but to keep our
noise from her ears. She seemed happier after that, but she is
still concerned . . . when we came to the final picture, she
tried to find evidence that the door was really open. [This
concern about whether a character is shut in, and whether he
can get out, occupied her, with decreasing emotional involvement, until its final recorded instance at 3.10.]

When she looked at the title opening she dithered about trying
to see if Max was happy or unhappy. Max's complex expression
on this page consists of two contradictory elements--smiling
mouth and frowning eyes. No wonder Anna dithered! She said he
was not wearing his hat (the head of his wolf suit); it is

covered by his crown. In Op. 10 she said of the Wild Thing to the extreme right . . . that he is eating grass. He is in grass up to his chin. She said of the beaked Wild Thing (Op. 11) "marvelous nose!"

Entry 6 (c. 24 August '74)

When I read "roared their terrible roars" in my fiercest manner, she cuddles close to me. [Note in later hand: "This passed soon."]

Entry 7 (25 August '74)

Yesterday she came to me in the garden and said "Wild Thing. Wild Thing. Mother Wild Thing." I don't know if this was an accusation or a partial quoting of "His mother called him Wild Thing."

Today she said of the beaked Wild Thing "like hen." She looks at these creatures and tries to sort them out--"feet," "ears," "red nose," etc.

Entry 8 (27 August '74)

Anna was being exceedingly bouncy about teatime (i.e., about 6.00 p.m.) and I called her a Wild Thing. She was jigging about and I said "Dance! Like the Wild Things!" So she did, doing a stamp, bounce routine which involved lifting her arms straight up, as the Wild Things do. This seems a new behavior pattern, but Anna may simply have been imitating Hugh, who had done such dances at appropriate points previously.

Entry 9 (30 August '74)

This morning Anna was looking at Tenniel's bespectacled lion, seen in profile on a catalogue. "Wild Thing" she said . . . I think the predominating feature responsible for this association is the size of the lion's head in proportion to its body. Another Wild Things influence came through later in the same catalogue, which is illustrated with pictures from Tenniel's Alice. Anna said "girl," so I explained that she was called Alice, and after a couple more examples she began referring to Alice by name as we went through. But she was foxed by a picture of Alice with crown and scepter and eventually produced "like Mickey" (i.e., Max). [Anna frequently confused the names of the two Sendak heroes at this time.] The two crowns are almost identical.

Entry 10 (12 October '74) Anna 2.3

Today Anna set off with her doll's stroller and on being asked where she was going replied "Going where Aunt Helen are," which must be formed on the pattern of "Where the Wild Things Are."

Entry 11 (21 November '74) Anna 2.4

Anna said of Op. 2 "he happy" and of Op. 3, where Max has been shut in his room, "he mother in kitchen washing up." At Op. 4 "Where he mother?" Of Op. 6 she said "he should go bed" and this she repeated at Op. 16. This last is a simple case of seeing Max as a child like herself with regular routines; Anna now is capable of predicting that she should have a bath, be read to, and go to bed.

Entry 12 (31 December '74) Anna 2.5

She now says carefully every word in the title Where the Wild Things Are.

Entry 13 (Undated)

Anna said of her teddy with a bracelet atop its head "Poor Winnie Bear's lonely" (cf. Sendak text, Op. 15). Again, the image of Max crowned seems crucial.

Entry 14 (22 January '75) Anna 2.6

Tonight she asked me "Where that night?" on each of the first two occasions where the word "night" was used [Ops. 1 and 4]. I seem to remember that she has asked this one before. . . . As Max arrived at the Wild Things' country, Anna asked tonight "Where his people?" which I found curious, and weakly asked if she meant his mother and father. She said yes, but one can't be certain if she was satisfied.

[We now feel pretty sure that Anna was asking after Max's toys (the toy dog strung up in Op. 1, with other hypothetical toys), the like of which we called Anna's "people" when in need of a plural. Whichever she meant, it is significant that Anna thought of them just at the point where Max is confronted by the large and menacing Wild Things.]

ANALYSIS

Because of the nature of the recorded data, there can be only a rough-and-ready indication of Anna's focus within the book. Nevertheless it is possible to see two clusters of reactions. One covers Ops. 1-4, with Op. 3 scoring four separate mentions; the other covers Ops. 10-12, with Op. 11 also scoring four times, which thus indicates an unusual degree of interest. These clusters could perhaps be designated "Max at home"

and "Wild Things." Max's journeys to and from the Wild Things'
land (Ops. 7-9 and 17) seem to engage her much less; nor do
the actual interactions between Max and the Wild Things or the
Wild Rumpus (13-14) provoke much verbal reaction.

It would be fair to describe Anna's concern in the "Wild
Things" cluster as being the identification of the creatures
and their absorption into her existing schemes of classifica-
tion. After some ten days of preoccupation with their appearance, Anna seems to have been content; the initial term
"pirates" had long since been dropped, and by 30 August '74,
Anna had sufficiently framed the "Wild Thing gestalt" (over-
sized head, shaggy mane, upright posture, large clawed paws)
to apply it to a novel creature, Tenniel's lion. We notice
that Anna's early labeling of the Wild Things as "dinosaurs"
or "hens" in no way means that she has disposed of their
individuality as "Wild Things."

Whereas the bulk of Anna's comments in the "Wild Things" cluster come in the first half of the record, those comprising the
"Max at home" cluster are distributed more widely. Anna's
concern about Max's door being shut surfaced in Entry 4; the
search for Max's mother began in Entry 11. In all of these
comments, as in the statements that Max "should go bed," we
can see a measuring of the fictional experience against Anna's
own and a wish to add to the book those details which Anna has
established as being part of a child's life.

While the Wild Things record exemplifies almost all the
forms of response we noted in A Lion in the Meadow, it also
contains significant new developments. Now Anna explicitly
questions, and most of her questions reflect an awareness of
the text, with an assumption that what it mentions should also
be illustrated ("where that 'night'?"). It will be another six
months before Anna's focus will shift decisively in the direction of the text. "Where he mother?" and "Where his people?"
also instance her apparent assumption that the book should in
some key respects mirror her own life, though there are times
(e.g., Entry 11) where a strong demand for consistency with
her own reality seems linked with a denial of potential
threat ("he happy"; "he mother in kitchen washing up") or an
injunction to the hero to behave otherwise ("he should go
bed") to avoid danger. Anna leaves us in no doubt of the
emotional impact of the story.

3

The Little Red Lighthouse

The Little Red Lighthouse, by Hildegarde H. Swift and Lynd Ward (1942), is a vintage example of that peculiarly North American genre, the picture-story book whose protagonist is a personified machine of some type. In this case, it is a lighthouse drawn with eyes and mouth. The pictures, in grays, blues, and red are representative of the style of their time; the text, despite a tendency to mawkishness, still reads strongly. The lighthouse believes itself outmoded by the great new bridge that has been built nearby across the Hudson River; on the night of a storm, its keeper is delayed and a "fat black tug" coming downriver from Albany is wrecked because the lighthouse, to its shame, cannot turn on its own light. It is only after the keeper arrives belatedly that the lighthouse realizes that it still performs a valuable function, for the light on the Great Gray Bridge is intended for aircraft rather than to warn ships on the river.

THE RECORD (ANNA 2.6-2.7)

Entry 1 (29 January '75)
Yesterday we borrowed . . . The Little Red Lighthouse and the Great Gray Bridge . . . which she demanded several times. She referred to it first as "that little red--er--," later as "flashing lights." (The phrase as such isn't used in the text but I used it to explain the idea of a lighthouse to her. She knows flashing lights on street-repair signs.) It kept her attention throughout. In spite of the numerous dramatic exclamations in the text the first phrase she quoted spontaneously

21

was "I thought you were never coming," which the lighthouse
uses to its keeper after he has been delayed and the lighthouse has thought itself abandoned. This is an _emotional_
peak rather than the temporary excitement of an ordinary
exclamation such as Anna tends to memorize readily in a new
book. She was puzzled by the many pictures showing partial
views of the Great Gray Bridge, wanted to know what was inside
the steel pylons (e.g., Ops. 16, 17)--in other words, what was
behind the steel latticework. I feebly said "Nothing." She
wanted to match the picture of the keeper on Op. 23 with the
earlier picture of him, Op. 7: "Where that other man?" That
is, she did not initially recognize the two pictures as being
of the same person. The keeper's appearance is similar on both
occasions, though his posture is fairly different, since he
walks in Op. 7 but runs, bent forward and striding, in Op. 23.
She puzzled mightily over the picture showing a barge with
four cable reels aboard, unreeling cable across the river (Op.
13). She also wanted to know several times where the _door_ of
the lighthouse was. The door is referred to only once in the
text (Op. 23). However, it seems fairly likely that she was
confused by Lynd Ward's decision to heighten the animism of
the lighthouse by drawing its door as a recognizable "mouth."
That "door" was already established as an emotionally significant concept for Anna is demonstrated by _Wild_ _Things_, Entry 5.

Entry 2 (30 January '75)

In later readings she more predictably picked up and repeated
"CRASH" (Op. 20) and "Warn-ing" (e.g., Op. 10), which I had
chanted in a bell-like tone.

Entry 3 (1 February '75)

Little _Red_ _Lighthouse_ continues to engage her attention. She
has spontaneously leafed through, stopped at the page showing
the black tugboat crashing onto the rocks, Op. 20, and told me
"I don't like this picture." Why? "I don't like this black
tugboat" (and later) "I don't like you say 'CRASH.'" The text
at this point reads: "CRASH! CRASH! CRASH! The fat black tug
ran upon the rocks and lay wrecked and broken." I have explained to her (on the first or second reading of the book)
that the tug had been very badly hurt. Tonight as I came to
the passage describing the storm that precedes the shipwreck
(Op. 18), she looked worried and began to cling. She put her
hands up near her ears in a curious stylized gesture as if to
indicate that she didn't want to hear what was coming next,
though she did not actually cover them. I decided to go ahead
anyway, but read with less drama than usual and cuddles for

reassurance. It is now clear to me that some of the impact
this episode has had on Anna has been due to my emotive
reading of it. But it interests me greatly that the way she
chooses to express the impact is oblique. If it is the fate
of the tug she's worried about, why does she say "I not like
that tug" or (today) "I don't like the tug coming from Albany"
. . . is it just inadequate vocabulary? I don't think so. I
think I can dimly remember reacting similarly to fearful or
emotion-laden pictures in my own childhood, somehow transferring the emotion generated by an action to the object or
person to whom the action happens. N.B. that Anna is quite
capable of saying, in other contexts, "I frightened by that--"

In the same reading tonight she reacted, for the first time,
with marked emotion to the later picture of the lighthouse
with its beam of light restored, Op. 24. The beam is drawn
more prominently than before, and she exclaimed with an expression of intense joy "Oh look at that!" A balance to the
earlier tragedy? Certainly the text asks to be experienced
this way: I find it hard to get through it without my own
voice shaking in one or two places.

Entry 4 (9 February '75) Anna 2.7
My parents have been here all week and reading has been down
to a minimum. . . . In The Little Red Lighthouse she has
commented several times on the "fat black tug" which is illustrated as being largely red. She points out that it isn't
black at all. . . .

Anna has memorized a surprising amount of the text of The
Little Red Lighthouse. Her dislike of the section of the
story which deals with the tug's wreck remains strong, so that
she will cross the room and cuddle up for just that page. Once
we reach the page where the lighthouse is operating once more
(Op. 24), Anna insists "Now the lighthouse can turn itself
on." No amount of explanation from us will convince her that
the lighthouse is incapable of action but depends entirely on
the keeper. Anna is in fact consciously reversing the earlier
statement made by the lighthouse on Op. 22: "My man will not
come. I cannot turn myself on. Very likely I shall never shine
again." Since both of the other two conditions have been
changed (the man has returned; the lighthouse is shining
again) Anna naturally expects the third will be reversed also.
When she talks of the lighthouse she puts her hands on her
head and says "This is where the lighthouse has its light. Up
here."

Entry 5 (10 February '75)

Yesterday . . . she remarked "That lighthouse toy lighthouse isn't it" (on Op. 22). . . . It may be the scale of the representation which is responsible here. Is it on the other hand a way of denying her sadness that the lighthouse is abandoned? If the lighthouse is only a toy, then why worry?

ANALYSIS

It is clear from the record that Anna's response to The Little Red Lighthouse in February 1975 was closely aligned with what we would judge to be the emotional "curve" of the book. Less richly ambiguous than Where the Wild Things Are, The Little Red Lighthouse is tightly and one-dimensionally cued to a preset pattern of reader response, a pattern which Anna could not wholly escape. Though the early entries contain evidence of visual problem solving unrelated to the plot, there can be no doubt that right from the beginning, and consistently throughout, her peak of involvement came at Op. 20, the wreck of the black tugboat. "Hurt" had been one of Anna's earliest fictional triggers of emotional response (The Pirates' Tale at 1.9), but even without this fact, the words of the text pull crudely but effectively at the heartstrings:

It was caught and blinded by the fog. It looked for the little red lighthouse but it could not find it. It listened for the bell, but it could not hear it. . . .
CRASH! CRASH! CRASH!
The fat black tug ran upon the rocks and lay wrecked and broken.

It is not till the third and fourth entries that Anna's explicit concern at this passage is balanced by clear signs of joy at the restoration scene (Op. 24), though perhaps we would be entitled to regard her early repeating of "I thought you were never coming" (Op. 23) as evidence for her comprehension that all has ended happily. It is worth noting (and odd, in view of the symmetrical structure of the text) that the "fat black tug" never is restored to "health" like the lighthouse.

Anna did not, in this series of readings, give any signs of recognizing the bridge as a character in the same way as the lighthouse is. Hence it seems probable that one of the book's implicit themes--small child overshadowed by adult competence and potency--was not within her grasp at this stage; Anna's conception of the story, so far as we are justified in reconstructing it from verbal comment only, when much may have remained understood but unarticulated, seems then to have been on the level of the lighthouse's abandonment by its keeper, its inability to turn itself on, the crash of the tug, the return of the keeper, and the restoration of the lighthouse's normal functioning.

We are fortunate in possessing a very full record of Anna's responses to The Little Red Lighthouse, dated almost exactly two years after the first, and occasioned by our having borrowed the book while writing this chapter. In the interval, Anna had now and then recognized its cover among books on display in the library but had never requested that it be borrowed. On seeing it this time, at 4.8, she remarked "I like this one--but at the end, I'm afraid." Among much comment that belongs to her four-year old sensibilities (interest in the geographical location of the story, intentions of going to New York, etc.) all her old emotional concerns are still present, with a significant rounding out of comment on Op. 15 which shows her awareness of the lighthouse's shamed feeling of inferiority. This second record shows how much more wide-ranging the pattern of comments is, and her language is now sufficiently confident to enable her to voice her empathic feelings at almost every relevant point.

Reading 2

OP. 15
Text: ". . . made the little red lighthouse feel very, very small." . . . Anna placed her index finger over the tiny lighthouse dwarfed by the bridge, saying "that small." . . . She repeated "that small" then added, in the words of the text, "very very small."

OP. 20
A: I--feel sorry for this tug.
M: Why?
A: Because I don't like boats--I don't like that sort of thing happening to boats.
(Thus neatly confirming our guess on 1 February '75 about the meaning of "I don't like this black tug.")

OP. 22
Text: "This is the end of me, it thought."
A: Poor lighthouse. (Heavy emphasis on "poor").
There is even a confirmation of our suspicion that the tug's nonrestoration may have set up problems for Anna. Whether it

did so earlier is impossible to say, but it certainly does so now.

Reading 4

OP. 24

A: <u>Does this book tell</u>--<u>about the tug</u>, <u>any more</u>?

M: No, all we know is that the tug lay wrecked and broken.

A: <u>But that's not real</u>--<u>I hope</u>.

M: Oh, it could have been real--that sort of thing does happen to tugs.

A: <u>But are other</u>--<u>is another tug made now</u>, <u>so I can go to Albany</u>?

Anna's distress for the tug's demise is obviously not wholly altruistic!

4

Rapunzel

Rapunzel, by the Brothers Grimm and Felix Hoffmann (1949),
one of the better known of the tales collected by the Grimms,
seems in fact to be partially literary in origin--something
which would certainly account for its elaborate concluding
section. It draws its power, though, from the age-old folk
motif of a child taken away by a fairy or sorcerer in punishment for its parents' transgressions. A man and his wife long
for a child: after she finally becomes pregnant, she develops
a craving for rapunzels, which her husband is obliged to steal
from the garden of a powerful witch. When he disobeys her
injunction never to come again, the witch takes the newborn
baby and shuts it up in a doorless tower deep in the forest.
Fifteen years pass, and the girl Rapunzel, who is accustomed
to let down her long hair for the witch to climb up to her
tower room, is discovered by a prince who plans to rescue her.
But the witch finds out their intention and cuts Rapunzel's
braid while the prince is climbing it, so that he falls into
thornbushes and is blinded. Rapunzel's tears of pity restore
his sight, and together they leave the forest; the witch is
trapped in her tower until eventually she shrinks and is carried away by a great bird of prey. Felix Hoffmann's litho-
graphs are appropriately somber: brooding faces, looming
walls, dark tones. The pictures illustrate, but they do not
carry, the narrative. In particular, the faces of Hoffmann's
characters are impassive or ambiguous in expression, which as
we shall see causes Anna some problems. Basically naturalistic
in style, Hoffmann's drawing incorporates some stylization,
especially of human figures, and there are frequent shifts of
perspective and focus.

THE RECORD (ANNA 3.0-3.1)

Readings 1 and 2 (16 July '75)

Hugh brought this home yesterday and Anna heard it through, saying only "read it again!" At this stage it is standard for Anna to make no verbal comments on her first hearing of a new book.

Earlier today the book lay open at the scene where the witch is running away with baby Rapunzel (Op. 5) and Anna asked if the witch was going to eat Rapunzel. She is very free with such suggestions, and clearly has no idea what is entailed.

OP. 1

Tonight she suggested that the man and his wife sitting on their balcony "should put on their light so they can see the dark." She then added something that sounded like "they should have rooms"; the text here reads: "They had a house with a small garden and balcony, where they would often sit in the evening and watch the sky grow dark." Anna's phrase "see the dark" was used by us to her from the time when she was much younger, to denote a visit to the garden at nighttime, the aim being to calm Anna before bed and help her to appreciate without anxiety the special features of air, sky, and scenery in the evening. Her seemingly illogical remark probably means "they should turn on their light inside, since it's getting dark, and then go outside to see the dark as we do." "They should have rooms" shows that she has heard "house with a small garden and balcony" as meaning literally, a house containing no rooms but only a garden and balcony.

OP. 2

She asked what the man held in his hand, and finally announced that it could be a knife; she doesn't know that people cut lettuces from their stalks.

We had to do some turning of pages to establish that the small witch in this scene is the huge menacing figure in the next (Op. 3). I showed her that the witch has large hands and feet, and so she must be a large person.

OP. 7

She objected that Rapunzel could not "let down her hair" because "it is hanging (?) up there." Because Hoffmann's picture does not show Rapunzel herself, but only the braid hanging from the window, Anna seemingly assumes the braid to be unconnected with her. Hence she cannot see the sense in the witch's

Rapunzel (Op. 1): "They mustn't sit on the balcony and watch the sky grow dark." Reproduced by permission of Oxford University Press.

cry. Though Anna is trying to connect text and picture, she is still (apparently) unable to use the text's information that Rapunzel is in the tower; the pictorial evidence, interpreted literally, takes primacy.

OP. 8
"Is that Rapunzel?" she asked of her first view of Rapunzel grown up; was she bewildered by the transition from baby to fully grown woman in two pictures? "Is that a door?" she asked, pointing to a dark patch behind Rapunzel, who leans from the tower window: the depth of the embrasure must have foxed her.

OP. 11
Of Rapunzel and the prince embracing, framed by this same window, but seen from directly in front, she said "They look as if they are in their house, but they're not." Anna's comments on both pictures (Ops. 8 and 11) are more explicable once we see that Hoffmann shows us only the topmost portion of the tower, which thus appears to be a circular stone hut with its window at a normal distance from the ground. In this reading, Anna is relying upon visual evidence for her conception of what is going on; only two of her remarks refer to the text.

Reading 3 (17 July '75)
She listened intently to most of the story, but her attention waned considerably where the prince and Rapunzel meet and agree to marry (Op. 10) and I only revived it by turning on a dramatic, malevolent voice for the return of the witch on the following page. It would be reasonable to guess that the drama of the witch and the stolen baby would interest her more than the wholly adult (and, in folktale manner, prosaic) account of the lovers' meeting.

OP. 1
Anna made a perceptual error, when she told me emphatically that "that" (the husband's pipe, shown in brown against the sleeve of his wife's blue dress) "looks a little bit like her skin is coming off." She persisted in this, although she has correctly identified pipes in many previous books. The brown patch could easily be seen as a rent in the dress (her wording wasn't clear, and I'm still not sure whether she meant that the dress or the skin was torn). This error exactly parallels her difficulty in identifying the man's knife in Op. 2 during the last reading. Both are cases where a small object protrudes beyond a human figure against a background whose color

is deeper and more eye-pulling than the object itself. The
latter is then seen as an interruption in the field rather
than as a figure on a ground.

OP. 5
Anna asked "Is there snow on that baby?" I explained that
because the sky was blue, no snow was actually falling, so
there couldn't be any on the child.

OP. 6
I asked her, to test her comprehension, who lived in the
tower. She answered correctly, "Rapunzel," but added "I think
the witch will take her home." I explained that the witch's
intentions were exactly the opposite. Has she completely
failed to follow the story, or is she looking for reassurance?
[Surely the latter--denial again.]

OP. 7
I read "the royal prince . . ." and Anna darted her finger at
his small figure, looking out from behind a tree: "There he
is!" (This identification had originated in Maureen's reading
the previous day, when she had said "Ooh, I can see the
prince, Anna. You look too. Can you find him?")

OP. 9
Anna's problem yesterday with the window ledge in Op. 8 was
paralleled today by a request to know what it was the witch
was standing on (a deep embrasure, its platform a step above
floor-level) as she confronts Rapunzel.

OP. 10
Where the text says "Rapunzel . . . had never seen a man
before" I added an explanation of why she had not.

OP. 15
Here the prince and Rapunzel walk out of the forest onto a
windy hilltop overlooking a seaport town, and Anna was puzzled
as to why Rapunzel had leaves in her hair. I explained that
they were to make her look pretty.

Reading 4 (18 July '75)
OP. 1
Tonight Anna asked about the historiated initial on the text
page of this opening "Is that Rapunzel?" The female figure
(presumably a mother or nurse telling stories to children) is
drawn so as to roughly resemble the wife in the colored illustration opposite, but she looks nothing like Rapunzel. Anna's

search for continuity in the book makes her think that this figure <u>must</u> be one of the characters in the story.

OP. 7
She again pointed to the prince. . . . She was engaged in eating a crumpet tonight, and her flow of questions may have been depressed by this.

OP. 14
"What is that thing?" <u>That</u> <u>thing</u> is in fact Rapunzel's left heel, right foot and lower right leg, its junction with the rest of her body obscured from view by a tree trunk. When asked, Anna could identify the left heel, the dress, and the right leg correctly in that order. This is clearly a similar perceptual difficulty to the two noted in earlier readings; here the tree isolates the legs from the remainder of the figure, so that they appear autonomous. [See chap. 10, "Order from Chaos," for further discussion of "overlapping."]

General Comment: She seems more able to listen to the whole story now, with interest.

Reading 5 (19 July '75)

OP. 1
A: <u>They mustn't sit on the balcony and watch the sky grow dark because they'd better turn the light on and they'd better have a house like this</u> [ours].
I explained that the man and his wife did have rooms and showed her where. I suggested they might have two rooms; Hugh and Anna voted for three. Putting her nose close to the book she decided the man was smoking a pipe. "Does he always have a pipe in his mouth?" This she sorted out by looking at the next two scenes.

OP. 6
Text: "When she was twelve, the witch locked her up in a tower deep in the forest. The old hag took away the staircase and walled up the door."

A: <u>Who is the old hag</u>? (not realizing that this phrase represents an alternative name for the witch.)
A: <u>Who took the staircase away</u>?
M: The old hag.

Maureen must have answered Anna's "Who is the old hag?" (we did not record the answer), but her second question "Who took the staircase away?" seems to indicate that she is still

confused by the (apparent) presence of two characters where
she expects one.

A: <u>Did</u> <u>she</u> <u>wall</u> <u>up</u> <u>the</u> <u>staircase</u> <u>too</u>?

OP. 7
She found the prince again.

OP. 9
"What is she [witch] doing?" The witch is standing confronting
Rapunzel, but without some visible sign of action, Anna needs
explanation. "Isn't Rapunzel big there!" It's the first full-
length picture of her grown up.

OP. 13
"Is that Rapunzel's hair?" The text supplies the answer, but
if Anna is working from the picture alone, the question is
fair enough, since the prince is hanging onto one end of the
braid, and the witch onto the other.

OP. 16
She showed me with her fingers (rather grubby they were) how
small the witch was become: just two of her fingers' breadth.
I asked her to search for the nestlings in this scene, and she
insisted that they looked like crows until Hugh pacified her
by claiming that lots of baby birds resembled each other.

The endpapers exert no pull on Anna at all.

Reading 6 (20 July '75)
She was quiet, concentrating mainly on drinking a whole mug of
milk during <u>Rapunzel</u> tonight. No questions at all, and her
comments were repetitions of previously learned responses.

OP. 5
She whispered "Yes, snow."

OP. 6
"She's the old hag," where the witch is walling up the door.

OP. 7
She pointed silently to the half-hidden prince.

Reading 7 (21 July '75)
OP. 1
Initial lack of involvement in this page turned to insistent

questioning as to what <u>they</u> were (the pinkish-gray blobs in the lower right-hand corner). Are they hydrangea bushes?

Reading 8 (23 July '75)
Anna, who is ill and now weak, was distrait through tonight's reading.

OP. 3
She asked for identification of the witch's walking stick, but could identify it herself when I had got her to tell me what was in the witch's hand in the previous scene.

OP. 10
A: <u>Why</u> <u>is</u> <u>the</u> <u>prince</u> <u>wearing</u> <u>all</u> <u>red</u> <u>things</u>?
M: Well, why do you wear red?

She couldn't answer this coherently; her mumble was not even properly audible, and she contented herself with declaring that she once had red shoes and the prince had red sandals.

OP. 13
"This is a frightening story" she said, as the prince fell "down, far down, and both his eyes were pierced by thorns as he fell." This is Anna's first explicit evaluation of <u>Rapunzel</u> as a whole.

Reading 9 (25 July '75)
OP. 1
"Is that a bird?" It is a mysterious object in the garden, which may be part of a hydrangea bloom, but is roughly bird-shaped and apparently perching.

OP. 3
"What is that brown?" Anna is referring to brown "shadows" cast by the hair of the man onto his forehead. They do not look particularly like shadows, being more the result of Hoffmann's tendency to blur borders between parts of objects, and Anna's problem is an understandable one.

OP. 13
"What is that?" (pointing to Rapunzel's hair; as we noted in recording earlier readings of this opening, Rapunzel herself is nowhere in sight, so that Anna cannot readily see the connection). Again, it would seem that her understanding of the text has not been sufficient to enable her to interpret the picture correctly.

"What is that black?" (a tiny spot near the prince's ear).
Again, this could be a meaningless dot of color or possibly an
impressionistic suggestion that an ear is to be glimpsed here.
See Anna's question for Op. 3 above. My actual answer at the
time was that it was a dirty spot. Notice that all Anna's responses in this reading are focused on visual identification.

Reading 10 (28 July '75)

OP. 1
A: What is that?
M: What could it be?
A: It could be the balcony--

(It is in fact the balcony wall)

OP. 2
A: She [the witch] should be like this! (baring her teeth and
looking fierce, as we have done when pretending to be a witch;
Hoffmann's hag is closemouthed, and Anna obviously expects her
to conform to the stereotype she has formed). Now, however,
she briefly denies the witch's evil nature.
A: She should be nice to them, shouldn't she--but she isn't.

OP. 6
A: Is that her tower?
M: Yes.
A: The witch's tower?
M: Yes.
A: A house is bigger than a tower--is that the doorway there?

I then pointed out the witch lifting up a stone to continue
walling up the door. Perhaps we can see, in Anna's comment
that "a house is bigger than a tower," some of the reasoning
behind her deduction in the second reading that the dwelling
depicted in Op. 11 must be a house.

OP. 7
A: Why did she "unwind her braid"?

The text here reads: "Rapunzel had beautiful long hair, like
finely spun gold. When she heard the witch's voice, she would
unwind her braid and tie it to a hook in her window; it would
tumble down and then the witch would climb up it." It looks as
though Anna simply did not follow the text: but a more likely
explanation is that her question, though couched as if to ask
for an explanation of cause, was in fact a request for the

meaning of "braid," a word that was unfamiliar to her at this time.

OP. 9
A: Is that [distaff] the witch's broom, or mop?
Her association is witch + broom(stick), complicated by the moplike appearance of the distaff.

A: Her hair [Rapunzel's] is like mine, because it is golden. It is like Lisel's too. (Lisel is a neighbor's child.)

A fascinating comment in the light of the fact that Rapunzel's "golden" hair is faintly gray-green in the illustration. Anna may well be relying on the text of Op. 7 ("Rapunzel had beautiful long hair, like finely spun gold"), or she may be demonstrating her ability to read Hoffmann's color scheme, which does not permit a clear yellow, in terms of its symbolic intention rather than its literal practice.

A (commenting on Rapunzel's bare feet): Maybe she doesn't want to wear shoes.

She has referred to Rapunzel's bare feet before, but I think I have forgotten to record it.

OPS. 14, 15, 16
Clear lack of interest in the last three scenes tonight.

Reading 11 (29 July '75)
OP. 1
Anna asked about a strip of greenish yellow--the light of the setting sun falling on top of a garden wall. When I asked her what she thought it was, she replied "Hay. And there is hay, too, in the light in the window." The latter is a lighted window, the same yellowish hue. Why she should see it as hay is hard to fathom, unless she is making an analogy and is unable to express her intention properly.

Text: "I know that I shall die if I cannot have any of the lettuce from the garden next door!" (read mournfully).
A: There is the wife [pointing her out]. Has she a handkerchief, to wipe away the tears from her eyes?

OP. 2
A: Will the witch put the lettuce into that bag?

The text has been presenting a picture of the witch threatening the man for stealing her lettuce. In Anna's terms, it
would now make sense for the witch to take back what is rightfully hers. There is no indication in the text that the bag is
the man's and not the witch's.

OP. 5
Of baby Rapunzel, red-faced and bawling as the witch bears her
off through the snow,
A: She is crying because she wants milk.

Presumably an observation from life!

OP.6
A: There is the old hag (confirming her earlier piece of
   learning).

OP. 9
A (embarrassed): Spinning wheel (trying to remember the
right word for the distaff).

OP. 10
A: That floor looks like--my dominoes. Why does it look
   like my dominoes?
(The paving stones of the tower room are rectangular and
appear to be separate tiles, not unlike dominoes.)
   Why are they stones? I want us to have a floor like that.
M: You'd find a stone floor cold.
A: I would walk on a stone floor in my socks. Why is that
   floor black? (prince's shadow).

I made her say whose shadow it was, and she could tell me
correctly.

OP. 14
This reading followed Farmer Barnes at the County Show, and
twice during that story Anna interrupted to show me "the
pretty pages" which turned out to be all the colored pages and
endpapers. As we opened Rapunzel she said "I shall show you
something--here is the pretty page." I took this announcement
with a grain of salt, suspecting a random choice purely in
order to continue the ritual established in relation to the
earlier book. But she chose this forest scene, which with its
soft oranges and greens, and its all-over color does seem
"prettier" than most illustrations in this stark volume.

Reading 12 (31 July '75)

I expected that we would return <u>Rapunzel</u> to the library today, but Anna said "Oh! not <u>Rapunzel</u>!" and we kept it, though
after we renewed it she seemed displeased. . . . Anna was still
playing with her toy rabbit, Mrs. Sneeze, as we read tonight.

OP. 1
A: <u>There</u> <u>she</u> <u>is</u>! (the wife again).

OP. 2
Text: "Then the witch . . . said to him . . . 'if you come
      again, you must give me the child that your wife is
      going to bring into the world. It will flourish under my
      care; I will look after it like a mother.'"

In some earlier reading Anna has (unnoted) requested to know
the meaning of "flourish," and I have glossed it as "grow
well." Hence Anna now interrupted:
A: <u>I</u> <u>want</u> <u>you</u> <u>to</u> <u>grow</u> <u>too</u>!
Text: "The man hurried away, quite determined never to come
back."
A: <u>Maybe</u> he <u>had</u>, <u>um</u>, <u>a</u> <u>cold</u>--

Having a cold is one reason Anna knows for hurrying away from
people!

The next three remarks were to correct my reading: details
unrecorded; normally such corrections referred to minor slips
of the tongue like "he" for "she"; to omission or alteration
of the special voices the reader had originally allotted a
given character; or to the semantically obvious miscues like
"wonderful witch" for "powerful witch" which Anna corrected in
Maureen's reading of <u>Rapunzel</u> on its reborrowing three
months after the record reproduced here.

OP. 10
Text: "Rapunzel . . . put her hand in his" (the prince's).
A: <u>Like</u> <u>this</u> (putting her hand on mine).

OP. 12
Text: "'Oh, you wicked child,' cried the witch . . .'"
Anna hugged me and according to Hugh, who was observing,
looked happy--a defense against the fear inspired by this
scene? We acted out the cutting of the hair in mime, on my
initiative; Anna then repeated the mime, saying "like this--
and she cut some ears off too!"

(Yesterday, while pruning our peach tree, I yelled at her "Get down off there this minute or I'll saw your ears off!" She was right in the line of the saw's thrust, and it was no idle threat I made.)

Anna's comment about ears provoked:
M: Oh no!
A (recanting): I don't want her to do that!
M: It would be horrid.
A: Horrors! Lowly [Lowly Worm in Richard Scarry's Please and Thank You Book] said "Horrors!"--Isn't she [witch] trying to be nice to her?

Again Anna, after her seemingly frivolous excursus, defends herself by a kind of doublethink against the impact of the witch's cruelty.

OP. 14
A: What is that thing?
To get an answer, I turned back to Op. 10, where the prince is seen full-length, facing the viewer; there it is clear that there is a crown on the front of his tunic, in the same position as the blur Anna is unable to identify here. "Crown," she said.

OP. 15
The seaport in this double-page spread has so far been simply background, unremarked by Anna. But tonight she asked, pointing to a square crenellated tower in the town, "Is that where the wicked old woman lives?" (The text on the following page refers to "the wicked old witch.") Not knowing whether this is a different town or the one in which Rapunzel was born, we couldn't be sure, but, looking back to what we could see of the witch's home in Op. 1, we tried to see where in this town her house could be.
A: Maybe there?
M: Maybe she owns lots of houses?
A: Maybe 1-2-3-4-5 (pointing to various buildings).

OP. 16
A: What is he [the bird] doing that for?
M: Well, why did he take her [witch] away?
A: To feed his birds (i.e., his baby birds).

Entry dated 6 August '75. Anna rejected our offer to read this tonight, because she was "tired of it." We'll return it to the library tomorrow.

Longterm Impact

<u>27</u> <u>August</u> <u>'75</u>. "Look Father, I'm wearing Rapunzel glasses."
She had looped a string of plastic beads over her ears—like
Rapunzel's braids of hair. The act may have set up a double
association—"beads" = "braids", in sound, and at a quick
glance, and against the ears, the beads-braids might recall
the earpieces of glasses.

<u>30</u> <u>August</u> <u>'75</u>. "The cat in <u>Rapunzel</u> wanted to eat Rapunzel's
eyes." She repeated this literal interpretation of the witch's
metaphor with cheerful confidence. The original text (Op. 13)
read: "But when [the prince] had almost reached the top, [the
witch] leaned out and cried in spiteful tones: 'Aha, you want
to fetch your beloved, but the pretty bird has left the nest
and will sing no more. The cat has eaten it, and she will
scratch your eyes out too.'" It is not hard to see how Anna
could have inferred from this syntax that Rapunzel's <u>eyes</u>
would be <u>eaten</u>.

<u>1</u> <u>September</u> <u>'75</u>. Anna asked where the witch was when she
was not with Rapunzel (good question!) and when she came to
Rapunzel. The latter question is best interpreted as an
attempt to rephrase her earlier request, having received a
reply she considered unsatisfactory.

<u>9</u> <u>September</u> <u>'75</u>. Apropos of nothing, "<u>Rapunzel</u> was a nice
book to have."

ANALYSIS

The overall prominence of the first opening, on which at least
one comment was made in nine of the twelve readings, is obvious; so is the much higher frequency of explicit response to
the first half of the book as against the second. Though there
is no clear correlation throughout between the length of the
text on a given opening and the amount of comment it generated, it cannot be fortuitous that Op. 1 has by far the longest single block of text in the book: Anna simply had more
time to gaze on the illustration, and hence to frame questions
and statements about it. Op. 3, with a two-line text, provoked
no comment at all in the entire period; but Ops. 5 and 8 and
11 (wordless) all elicited more than Op. 3.

The nature of the <u>Rapunzel</u> record is such that Anna's exact
words are nearly always quoted; so although there are some
difficulties involved in deciding what constitutes a single

utterance (practically, we have defined this as any clause or
sequence of words which can be taken as a meaningful whole,
and which is separated by a pause from what precedes and follows it), we can make a fairly accurate count of comments and
questions. Of these, 47 refer clearly to the illustrations
alone, 12 to the text alone; 9 referred to both, matching the
words with what was pictured, and 5 were ambiguous, or impossible to classify within this scheme. What can we learn from
this? First, that Anna is still responding to pictures more
than to text and, to a certain extent, still relying on the
pictures to carry a meaning that is independent of the text.
Over the twelve reading sessions, the text seemed to claim an
increasing amount of Anna's attention, and the final session
yields more responses that depend on text alone, or text and
picture in combination, than purely on the pictures.

It is in any case a delicate matter to categorize a particular
utterance as occasioned primarily by picture alone, since the
verbal labels which enable Anna to refer to features of the
illustrations are ultimately derived from the text. A more
profitable mode of approach to the Rapunzel data would be to
look at the various comments and questions in terms of content
preoccupations, and this we now intend to do.

It will already have struck the reader how high a proportion
of Anna's responses seem occasioned by visual problems of a
fairly minor nature. Many of these are really caused by
Hoffmann's mode of drawing, his palette, or both. What is
interesting about Anna's desire to identify these insignificant strips and spots of color is that so many of them are
associated with the human body. With the notable exception of
the balcony wall, "hydrangeas" and "hay" of Op. 1, almost all
of Anna's questions or ventured identifications referred to
the human face, clothing, feet, or to objects held in hands or
(in the case of the pipe) mouth. Her focus of concern extends
as far as the distaff in Op. 9, the floor on which the characters stand (Op. 10), or the shadowed area immediately behind
them (Ops. 8, 9), but never to the background proper except in
her request to know whereabouts in the seaport town the
witch's house is. Yet the backgrounds of several of the illustrations abound in visually ambiguous spots and shapes of the
kind which drew Anna's comment when they formed part of the
human figure. Clearly her understanding is that it is people
who matter in this book.

While one set of visual problems is raised for Anna by figure/
ground relationships, another group of responses owes its

origin to the standard picture-book practice of varying the size of characters (or objects) from one page to the next, either arbitrarily or as a result of perspective changes. In Rapunzel this is complicated by the plot itself, which requires the baby Rapunzel to grow into an adolescent almost from one page to the next, by passing over fifteen years in a couple of sentences. No wonder Anna must confirm "Is that Rapunzel?" "She is big there."

Careful study of the pattern of Anna's response in successive readings can supplement the more general perceptions of which we have been speaking. Thus Reading 9 showed Anna commenting solely on visual stimuli; Reading 12, as we have already noted, is heavily cued to the text. That Anna appears to have a kind of preset response grid for some readings is strengthened by the strongly similar content preoccupations of Readings 2, 5, and 10. This may be tabulated as follows:

Reading 2	Reading 5	Reading 10
Op. 1. evening on the balcony	1. evening on the balcony	1. request to identify balcony wall
2. man's knife		2. appearance of witch; witch "should be nice to them"
2-3. size of witch		
	6. "old hag"/witch	6. house/tower, doorway of tower identified
7. Rapunzel's hair	7. identifies prince	7. "why did she 'unwind her braid?'"
8. Rapunzel's size; "door" behind Rapunzel		
	9. what is she [witch] doing? Rapunzel's size	9. witch's broom (distaff); Rapunzel's hair (color); Rapunzel's bare feet
11. house/tower confusion		
	13. Rapunzel's hair	
	16. witch's size	

In each of the three sessions, Anna's focus in Op. 1 was on the puzzling balcony; in the second and the tenth session she tackled the house/tower problem. In all three, she made some comment on Rapunzel's hair and, in Readings 2 and 5, on Rapunzel's size as well. It looks as though Anna's response to the book is cyclic, leaving certain preoccupations for a few readings only to return to them, perhaps to explore the same problem in different words or to focus on a new aspect of a previous area of interest.

If we turn now to those of Anna's reactions which relate broadly to the story and its characters rather than to the illustrations alone, we can attempt to piece together the story of Rapunzel as she has remade it for herself. Clearly, her attention is engaged far more by the theme of threat, suffering, and violence than by the love of Rapunzel and her prince; her consistent focus on the witch and her doings is the source for almost all the purely affective comments Anna made: "She should be nice to them--but she isn't." "Is the witch going to eat Rapunzel?" "Isn't she trying to be nice to her?" "I think the witch will take her home." "I don't want her to do that." "This is a frightening story."

For Anna, we can guess with some certainty, this is a story of a defenseless girl and an evil witch: the forces of good are pale by comparison. Moreover we notice, when all these comments are placed together, how Anna tends to respond to threat in terms of denial, a type of response which we saw in embryo in the record for Where the Wild Things Are. It is also worth noticing that the climax of the story, in emotional terms, comes on Ops. 13-14, and that Anna's first direct registering of this fact did not come until Reading 8 ("This is a frightening story" on Op. 13); rather, her emotional involvement seemed highest in the earlier portion of the tale; her attention is twice described in the record as wandering--once after Op. 10, once during the "last three openings." Thus, while Anna's cognitive focus was potentially engaged throughout the entire book, solving visual and textual problems, her emotional grasp of the story seemed to grow forward from the beginning of the book, only later encompassing the dramatic events of the climax and denouement.

Though we were unaware of it when we wrote the diary entries, it now seems probable that Anna's obscure injunctions in Op. 1 ("they'd better have a house like ours") in fact reflect not so much specific unease about a house that is unlike the one she knows but a more generalized wish that the story itself should be other than what it is--frightening. When she made the first of these comments (Reading 2) she had already heard the book through once and presumably registered its threat, if silently. Particular, "factual" reactions must, we now realize, be read in the light of this underlying affective response.

5

Finn Family Moomintroll

Tove Jansson's 1946 classic appeared in English for the first time in 1950. The author, who had been a cartoonist, illustrated her own books with pen and ink drawings of the rotund, prominent-snouted Moomins and their queerly shaped friends and associates. Her backgrounds show exaggeratedly dark forests, craggy mountains, or looming waves, thus balancing the semicomic effect of the little creatures with a note of melodrama. The same subtle blend characterizes the text, where hints of real adventures and genuine terrors lurk at the limits of the Moomins' cozy, fun-filled world, never permitted (in this book at least) to come uncomfortably close to the center of the stage for very long.

Anna first saw <u>Finn Family Moomintroll</u> in the Puffin paperback edition; we had fetched it from the shelf in order to assess its suitability for reading to her in a few months' time. Anna, interested by the brightly colored jacket, insisted that it be read immediately. We were somewhat surprised at how readily she listened to a text of this length, and by the initial and continuing impact made on her by Tove Jansson's imaginary world. For the actual reading, we used a more durable hardback edition (1950; reprint ed., London: Benn, 1958) and all page references in the record that follow are to this volume.

THE RECORD (ANNA 3.7-4.0)

<u>Finn Family Moomintroll</u> was read <u>in toto</u> twice--Readings 1 and 2; Reading 3 reached p. 88 before Anna lost interest. It

was, like Anna's earlier books, read concurrently with other
titles and was not necessarily read on consecutive days.
Because of the amount of material involved, and the length of
time spanned by the readings, we have elected to reproduce the
diary in such a way that it shows the developing response to
one chapter at a time.

Prologue and Chapter 1 (pp. 11-32)

After the prologue, in which the Moomins are shown settling
down for their long winter sleep, their tummies comfortingly
stuffed full of pine needles, the story proper begins with the
coming of spring six months later. Moomintroll and Sniff,
wandering outside as the world awakens into new life, find a
curious tall black hat atop a hill and bring it home. The hat
then begins to effect transformations on objects placed in it:
discarded eggshells turn into soft, maneuverable little clouds
on which the younger inhabitants of Moominhouse ride gleefully
for a day, meeting in the course of their games the doleful
Hemulen whose plaint it is that having completed his stamp
collection, he has nothing left to collect--a problem easily
solved by the suggestion that he begin a plant collection.

READING 1

6 February '76. Anna listened deadpan until p. 24:

Text: "'No, no,' said the Snork Maiden. 'We'll try them out
ourselves,' and she dragged a cloud onto the ground and
smoothed it out with her paw. 'So soft!' said the Snork
Maiden, and the next minute she was rocking up and down
with loud giggles.

'Can I have one too?' squealed Sniff jumping onto
another cloud. 'Hup-si-daisy!' But when he said 'hup'
the cloud rose and made an elegant little curve over the
ground.

'Golly!' burst out Sniff, 'It moved!' Then they all
threw themselves onto the clouds and shouted 'Hup! hup,
hup-si-daisy.' The clouds bounded wildly about until the
Snork discovered how to steer them. By pressing a little
with one foot you could turn the cloud. If you pressed
with both feet it went forward, and if you rocked gently
the cloud slowed up. They had terrific fun, even floating up to the treetops and to the roof of Moominhouse.

Moomintroll hovered outside Moominpappa's window and
shouted 'Cock-a-doodle-doo!' (He was so excited he
couldn't think of anything more intelligent.)

        Moominpappa dropped his memoir-pen and rushed to the
        window.

        'Bless my tail!' he burst out. 'Whatever next!'"

Anna giggled at the jumping onto the clouds, and especially at
the exclamations "hup-si-daisy" and "cock-a-doodle-doo." At
the end of the chapter she asked "Where can we get some of
those clouds?" a request that does not necessarily mean that
she accepted the magic clouds as literal truth; rather, it
fits in the category of "I wish I could . . ." applied to
such things as visits to America, Sweden ("where Lotta lives")
or Finland (where the Moomins live)--all rather remote possibilities and known by her to be so.

READING 2
25 February '76. Anna asked for this tonight. We read pp.
11-20. No comment on the reading.

26 February '76. Apropos of nothing, Anna said "Bless my
tail! I said what Moominpappa says: 'Bless my tail!'" While I
was cooking, Anna was looking at Finn Family Moomintroll by
herself, raising her voice to say to me "I don't know why the
man Hemulen wears a dress--there's no sense in that." She was
probably referring to the illustration on p. 27, although she
may be remembering the laconic Author's Note from p. 31: "The
Hemulen always wore a dress that he had inherited from his
aunt. It seems strange, but there you are."

She asked for more of the book tonight, and I read pp. 20-26.
She chuckled at "'Golly!' burst out Sniff. 'It moved!'"; at
"Hup, hup-si-daisy" (followed by a second, delayed chuckle);
at "cock-a-doodle-doo," repeating the exclamation herself and
explaining "I was trying to do what he did! [Giggle] Then
Moominpappa said 'Bless my tail!' [Giggle]" A final giggle was
reserved for the Hemulen's gasp "ouch! oh!" on p. 26.

It will be readily seen that Anna's response follows almost
exactly the contours of her earlier one, concentrating principally on the single exclamation-studded passage on p. 24, but
this time enriched by attempts to prolong the amusement by
repeating the words she found funny herself.

29 March '76. "Bless my tail!" said Anna as she sat down at
the table.

2 April '76. About three times lately Anna has asked for
Finn Family Moomintroll but has changed her mind in favor of

something else. Tonight we read pp. 26-32. No comments, but I noticed the great concern on Anna's face as we read about the Hemulen's problem, and the pleasure as we reached p. 31.
Text: "When they got home to dinner they met the Hemulen on the steps. He was beaming with happiness."

It seems likely that the cue word "happiness" was responsible for Anna's reaction here. (See chap. 12, "Funny Ha-Ha and Funny Peculiar," for more on cue words.)

READING 3
9 June '76. We read pp. 11-20 with no comment.

10 June '76. We read pp. 20-26.
Text (p. 20): "When Moomintroll, Snufkin and Sniff went out onto the verandah the others had already had their breakfast and gone off in various directions."
A: Where have the others gone?
M: "In various directions."
I then found that Moominmamma was in the kitchen, and I guessed where Muskrat and the Hemulen were. Some months later, 26 March '77, we tested whether Anna actually understood the phrase "in various directions" outside the Finn Family context: she did.

Text (p. 21): "Moominpappa looked at himself in front, behind and from both sides, and then he put the hat on the table with a sigh.

'You're right,' he said. 'Some people look better without hats.'"

A: Grandpa Richmond and Grandpa Crago don't wear hats!
Anna's statement sounds like the archetypal irrelevant response of the egocentric child listener. But is it? Is Anna merely stating, in a concrete way, that she can vouch for the truth of the statement "some people look better without hats"? Surely such measuring of statements heard in fictional contexts against our own experience goes on (albeit silently) in the adult mind as well?

On p. 24, a giggle for each of the established cues: "Golly! . . . it moved!" "Hup, hup-si-daisy!" "Cock-a-doodle-doo!" "Bless my tail!"

20 June '76. Anna requested this, and we read to the end of the chapter, with no comment.

ANALYSIS OF CHAPTER 1 RESPONSES

At no stage in any reading did Anna comment on the Prologue or
the part of the chapter before the Hat is brought home: the
center of the chapter, judging by her overt response, was the
amusing episode where the powers of the little clouds are discovered. Notice how exactly the giggles come on cue, in the
pattern laid down at the very first reading and slightly
extended at the second. From this center, Anna's explicit
reactions moved outward in two directions--back to the directly preceding incident of Moominpappa trying on the Hat and
forward to the Hemulen and his problems--exploring his appearance first and then (silently) the pathos of his plight, which
Anna seemed to take completely seriously.

Chapter 2 (pp. 33-52)

This chapter contains three episodes. In the first, Moomintroll hides under the Hat (at this stage the Moomins have not
realized that it was the Hat which produced the magical
clouds) and is transformed into a distorted creature; his
playmates reject him and he is only restored to his rightful
shape when Moominmamma recognizes him despite his altered
appearance; having deduced that the Hat is responsible for
changing whatever goes into it, Moomintroll and the Snork
capture the hated Ant-Lion and deposit it in the Hat as an
experiment, placing a Dictionary of Outlandish Words on top to
keep it there. The Ant-Lion, surprisingly, is transformed into
a tiny hedgehog, not at all menacing; the Outlandish Words
crawl from among the pages of the Dictionary, and the sand
that covered the Ant-Lion becomes water. In the final episode,
the Moomin parents decree that the Hat is potentially dangerous, so it is rolled into the river. However, Moomintroll and
Snufkin discover that it is now transforming the river-water
into raspberry juice, rescue it and hide it in their cave by
the beach.

READING 1

6 February '76, 7 February '76. No comment, but a tiny
ghost of a chuckle at Moomintroll's exclamation "goodness
gracious me!" on p. 45.

24 February '76. "Now can I have another passion fruit
please?" uttered in a strong and decisive tone, and followed
by: "I'm pretending to be those words that come out in Finna
[sic] Family Moomintroll."
She means the words transformed into odd creatures by contact
with the Hobgoblin's Hat.

Finn Family Moomintroll (p. 45): The "Outlandish Words"
come alive. Reproduced by permission of Ernest Benn.

1 March '76. Anna (looking at the volume on her own) sat
examining the Outlandish Words emerging from the Hobgoblin's
Hat (illustrated on p. 45): What are those little creatures
called? . . . We'd better call this one Towel--no, we'd
better call this one Brush-mouth because he has a brush-mouth,
see! And we'd better call this one Donkey because he's the same
size as a donkey--and we'd better call this one Chair because
he's the same size as a chair--and we'd better call this one
Person, because he's the same size as a person--we'd better
call these two Funny Names because they are funny--and we'd
better call this one Egg because he's the same size as an egg.

If we assume that "size" is Anna's slip for "shape," all her
identifications make sense and are readily located in the
illustration.

Tonight Anna asked for the weirdly transmogrified Moomintroll
to be identified in the illustration at the head of the chapter. No comment was recorded for pp. 39-43.

READING 2
10 April '76. No comments on pp. 33-39 (transformation of
Moomintroll).
15 April '76. No comments on remaining pages of chap. 2.

<u>2</u> <u>May</u> '76. Anna had announced her intention of having <u>Finn</u>
<u>Family</u> <u>Moomintroll</u> tonight but during dinner which preceded
the reading, she asked:
  <u>Why</u> <u>didn't</u> <u>Moomintroll</u> <u>and</u> <u>Snufkin</u> <u>let</u> <u>Sniff</u> <u>see</u> <u>the</u> <u>rasp-</u>
  <u>berry</u> <u>juice</u>?
M: They thought Sniff was too small to be told a secret.
A: <u>Which</u> <u>he</u> <u>was</u>. [Pause] <u>Only</u> <u>Moomintroll</u> <u>and</u> <u>Snufkin</u> <u>know</u>
  <u>the</u> <u>secret</u> <u>don't</u> <u>they</u>.

READING 3
<u>21</u> <u>June</u> '76. No comments on pp. 33-39.
<u>28</u> <u>June</u> '76. We read pp. 39-46.
Text (p. 40): "'Perhaps we could lure somebody else into it,'
                suggested the Snork . . .
              'What about an enemy?' . . .

              'Hm,' said Moomintroll. 'Do you know of one?'

              'The Pig-Swine,' said the Snork.

              Moomintroll shook his head. 'He's too big.'

              'Well, the Ant-Lion then?' the Snork sug-
              gested . . .

              So they set out to look for the Ant-Lion and
              took a big jar with them."

A: <u>Could</u> <u>I</u> <u>see</u> <u>an</u> <u>Ant-Lion</u> <u>and</u> <u>a</u> <u>Pig-Swine</u> <u>in</u> <u>the</u> <u>real</u> <u>village</u>?
Could we translate "in the real world"? (The standard way Anna
found at 5.0 for expressing what appears to be the same concern was "in our world." We can now confidently translate her
question as "Do Ant-Lions and Pig-Swine really exist?")

<u>3</u> <u>July</u> '76. Hugh read pp. 46-52, while Anna studied the illus-
trations in one of her library books; she did however beam
happily when Moomintroll exclaims "raspberry juice!"

<u>7</u> <u>July</u> '76. Anna heard to yell Moomintroll's war cry while
riding her new bike: "Pee-Hoo!" (See p. 50.)

<u>9</u> <u>July</u> '76. Read pp. 52-60. No comment.

ANALYSIS OF CHAPTER 2 RESPONSES
Two exclamations apart, the theme of Anna's meager response to
this chapter might reasonably be described as identification--
of the Outlandish Words, of the transformed Moomintroll, and

of the Ant-Lion and Pig-Swine (asking to see a new creature being one of Anna's ways of locating it within reality).

Chapter 3 (pp. 53-78)

In this chapter the Muskrat falls out of a hammock when its strings part with age and departs huffily to philosophize in peace in the cave. Still unaware of the Hat's powers, he puts his false teeth in it, goes to sleep, and is later observed by the Moomins running in indescribable terror from the cave, though it is never discovered what the teeth turned into. (Author's Note: "If you want to find out . . . you can ask your Mamma. She is sure to know.") Meanwhile the rest set out on a picnic in a new boat, found floating near the shore and named with the aid of the raspberry juice which Moomintroll is able to produce by filling the Hat with seawater. In the boat, "The Adventure," they reach Lonely Island and make a camp against a coming storm. The Hemulen wanders off into the interior of the island and is surrounded by menacing Hatti-fatteners who believe he is a threat to their barometer, a semisacred object which is hanging from a pole in their midst; Snufkin rescues him and together the Moomins and their friends sit out the storm: "Outside the storm redoubled its fury. The voice of the waves was now mixed with strange sounds: laughter, running feet and the clanging of great bells far out to sea" (p. 78).

READING 1
8 February '76. Read to p. 67.
Text (p. 65): "Wild and tempting the Lonely Island rose from
                the sea, wreathed in white breakers and crowned
                with green trees as if dressed for a gala."
A: Did it break? (The word "breaker" is new to her.)

10 February '76. Anna came running to me, showing me her hat full of "raspberry juice" which she had made "from the sea."

12 February '76. "And I want a book from the lounge room that I haven't had before." Her face lit up at my suggestion of Finn Family Moomintroll. We finished chap. 3 and a minute afterward as we were reading her other choice, The Selfish Giant, Anna said: When I am a bigger girl, we will go to the beach and make a tent out of blankets, (as the Moomins do on Lonely Island).

29 February '76. Last night when she was reading in bed, Anna asked me to tell her what Moominpappa was saying to Muskrat when the hammock collapsed. She then treated Hugh to

it this evening: "Oh dear--I hope you didn't hurt yourself" (p. 53), along with "Bless my tail!" The former was repeated in bed tonight.

1 March '76. Anna's waking monologue this morning included "Oh dear, I hope you didn't hurt yourself!" along with "Cock-a-doodle-doo!" and "Bless my tail!" established by earlier chapters.

READING 2
22 April '76. Anna asked for this tonight. We read pp. 53-63.

24 April '76. Anna rushed into the room and announced in an affected voice: The Hattifatteners have come! They've turned into Moomins. This reference depends on her memory of the previous reading, but was probably sparked off by her habit of leafing ahead to look at the illustration (p. 66) accompanying the section next to be read. The remark itself sounds initially like nonsense, but we have learned that this is rarely the case with preschool children's nonsequiturs. "Turning into" is recognizably the theme of the whole first part of Finn Family Moomintroll, with its succession of magical transformations. That the menacing Hattifatteners should "turn into Moomins" is one way for Anna to recognize and deny their menace, like her hopeful speculation that the witch might be kind to Rapunzel.

Again this afternoon Anna announced the arrival of the Hattifatteners. She asked for more of the book tonight, but then changed her mind in favor of an old Babar we keep in the lounge room (safer than hearing more of the Hattifatteners?).

2 May '76. We read pp. 63-73.
Text (p. 65): "Far out to sea lay the Hattifatteners' Lonely Island surrounded by reefs and breakers. (Once a year the Hattifatteners collect there before setting out again on their endless foraging expeditions round the world. They come from all points of the compass, silent and serious with their small, white empty faces, and why they hold this yearly meeting it is difficult to say, as they can neither hear nor speak, and have no object in life but the distant goal of their journey's end. Perhaps they like to have a place where they feel at home and can rest a little and meet friends."

I had glossed "foraging expeditions" as "they pick up things
as they go".
A: <u>Do</u> <u>they</u> <u>pick</u> <u>up</u> <u>rubbish</u>? (one of her own occasional activities when out walking, although she calls her finds "trea-
sure").
M: I don't know what they pick up--oh! we know they pick up
   things like barometers!
After the phrase "meet friends":
A: <u>Do</u> <u>they</u> <u>have</u> <u>Hattifattener</u> <u>friends</u>?

On p. 67, as we turned the page and Anna saw the picture of
the Hemulen with his magnifying glass, she asked: <u>Did</u> <u>the</u>
<u>Hemulen</u> <u>come</u> <u>too</u>?

The Hemulen's presence on the boat has not been noted in the
text; he was last mentioned in the account of the boat-naming
ceremony on the beach. So Anna's question does not necessarily
point to inattention. Jansson rarely marks entrances and exits
for all her characters; often the only way of knowing whether
one of the Moomin entourage is on stage is to wait until his
name is mentioned.

Text (p. 73): "'A big storm?' asked Sniff anxiously.

                'Look for yourself,' replied Moominpappa.
                The barometer points to "00" and that is the
                lowest a barometer can point to--if it isn't
                fooling us.'"
A: <u>Why</u> <u>does</u> <u>the</u> <u>barometer</u> <u>point</u> <u>to</u> "00"?
She has had no acquaintance with barometers, so the connection
between Sniff's question and Moominpappa's citing of the "00"
reading escapes her.

Text (p. 78): ". . . and the clanging of great bells far out
                to sea . . ."
A: <u>I</u> <u>think</u> <u>that</u>--<u>big</u> <u>bells</u> <u>was</u> <u>a</u> <u>ship</u> <u>sinking</u>.
H: Do you? whose ship?
A (embarrassed): <u>Maybe</u>--<u>a</u> <u>sailor's</u>.
M: Maybe Anna means like the one in <u>The</u> <u>Water</u> <u>Babies</u>.
A: <u>Mmm-hm</u> (not entirely convinced).

READING 2
<u>8</u> <u>May</u> <u>'76</u>. No comment.

READING 3
<u>28</u> <u>July</u> <u>'76</u>. Anna requested this. We read pp. 79-88.

Text (p. 86): "But the Snork ran to the top of the highest
            hill and looked round. He could see from shore
            to shore--"

A: <u>Is the Snork a boy</u>?
H: Yes. But the Snork Maiden's a girl.

Anna made no reply, but looked most put out. Maureen asked if
she had wanted both of them to be girls, and she said "yes." I
found for her the illustration on p. 120, which shows Moomintroll, the Snork, and the Snork Maiden all at once. Picking up
the lesson, Anna proceeded to identify the p. 87 picture of
Moominmamma asleep: <u>And that's a lady one</u>.

It should be remembered that the Moomins and Snorks have no
obvious physiological differences, in Tove Jansson's illustrations, and that Anna may well have been treating the
phrase "the Snork" as a shortened form of "the Snork Maiden"
(that "maiden" refers to females she is well aware). Moreover,
this is one of the very few places in the entire book where
the pronoun "he" is used of the Snork, thus insisting un-
equivocally on his gender. See chap. 14, "Heroes and Villains," for Anna's consistent preference for females over
males.

READING 3
No comment recorded on any section in this chapter.

It would seem that the Hattifatteners constitute Anna's major
concern in this chapter. Witness the several detailed questions referring to the description of them on p. 65, and the
two announcements of their "arrival." Notice, though, that
this interest does not seem to surface until Anna hears the
episode for the second time. In the first reading, she follows
her standard pattern of response in focusing on the slapstick
of "I hope you didn't hurt yourself" and the gratifying play
image of the makeshift blanket tent.

Chapter 4

A much briefer chapter than its predecessor, this one contains
an account of how the Hattifatteners invade the Moomins' tent
later during the night of the storm and wrest back their
treasured barometer from the Hemulen; they depart from the
island, leaving the Moomin party to hunt for treasure inland
or among the flotsam and jetsam thrown up by the storm. Each
discovers something of considerable significance to him or

herself, and in the evening they sail home laden with their
finds. Only the Snork Maiden is disconsolate, the Hattifatteners episode having resulted in her losing her much-
prized fringe of hair.

READING 1
12 February '76, 14 February '76. No comments during the
reading of the text, but at the end of the chapter, Anna
pointed to the illustration on p. 89:
A: Is that Lonely Island?
M: Yes--they're sailing away from the island now.
A: Why?
The text itself gives no reason why the Moomins choose to
leave at this particular time, and hence Anna's question is
justified. But it seems unlikely that she would have asked at
all had Maureen's comment not opened a discussion of the
incident.

READING 2
15 May '76. On p. 94--
Text: "Their cargo consisted of the gold and the little snow
      storm, of the gorgeous big buoy, the boot, the dipper,
      the lifebelt and the raffia mat, and in the prow lay the
      figurehead gazing out to sea."

A: What's a raffia mat?

Chapter 5 (pp. 97-123)
Bored in the summer heat, the younger ones are packed off by
Moominmamma to live in the beach cave for a few days. They go
fishing in the rain and catch a gigantic creature called the
"Mameluke," but on their triumphant return with it, find
Moominhouse has turned into a jungle as a result of Moominmamma's depositing in the now-reinstated Hat "some poisonous
pink perennials" collected by the Hemulen in the course of his
botanizing. The family plays jungle games amidst the foliage
until at nightfall it withers away. Earlier, during the first
night in the cave, Snufkin has told the others about the original owner of the Hat, the Hobgoblin, who flies out each night
on a black panther, collecting rubies. It is revealed that he
lost the Hat while searching for a giant stone called the
King's Ruby among the craters of the moon.

READING 1
14 February '76. In reading pp. 105-6, I thought the Snork's
annoyed retreat into the stern after Sniff has tangled the
fishing line in an attempt to help Sniff too allusive for

Anna, and explained that the Snork had moved because he didn't want to have to untangle the line.

A: Why?

Once again, an adult explanation designed to ease Anna's passage through the narration results in her requesting further explanation. It seems to us here, as before, that Anna treats our glosses or comments as in some sense independent of the text, almost as if they tell a different story from the one she has just heard. In view of the sophistication of this particular text, such behavior isn't surprising.

15 February '76. On p. 107 she interrupted to ask the meaning of "snooze." On p. 114 (they have discovered the "disappearance of Moominhouse") the text reads: "'Yes, but where's the house?' asked the Snork."

A: Where are their mother and father?

Because I intended to leave off reading at the beginning of the jungle games episode, we looked ahead to the illustration on p. 120, explaining roughly what each of the characters was doing. She was fascinated by the Muskrat, unable to understand why he should fear that the plants might grow into his ears, and in the end evidently decided that it must be a joke, and kept chuckling.

16 February '76. Anna's request. We read to the end of chap. 5. I read (p. 119): "It was a thrilling afternoon. They played a jungle game in which Moomintroll was Tarzan and the Snork Maiden was Jane. Sniff was Tarzan's Son, and Snufkin was the chimpanzee Cheeta, while the Snork crawled about in the undergrowth, with huge teeth made of orange peel, pretending to be the Enemy." I traced the illustration with my finger to show which was Moomintroll and which was the Snork. In the pause, Anna chuckled. I'm not sure at what.

Text (p. 121): ". . . nobody even thought about the poor Hemulen. He still sat, with his wet dress flapping round his legs . . ."

A: Is that Hemulen a man? (pause).

M: He's a creature. Are you asking me if he's a man creature, a boy creature, or a he creature?

A: Mmm--but why is he wearing a dress?

Anna was clearly confused by Maureen's reply, but her second attempt reveals her reason for puzzlement clearly enough: she is still perplexed by a male creature in female attire (see sec., "Prologue and Chapter 1," Reading 2, above). In Anna's pictorial experience, male and female stereotypes were established very early, and at 1.6 the diary records her persistent refusal to accept that men pictured in long robes were not "girls." Jansson's Hemulen positively invites her to resurrect this archaic response. (See chap. 14, "Heroes and Villains.")

(Later) looking at the illustration on p. 116:
A: Is she [Moominmamma] happy that things are growing through the ceiling?

As drawn, the Moomins have no obvious mouth line; since Anna's (and our) usual mode of determining a character's emotion depends on the mouth--upturned for happiness, downturned for dejection--she is thus deprived of her normal visual cue.

18 February '76. Hugh bathed her and was pulling faces at her. She commanded: "You be a lion with orange peel teeth," attempting to duplicate the jungle game in the story.

19 February '76. Today she has continued to "be Muskrat" in play, and putting Special Blanket over her head, she said: I did this so nothing could grow into my ears like the Muskrat (see p. 119).
Text: "'Well, things can't get much worse--that's one consola-
        tion,' the Muskrat groaned. He had hidden himself in a
        forest of bracken in the bathroom, and had wrapped his
        head in a handkerchief so that nothing should grow into
        his ears."

4 March '76. Anna comments: I am going to dream about nice things tonight--and the Hobgoblin (implying that the Hob-goblin is not nice? impossible to be sure).

15 May '76. At dinner we were fooling about with mandarin peel, and Hugh offered to make Anna some mandarin peel teeth. This seems to have prompted Anna to request a reading of Finn Family Moomintroll later.

READING 2
16 May '76. On p. 105 the text reads: "'Must we fish?' asked the Snork Maiden. 'Nothing ever happens when we fish, and I'm so sorry for the little pike.'" I glossed "little pike" as "fish."
A: What is it? Is the "little pike" a fish?

On p. 106 in the passage describing events back home at Moomin-house, contemporaneous with the fishing expedition, Moomin-mamma only is mentioned.

A: <u>Where</u> <u>is</u> <u>Moominpappa</u>?
Anna may be remembering from the previous reading that Moominpappa proves later to be in the house too, and wondering why
nothing is said of him at this stage. Or, she may have built
up an expectation that the two normally appear and act as a
duo. At all events, the concern persisted as we read on.

<u>20 May</u> <u>'76</u>. On p. 114 the text reads: "'Yes, but where's the
house?' asked the Snork."
A: <u>Where's</u> <u>Moominmamma</u> <u>and</u> <u>Moominpappa</u>?
This repeats her reaction during Reading 1.

Soon we were reading the long paragraph which recapitulates
how the jungle came to appear in the house, mentioning only
Moominmamma.
A: <u>Where's</u> <u>Moominpappa</u>?

Text (p. 121): "'Well, well!' [Moominmamma] said, 'it seems to
                me that our guests are having a very good
                time.'

                'I hope so,' replied Moominpappa. 'Pass me a
                banana, please dear.'"
A: <u>Why</u> <u>did</u> <u>Moominpapa</u> <u>say</u> "<u>Pass</u> <u>me</u> <u>a</u> <u>banana</u>, <u>please</u>"?
This question prompted by Moominpappa's sudden change of
subject. We completed the chapter.

<u>7 June</u> <u>'76</u>. We were walking out the gate in the evening on our
way to buy the milk, and Anna told me to look at the moon in
the sky: <u>I</u> <u>think</u> <u>there</u> <u>is</u> <u>a</u> <u>ruby</u> <u>in</u> <u>the</u> <u>moon</u>! This is a
reference to Snufkin's story of the Hobgoblin.

Chapter 6

From the beginning of her acquaintance with our paperback
edition of <u>Finn</u> <u>Family</u> <u>Moomintroll</u>, Anna had been fascinated
by the cover illustration and in particular by the two small,
red-clad figures of Thingumy and Bob. During the first reading
of the book, she had several times asked for a story about
"those creatures"; they finally make their appearance in chap.
6, carrying a large suitcase and speaking a special language
which the English translator renders by reversing the initial
letter(s) of the principal content words in each phrase (thus
"foke means smood" = "smoke means food"). The Hemulen reveals
that the Groke is pursuing them because they have stolen her
suitcase. In the course of a "trial" arranged by the Snork, it
is learnt that in fact the suitcase is theirs, but the contents (the nature of which is not disclosed in this chapter)

are rightfully the Groke's. The Groke, a frightening creature
of the Winter who freezes the ground wherever she rests, turns
up to claim her property, but is satisfied with Moominmamma's
offer of the Hobgoblin's Hat instead, and departs.

READING 1
18 February '76. No comment on the reading of chap. 6, although she looked worried about the Groke.

20 February '76. She mentioned "smooth" to me once, and again
to Hugh while in the bath, in connection with Thingumy and
Bob. We asked her about it, and she now linked it with "food."
This enabled us to trace it to p. 127, "Did I fell smood?"

26 February '76. Anna came running to me: I'll tell you something Thingumy and Bob could say: "Finna Family Moominmoll."
"Finna" is her own previously used "metrical form" for "Finn"
in the title, but "Moominmoll" is not a bad attempt at a rever-
sal of consonants à la Thingumy and Bob.

READING 2
21 May '76, 24 May '76, 29 May '76. No comment on this chapter,
except to correct Maureen when she read the Hemulen's words
without the quavering voice we customarily accord him.

Chapter 7 (pp. 140-70)
The final chapter of Finn Family Moomintroll begins with
Snufkin's departure from Moominvalley, witnessed only by
Moomintroll, who feels so sad that Thingumy and Bob try to
comfort him by revealing the contents of the infamous suitcase
--the King's Ruby, for which the Hobgoblin has been searching.
Moominmamma's handbag disappears and is "found" by Thingumy
and Bob, who had quietly appropriated it as a sleeping place;
its rediscovery seems sufficient cause for a party, at which
the Ruby is once more displayed. Its vivid pink glow brings
the Hobgoblin down from the moon, but he proves well disposed,
and the book ends with a free-for-all, in which everyone has a
wish granted by the Hobgoblin.

READING 1
20 February '76. We read from where Hugh left off last night.
When we reached Moominpappa's thanks to Thingumy and Bob for
"finding" Moominmamma's bag, Anna asked: Did Thingumy and Bob
climb the tree to get it?

The two little creatures had of course taken the bag in the
first place, but it is their collecting it from the rose tree

that has lodged in Anna's mind. I explained that they had
taken it from Moominmamma.
A: Why?
M: Because they needed it.
A: Why?
Again, as so often, the explanation that seems self-evident
to us is insufficient for Anna.

The illustration on p. 156 is a crowded scene of merrymakers
at the party celebrating the return of the handbag. Silhou-
etted in a patch of light, above and to the left of the main
table at which the Moomins sit, is the Hemulen. Anna picked
him out: There's--there's--there's--him.
M: The Hemulen?
A: Mmm.
She is still forgetting his name, and of course his female
dress makes him memorable to her.

21 February '76. Today we finished the book. On p. 168
Thingumy and Bob use their wish to create another Ruby so that
the Hobgoblin can have it for himself.
Text: "'We've decided to wake a mish for you because you are
        nice. We want a booby as rootiful as ours.'"
A: What does "booby" mean?

And on p. 170--
M: That's the end of the book, dear.
A (wistfully): We can read it again.
M: We can start from the beginning and read it again.
A (with confidence): We can read all the things again?
M: Yes.
A: Aah!--Again and again and again!
Anna's enthusiasm for the book at the end of this reading was
further borne out by her play that afternoon: she gave her
dolls a great "feast," elaborately spread out on the floor of
her bedroom.

READING 2
2 June '76. I spun out the brushing of Anna's hair longer,
so that we finished the book. Thingumy and Bob disclose that
they have been using Moominmamma's handbag as a place to sleep
in.
Text (p. 150): "said Bob . . . . : 'Pot a wity! It was so nice
                to sleep in the pittle lockets.'"
A: What are "pittle lockets"?
I wonder how much of this patter from Thingumy and Bob escapes
her?

6 June '76.
A (following a passage of conscious nonsense syllables):
  That's how Mrs. Sneeze [her toy rabbit] talks.
M: She's talking rabbit language.
A: She uses the language that Thingumy and Bob have.

From the evidence we have, Anna's principal focal point in this
final chapter seems to be her already established fascination
with Thingumy and Bob's language; the acted "feast" is the only
other feature for which her behavior gives evidence of impact.

Identification of the Characters

Apart from those of Anna's responses which can be demonstrated
to have been provoked by individual chapters, there remains a
body of comment occasioned principally by Anna's wish to identify and assimilate the host of novel and confusing characters
with which Finn Family Moomintroll confronted her. A number of
these remarks were made as Anna looked at particular illustrations while perusing the book on her own, and seem better
treated here than artificially included under the readings in
which those illustrations were first viewed.

21 February '76. Anna came in from the garden.
A: I said something clever--I sat down on the seat beside the
   Hemulen and I said "Goodbye Moon!"
Later she came in excitedly to tell Maureen that the Hemulen
was outside to help her play doctors and nurses.
M: What color is his dress?
A: Red, apparently (Maureen was wearing red that day). . . .
A: I'm pretending to be a nurse, and Hemulen is pretending to
   be a doctor!

23 February '76. Anna had the book today, chatting happily
about the illustrations.
A: The Hattifatteners look like this (demonstrates). They
   have eyes, but no ears--Did the Hattifatteners steal
   the---the--the
M: Barometer? (Obviously this was the word Anna sought.)
A: I would like the Hemulen to come and live with us.

24 February '76. Yesterday Anna came and asked for something
in a high-pitched voice; Maureen guessed that Anna was being
the Snork Maiden and she agreed that she was. Maureen customarily read the Snork Maiden in such a voice.

26 February '76. Yesterday she came to me and quavered something, adding: That's like the Hemulen's voice (again imitating

the distinctive voice we had given him). She also said she was
"facing like the Muskrat," i.e., pulling a face like the
Muskrat.
A: Does Moomintroll wear clothes?
M: No, I think he doesn't.
A: Like the Rhinemaidens--they don't wear clothes.

Anna is referring to the Rhinemaidens in Wagner's Rheingold,
part of which she has heard on record, accompanied by a much-
simplified version of the story. We have also shown her Arthur
Rackham's color illustration of the Rhinemaidens, in which
they are, of course, naked.

1 March '76. Illus., p. 87 (Moominmamma asleep, overhung by
grass)--
A: That shows us that Moominmamma is a small mother.
This was probably an attempt of Anna's to indicate her comprehension of what Maureen had at some stage previously told her
about the small size of the Finn Family Moomintroll creatures.

She has several times chanted "Moomintroll, Snufkin, and
Sniff." The names of the three creatures have, in this order,
a nice metrical ring, making the phrase a natural one to
recall and quote.

4 March '76. Maureen was washing the front porch and Anna
started talking to her in the quavering voice we use for the
Hemulen, then insisted that Maureen call her "Hemulen" rather
than "Anna" or any of the regular endearments. The content of
the Hemulen talk then fled Maureen's mind.

5 March '76. Anna was Sniff this morning.
A: Why is he called Sniff? Because he sniffs? (demon-
    strating)
M: Because his mother wanted him to be called Sniff.
A: Well, why is Moomintroll called "Moomintroll"?
We could only surmise a Moomin liking for the name "Troll."

7 March '76. For about an hour this morning, and then again
during her rest, Anna was "being" the Snork Maiden, using the
high voice that Maureen uses when reading her lines. She asked
Hugh to be the Hemulen and expected him to quaver all his
responses. He kept it up for a while. She came to Maureen at
one point and suggested that she would be a suitable Hemulen
because Hemulens wear dresses. But for most of this hour,
Maureen was Moominmamma, "because you do what Moominmamma
does." She then assigned other parts to the family who live

next door: Col can be Moominpappa and Gavin and Craig can be
Sniff and Snufkin.
M: What about Peg?
A: She can be Moominmamma (altering her earlier decision
that Maureen would fit into this role). All these roles were
aptly chosen, Col and Peg being adults, and Gavin and Craig
children.

7 April '76. Anna asked Maureen to tell her about the "rooms"
in Finn Family Moomintroll, evidently remembering that the
ground plan of Moominhouse in the illustration to which she
was pointing had to do with rooms. Maureen then explained all
the rooms but had to admit failure in identifying the little
creatures opposite.

22 April '76. Unprompted, Anna asked: Why was Sniff only small?
Snufkin, Sniff, the Snork Maiden--I was counting the Moomins--
Thingumy and Bob, the Hemulen, Moominpappa, Moominmamma, the
Groke--the Groke wasn't a Moomin, was he!--Why was Moomintroll
a Moomintroll?

The last question has point because one of Anna's current
library books is The Adventures of Mole and Troll, which has
enabled her to isolate the formative "-troll" in Moomintroll's
name. It is interesting that Anna refers to the Groke as "he,"
even though Jansson always uses the feminine pronoun. Sniff's
smallness is a characteristic constantly reinforced by the
text's use of the formula "Sniff, the little animal."

6 May '76. We had our lunch on the back porch in the sun. As
Maureen went off to get food, Anna said: You and me can be
Moominmamma. You can be Moominmamma getting food, and I'll be
the Snork. Presumably she meant the Snork Maiden (see entry of
28 July quoted above).

23 July '76. Yesterday she showed Finn Family Moomintroll to
Iain M., explaining that she had a book with creatures who
"wafted about on clouds and bumped into each other" (words not
exact--the tape was inadvertently erased). She then listed a
number of the characters: Moomintroll, Snufkin, Sniff, the
Snork Maiden.

21 January '77. Anna, playing an obscure game, was heard to
mutter: There you are, I've put--a Hattifattener into the box.

As we have already seen, the strength of Anna's wish to identify and assimilate the characters of Finn Family Moomintroll

is explicable in terms of the difficulties posed by the allu-
siveness of the text itself and the visual similarities between several of the creatures. Chronologically, we can see a
development from an early obsession with the Hemulen (perhaps
attempts to cope with his anomalous garb?) to a later focus on
Sniff, Moomintroll, the Snork Maiden, and Moominmamma. While
she was on two occasions prepared to take the role of the
Hemulen, she more often seemed to see him as external to
herself, like Moominmamma, whose role she always insisted
should be played by others. Similarly, she took the role of
Sniff and the Snork Maiden, but never that of Moomintroll,
despite the fact that he is clearly the central character.

ANALYSIS

Text and Illustrations

It will already be evident that a considerable number of
Anna's responses to Finn Family Moomintroll were dependent
on the pictures, despite the fact that this is not a picture
book but a novel which happens to be illustrated every few
pages with line drawings of modest size and visual impact.
Undoubtedly Anna's concentration on them has a lot to do with
her relative inexperience of "chapter books." Faced with a
long and at times baffling text--sophisticated in vocabulary
and often subtle in concept--Anna not surprisingly fastens on
the pictures as her way in, just as she seizes upon and reproduces the dramatic voices which we assigned to each of the
major characters. Even those of her questions which do not
refer directly to an illustration often refer to the appearance or attributes of one of the characters, who, drawing
substance from their visual representations, are her primary
point of interaction with the fictional world. In this respect, Anna's response is very little different from what we
observed in the case of Rapunzel. For the rest, Anna responded
to the text with lexical questions--concentrating especially
on Thingumy and Bob's special language--and asking questions
about events and their motivation almost solely when given an
entrée by Maureen's ad hoc explanations. In spite of the
limited range of her text-oriented comments, however, these
are still more numerous than those that depend purely on the
illustrations.

Focus

With a book the length of Finn Family Moomintroll, it is not
easy to give an indication of density of response that is
meaningful or suggestive of further analysis. Where each

opening of a picture book is readily identifiable as a discrete unit, to which volume of response can be noted, a novel
falls into much more extensive divisions perceived by author
and by more sophisticated readers, but arguably not by a child
as young as Anna. However, chapters, if arbitrary divisions,
are the only ones readily available, and we have attempted to
chart response using them, but taking into account also the
illustrations contained within each.

Clearly it is chaps. 3 and 5 which stand out in terms of the
quantity of response they evoke; both are relatively long and,
hence, provide plenty of valid opportunities for comment. But
if we reexamine the content of Anna's remarks, we will find
that large areas offered by the text go unheeded, and that her
verbal responses cluster notably around the Hattifatteners in
chap. 3 and around the disappearance of Moominhouse (and the
possible disappearance of Moominpappa) in chap. 5. In the
former case it is the threatening/unfamiliar which is in question, as embodied in the mysterious and menacing Hattifatteners, and in the latter, a threat to the ultimate embodiment
of domestic security: home, mother, and father.

There is nothing in Anna's pattern of response to suggest that
she conceived of Finn Family Moomintroll as a single continuous story. The fact that it had to be broken up for oral reading purposes into separate chunks would have hindered this in
any case, but more to the point, the novel is itself strongly
episodic. In responding to it as a series of isolated dramatic
or humorous incidents, Anna was doing no more than the book
itself invites its readers (child or adult) to do.

6

The Story of Doctor Dolittle

Hugh Lofting's 1920 Story of Doctor Dolittle is the oldest of
the six books chosen for inclusion in this section and one of
the oldest books Anna has heard. Its age, however, does not
show in any ways Anna was likely to notice: the patronizing
treatment of the black Africans in Jolliginki went unperceived.
Stronger and simpler in its story line than many of the later
"Doctor Dolittle" books, it seemed appropriate for Anna both
in language and content.

Lofting's drawings, more spidery and detailed than they later
became, are very much the drawings of an amateur and posed few
artistic challenges. They did, however, illustrate the key
incidents in the story in the way Anna had come to expect, and
as we shall see, she used the pictures as a means of predicting the future course of the story on several occasions.

The innocent Doctor, having chosen to work with animals in
preference to human patients, is summoned to Africa where
monkeys are dying of a terrible plague. Shipwrecked off the
African coast, he and his party of animal friends are taken
prisoner by the King of the Jolliginki, but contrive to escape
and reach the land of the monkeys. There the Doctor's medical
efforts prove successful and his grateful patients send him
off with a banquet and a gift of a rare animal, the two-headed
Pushmi-Pullyu. However, the Doctor's return is far from un-
eventful. Once again he has to escape from the Jolliginki,
this time finding an unexpected ally in Prince Bumpo, whose
secret desire it is to turn white. On the homeward voyage,
there are Barbary Pirates to be outwitted and their victims to

be rescued before the much-traveled party again reach "the little house with the big garden" in Puddleby-on-the-Marsh.

THE RECORD (ANNA 3.11-4.5)

Reading 1

<u>11 June '76</u>. We offered this to Anna last night . . . she heard chap. 1 with attention. Tonight I read chap. 2.
Text (p. 31): "'Now listen, Doctor, and I'll tell you some-
thing. Did you know that animals can talk?'

'I knew that parrots can talk,' said the Doctor.

'Oh, we parrots can talk in two languages--
people's language and bird-language,' said
Polynesia proudly. 'If I say: "Polly wants a
biscuit," you understand me. But hear this:
<u>Ka-ka oi-ee</u>, <u>fee-fee</u>?'

'Good gracious!' cried the Doctor. 'What does
that mean?'

'That means, "Is the porridge hot yet?"--in
bird-language.'"

Anna giggled after "Good gracious . . . what does that mean?" (As so often before, the first explicit response to a new book is to an exclamation. In this case, the obvious background to Anna's choice of "good gracious" is Moomintroll's "Goodness gracious me!" Notice too, how the phrase occurs directly after a passage of "animal language" quoted to the Doctor by Poly-nesia the parrot. Soon Anna's attention will encompass this concept as well.)

<u>12 June '76</u>. Anna asked for this this morning. We read chap. 3 without comment; in this chapter the Doctor quarrels with Sarah over his insistence on keeping the crocodile as a house guest, and in the course of their debate Sarah refers to the beast as an alligator. The Doctor replies (p. 46), "It isn't an alligator--it's a crocodile." Anna must have absorbed this and worked on the distinction privately, because a few hours later she came up with: <u>Alligators aren't crocodiles</u>, <u>are</u> <u>they</u>?
H & M: No.
A: <u>Their faces are much more frightening than crocodiles'</u> <u>faces</u>.

Certainly the crocodile drawn by Lofting is egregiously mild and ingratiating in appearance; but then the principal alligators in Anna's artistic heritage--Sendak's in <u>Alligators</u> <u>All</u> <u>Around</u>--are not particularly menacing either. All the Doctor is doing is correcting Sarah's imprecision in calling a crocodile an alligator, but the frame "It isn't a ------, it's a -------" very often seems to imply the superiority of the second element. In this case "superiority" is greater suitability as a domestic pet, i.e., less fierce.

Before her afternoon rest I read chap. 4. No comment, but during the afternoon she said to me "I'm Polynesia." We didn't pursue this, but rather her mispronunciation of "Polynesia" (she'd heard "l" as "d").

Tonight she again accepted <u>Doctor</u> <u>Dolittle</u> in response to her ritual request for "a book from the lounge room" (i.e., one of ours) and we read chap. 5, chronicling the voyage to Africa of the Doctor and his companions.

Text (p. 64): "Polynesia asked them how many miles they had yet to go; and the flying-fishes said it was only fifty-five miles now to the coast of Africa."
I stopped reading and tried to explain how long it would take to do fifty-five miles in a car.
A: <u>Can</u> <u>I</u> <u>go</u> <u>there</u> [i.e., Africa] <u>when</u> <u>I</u> <u>am</u> <u>a</u> <u>big</u> <u>girl</u>?

By age 4, Anna has formed the belief that places named in stories are likely to be real and that she may be able to visit them, if not now, then later "when I am a big girl." But as we noted earlier, a request to visit a fictional place needs to be seen not simply or even principally as exemplifying a growing consciousness of the geography of the real world but as part of a wider process in which Anna makes a fictional item her own--asking for fictional food, making a "magic pencil" for herself, or announcing that she will visit Africa are all instances of this.

Shortly afterward came the account of the wreck of the Doctor's ship and the escape ashore.
Text (p. 68): "But the ship was no good any more--with the big hole in the bottom; and presently the rough sea beat it to pieces on the rocks and the timbers floated away."
A: <u>Was</u> <u>all</u> <u>their</u> <u>things</u> <u>gone</u>?

The record does not specify whereabouts on the page Anna asked this question.

Since The Little Red Lighthouse, shipwrecks have figured several times in Anna's reading experience, with a growing consciousness in her of their consequences--death by drowning and loss of possessions. Lofting's illustration of the catastrophe shows the boat, stem forced upward, in a very similar position to that of the wrecked tug in Little Red Lighthouse. Maybe we are dealing with an instance of visual memory triggering an emotional response (see chap. 11, "The Genesis of Taste," for more on this). She was obviously sad about the losses of the Doctor and his friends, and we tried to reassure her that they were all too poor to own much. She was also much involved in the adventures of the White Mouse, and her face showed anxiety as he told his story: "'When the ship sank I was terribly frightened--because I cannot swim far. I swam as long as I could, but I soon got all exhausted and thought I was going to sink. And then, just at that moment, the old man's hat came floating by; and I got into it because I did not want to be drowned'" (p. 69).

On p. 71 a black man comes out of the woods to tell them that they must all come before the King of the Jolliginki. At this point the reading was interrupted when Hugh asked whether I had pronounced "Jolliginki" correctly (he had remembered it inaccurately from childhood), and I leafed ahead to prove that the spelling remained constant. Anna seized her chance to point to the King in the picture on p. 74.
A: I think that's the King. [Pause] Then why isn't he wearing anything? Why isn't he wearing anything?
We discussed loin cloths. The King's is not actually visible.
A (leafing ahead): Let's see the King--is this where he comes? (p. 78).
M: There--he has a bed.
A: Is that--is that his cave? (She seemed to be indicating the dark space beneath the bed where Polynesia is hiding.)
Anna has built up an expectation that kings (along with queens and, especially, princesses) are likely to be important. Hence her desire to establish in advance "where he comes."

13 June '76. I read chaps. 6 and 7, in which Polynesia tricks the King into allowing the Doctor's party to escape from the prison where he has placed them. There was no comment, nor any on chap. 8, but prior to this reading while Anna was looking through a pile of books of which Doctor Dolittle was one,

Shipwreck. <u>Above</u>, <u>The Little Red Lighthouse and the
Great Gray Bridge</u> (Op. 20): "CRASH! CRASH! CRASH! The
fat black tug . . . lay wrecked and broken." Reproduced by
permission of Harcourt Brace Jovanovich Inc.
<u>Below</u>, compare detail redrawn from <u>The Story of Doctor
Dolittle</u> (p. 67). The decorative curl at the prow of the
Doctor's ship resembles an "eye"; and the loose rigging is
windblown in a similar curve to the tug's smoke.

she asked: <u>Why</u> <u>did</u> <u>the</u> <u>black</u> <u>man</u> <u>say</u> "<u>The</u> <u>King</u> <u>of</u> <u>the</u>
<u>Jolliginki</u>"? Perhaps it was our dispute about the pronuncia-
tion of "Jolliginki" the day before that had caused the phrase
to stick in Anna's mind? In any case, it seems likely that she
is in fact asking the meaning of "Jolliginki" rather than the
man's motivation for mentioning the King.

<u>14</u> <u>June</u> <u>'76</u>. We read chap. 9 at Anna's request, before her
rest. The Doctor having cured the lions and the monkeys of
their illness is now preparing to depart and the monkeys hit
on the idea of giving him a pushmi-pullyu as a farewell gift.
I voluntarily turned ahead, looking for a picture of the two-
headed animal. Anna pointed to the Doctor, who is scratching
his head (p. 115), and asked "Why is he doing that?" It is the
unfamiliar pose of a known character, rather than the exotic
pushmi-pullyu, that has drawn her attention.

Tonight at Anna's request I read chap. 10 and (as I often do)
announced the next chapter in advance, "The Black Prince," to
which Anna responded: <u>Let's</u> <u>see</u> <u>it</u>--<u>let's</u> <u>see</u> <u>him</u>.

Looking ahead for a key character who has not yet appeared has
become established now as a ritual. Doubtless it also gives
Anna a point of reference around which to organize her picture
of the events in each new chapter as they unroll.

Prior to this reading Anna had come to us while we were
cooking and offered to "read" to us "the story of how Doctor
Dolittle became an animal doctor." What followed was inade-
quately preserved, since the tape recorder was not handy, and
my scribbled notes could not keep pace with her. Enough remains for us to note that in her story (based on chaps. 1-3)
the Doctor "gave up being an animal doctor and became a people
doctor again" because if he was an animal doctor, "he couldn't
exist . . ." (embarrassed mutter--she is not too sure of having used "exist" correctly). The single change of the original
has been transformed by Anna into a potentially endless sequence: people doctor--animal doctor--people doctor--animal
doctor . . ., reworked later in her story in which she has the
Doctor actually turn into a pig, a crocodile, a sheep, a lamb,
etc., to become an "animal doctor" in another sense--at which
point her invention failed and the tale was deemed to have
ended.

<u>16</u> <u>June</u> <u>'76</u>. Anna wanted a chapter tonight and we read chap.
11. No comment, but rapt attention and a wish to look through
the pages of chap. 12 once she heard its title "Medicine and

Magic." "Magic" was, of course, the lure (see chap. 13, "The Limits of Reality").

<u>18</u> <u>June</u> '76. Doctor Dolittle sets sail for home.
Text (p. 144): "When the ship moved out upon the water, those who stayed behind, Chee-Chee, Polynesia and the crocodile grew terribly sad."
A: <u>Why</u> <u>were</u> <u>they</u>--
I interrupted Anna before her question was completed because I could see that the explanation she wanted would be supplied by the next sentence.
Text: "For never in their lives had they known anyone they liked so well as Doctor John Dolittle of Puddleby-on-the-Marsh."

We read chap. 13, "Red Sails and Blue Wings," which introduces the names of the Barbary Pirates, and I began chap. 14.
Text (p. 146): "Now one sunshiny day the Doctor and Dab-Dab were walking up and down on the ship for exercise . . . Presently Dab-Dab saw the sail of another ship a long way behind them on the edge of the sea. It was a red sail.

'I don't like the look of that sail,' said Dab-Dab. 'I have a feeling it isn't a friendly ship. I am afraid there is more trouble coming to us.'"
A: <u>I</u> <u>think</u> <u>it</u> <u>was</u> <u>taking</u> <u>their</u> <u>ship</u>.
Anna's tense betrays her: her intention was almost certainly to predict the action of the red-sailed ship, on the basis of the information about the Barbary Pirates given a page before.

Twice, later in the morning, Anna was heard to use the word "Barbary" (quite inappropriately) in her fantasizing.

Anna asked again for this in the evening, and we read chap. 14. When we came to the word "disgraceful" on p. 155, Anna made a startled movement, then a tiny noise, and both times I stopped, the second time observing privately with annoyance that there was nothing to show for these interruptions. Her comment, when it did come, was poured out as an exciting revelation: <u>Oh</u>! "<u>Disgraceful</u>"'s <u>in</u> <u>the</u> <u>book</u> <u>with</u> <u>the</u> <u>bear</u> <u>and</u> <u>the</u> <u>fish</u> <u>in</u>! Immediately, Hugh remembered "grace" from <u>Wish</u> <u>Again</u>, <u>Big</u> <u>Bear</u>, borrowed (for the second time) in January 1976. In this easy reader, the fish, endeavoring to escape Big Bear's appetite by claiming magic powers, had chanted a rhyme intended to make Big Bear graceful.

A: <u>Small Bear</u>--(confused, she hesitated)
M: <u>Wish Again</u>, <u>Big Bear</u>?
H & M (quoting): "Let Big Bear chase
                      The bird of grace."
M: I don't think "disgraceful" was in there--
A: "<u>Disgraceful</u>" <u>was in there</u>, <u>yes</u> (decisively).
In fact the word "disgraceful" does not appear, but "graceful"
does--seven times in thirty-four short pages.

Though not strictly relevant to <u>Doctor Dolittle</u>, Anna's reaction is a vivid example of her long-term recall. What was it
about the word "grace" which so struck her that she has carried it, together with its fictional context, for so many
months? Maureen believes that without noting it, she must have
spontaneously glossed it for Anna, in reading <u>Wish Again</u>,
<u>Big Bear</u>, and found the exercise difficult. Another factor
may be that Anna has occasionally been told that her name
"Anna" signifies "grace," and this may have made the word
disproportionately important to her.

I read the chapter title "The Barbary Dragon" (on p. 161).
A: <u>What is it</u>? <u>Can we see it</u>?

The "Dragon" is actually a pirate chief with a flowery name,
but Anna clearly thinks of some specialized ("barbary") form
of winged monster! Notice that here Anna's old and new ways of
identifying a novel thing in a book are juxtaposed: "What is
it?" is the question she has been utilizing for years; "Can we
see it?" with its variants "Can I have one?" or "Can I go
there when I'm a big girl?" are more recent.

On p. 163 the illustration shows Too-Too, Gub-Gub, and the
Doctor looking over their bulwark toward the Doctor's old
ship, which the Pirates have commandeered.
A: <u>Why--why--why--are they looking like</u> that? <u>Why are they</u>
   <u>looking over the edge of that thing</u>? [I.e., bulwark.]
(Hugh explained that they were standing at the ship's side,
looking toward the other ship.)
A: <u>Is that the Doctor's ship</u>?
(We explained that it was, but that he now has the pirates'
ship because his own had been going to sink.)
A: <u>Yes--that was good</u>.
From the confidence of her tone, and the general level of
understanding she seems to have in this book, we are sure that
she meant that it was good that the Doctor had found a safer
vessel.
A: <u>Why are they</u> "<u>Barbary Pirates</u>"?

From her earlier toyings with "Barbary" it is now clear that
she wanted that word to be explained rather than to have an
account of what had motivated Ben Ali and his crew to become
pirates!

<u>19</u> June '76. This morning at Anna's behest I read chaps. 15
and 16 (no comment), and tonight chap. 17. Later she asked:
<u>Why</u> <u>was</u> <u>his</u> <u>name</u> <u>Ben</u> <u>Ali</u>, <u>do</u> <u>you</u> <u>know</u>? I explained that Ben
Ali, the "Barbary Dragon's" real name, was the "son of Ali,"
but she said firmly <u>He's</u> <u>Ben</u> <u>and</u> <u>he's</u> <u>Ali</u>. In other words she
is asking why he has two names ("Ben" as a boy's name is
already known to her). Ben Ali is actually last seen in chap.
15, though referred to again in chap. 17; Anna is still allud-
ing to the Pirates after they have ceased to be part of the
ongoing cast of characters. (Remember that <u>The</u> <u>Pirates'</u> <u>Tale</u>
was one of her earliest books.)

<u>20</u> June '76. Chap. 18 this morning--no comment. During the
current yo-yo craze, Anna regularly refers to the toys as
"Too-Toos," using the name of the Doctor's owl companion.

<u>30</u> June '76. Anna asked twice today for "a book from the
lounge room" and was satisfied with our nomination of <u>Doctor</u>
<u>Dolittle</u>. No comment on either occasion, though her face
expressed emotions: chap. 19 contains a dramatic account of
the rediscovery of the boy's uncle, marooned by the Pirates on
a bare rock in the middle of the ocean.

<u>1</u> <u>July</u> '76. We read the final chapter.
A (p. 223): <u>That's</u> <u>the</u> <u>end</u> <u>of</u> <u>the</u> <u>book</u>!
  (illus., p. 221) <u>What's</u> <u>that</u>? [a weeping willow with a
  table beneath it]
<u>What's</u> <u>he</u> [Gub-Gub] <u>doing</u> <u>there</u>? [digging]

Longterm Impact
Though Anna heard the first few chapters of <u>Doctor</u> <u>Dolittle</u>
again on several occasions, she never persevered with the book
long enough to request a complete reread. Apart from an identification of herself as a pushmi-pullyu in the course of playing "animals" (2 July '76) and an allusion to the Barbary
Pirates' red-sailed ship (3 July '76) in the course of a
conversation with us about Vikings, all of Anna's later references were to the events of the first couple of chapters. She
explained to her grandmother, who had just read the incident
where one of the Doctor's lady patients is about to sit on a
porcupine: <u>And</u> <u>anyway</u>, <u>she</u> <u>never</u> <u>came</u> <u>back</u> <u>because</u> <u>he</u> <u>was</u>
<u>going</u> <u>to</u> <u>be</u> <u>an</u> <u>animal</u> <u>doctor</u> <u>instead</u> (5 November '76).

On 3 September '76, during a reading of chap. 1 she attempted
to reproduce Polynesia's utterance in bird language, and asked
(p. 33) "How do I talk with my ears?" after Polynesia has told
the Doctor that dogs communicate in this way.

The notion of animal language was the only part of the book
which persisted in play and conversation outside the reading
sessions themselves. Anna's standard game was to utter a
string of nonsense syllables (often in a high screechy voice
such as we had employed in reading Polynesia) and then ask us
what this meant; alternatively, she would "translate" herself
for our benefit. This game is recorded no less than five
times, with slight variations, between July and December 1976.

ANALYSIS

In some ways the record for The Story of Doctor Dolittle
more closely resembles a series of early entries for a picture
book than one would expect. This could be because (apart from
simple identification of figures and objects in the illustrations, which can be regarded almost as an archaic survival,
unrelated to the impact of the narrative itself) Anna's responses are still at the "first reading" stage which normally
precludes complex speculations, statements of like and dislike, and plot-related questioning. On the other hand, it is
also true to say that the chronological period from which the
Doctor Dolittle entries come is marked by lack of explicit
verbal comment. For almost six months, much of Anna's response
to the books she heard went underground; her comments and
questions during reading sessions were few and brief, and we
could safely omit the tape recorder on many occasions. It may
be significant that Anna's baby sister Morwenna was born in
September of this year.

In spite of the relative thinness of Anna's articulated commentary, it is possible to discern something of the shape of her
response. The events of chaps. 1 and 2, which narrate the
Doctor's initiation into animal languages and his decision to
become an animal doctor, provoked comment and creative reworking both at the time she encountered them and thereafter. The
shipwreck represented an emotional peak, but there were no
later references to it, whereas the Barbary Pirates remained
important for some time; we may reasonably assume that Anna's
playing with the word "Barbary" and our suspicion that she did
not in fact have any clear idea of the meaning are merely the
surface indications of a deeper concern with the menace posed

by the pirates, as with her need to identify the Wild Things at 2.0-2.6. Certainly to Anna the Jolliginki episodes in _Doctor Dolittle_ provided plenty of opportunities for juggling with names and identities if Anna had chosen to take them. We may surmise that Anna was disappointed to find kings, queens and princes who wore no robes, lived in very ordinary grass huts, and did few of the spectacular things she has learned to associate with royalty.

7

The Shape of Anna's Response

There are two ways in which we can look at the material
collected in the preceding sections. We can examine the shape
of Anna's response in itself, concentrating on the strategies
she employed to take hold of the books, her content preoccupations, and the extent to which these things remained constant
over the period covered. Alternatively, we can consider Anna's
response in relation to the full field of experience offered
by each book. In other words, we can concentrate our attention
either on what Anna said, saw, and did or on what she did not
see, failed to mention, failed to act out. Ultimately the two
approaches are necessarily complementary, and we propose to
employ both. A study of Anna's explicit responses in isolation
from the field from which they were selected runs the considerable danger of presuming that what was unspoken did not exist.
While we can reasonably assume that some areas of experience
offered by the books remained mysterious to her, it is equally
clear that others, on which Anna offered only minimal comment,
had an effect far out of proportion to the amount she said. As
previously, we will need to interpret, to make discriminations
based on what we hope is a full and sharp awareness of Anna's
overall perception of each story; these interpretations cannot
really be objective, but at least they can be measured against
the evidence of Anna's overt reactions, and readers can make
their own appraisal of our accuracy.

In toto, the picture offered by our six case studies may not
differ greatly from what many readers may have expected. It
would be reasonable to predict that a preschool child, even
one with a wide knowledge of pictures and stories, would spend

much of her time asking questions designed to extend her comprehension of factual aspects of the experiences offered by
books--the identification of unfamiliar pictured objects or
words; the placing of details of an illustration in relation
to its main subject, the querying of already known figures in
unfamiliar poses. Similarly, it might be expected that a child
below the age of five would not voice many specific reactions
to the emotional aspects of a fiction or make many evaluative
statements. Rather, we would expect to look for evidence of
emotional impact, or favorable evaluation of a book, in the
number of times its rereading was requested or in incidental
play or talk relating to particular characters or incidents.
All of this does in fact happen with Anna. But, as we have
already seen in examining her responses to individual books,
it is neither necessary nor desirable to separate off the seemingly factual, cognitively oriented responses from the much
smaller number of overtly affective ones. Rather, when we look
closely at a series of responses over time to a particular
character or incident or illustration, we begin to see how
many of the remarks that seem purely concerned with the mun-
dane business of comprehending are the surface indications of
underlying concerns and preoccupations.

Not solely in Rapunzel, but throughout the six extracts from
the record, a very large proportion of the details on which
Anna requested information, or which she wanted to name or
classify, related to people (or to nonhuman but recognizably
animate protagonists like the Wild Things, the Moomins, and
the Little Red Lighthouse), to their faces, their clothes,
their footwear, and to objects carried in their hands or pro-
jecting from their bodies. From the purely visual point of
view, this reflects a principle early learned by Anna that the
human (or animal) figure is the focal point of a picture that
contains it; in terms of Anna's orientation toward narrative,
it is also laying the foundations for an approach in which
characters are very important.

In approaching the characters of a new book, Anna employed a
number of strategies, each simple enough and yet together
amounting to a multifunctional instrument for grasping and
assimilating the essential features of protagonists just
encountered. We have seen how Anna's habit of looking through
her books before they were ever read to her enabled her to
pinpoint in advance characters who might later be significant
and to establish their identity. When "chapter books" became
the norm, the process was extended to searching ahead for
anyone named in the title of the next chapter. In the case of
some characters, it was sufficient for Anna to be able to name

them, either in advance or during an actual reading; for others, she required more information--their physical appearance first and foremost but sometimes also their context. Did they have a home? a mother and father? friends? In this process Anna establishes to what extent fictional characters fit the mold of her own life or of fictional people who resemble her.

Next, and again applied only to a select range of characters, are a series of procedures in which Anna does not ask adults for information but enters into the fiction by duplicating fragments of the character's appearance or behavior--"facing like the Muskrat," exclaiming "Watch my rocks--keep away" like the lighthouse or "Pee-Hoo!" like Moomintroll, attempting to reproduce a special language as in Doctor Dolittle and Finn Family Moomintroll, role playing an incident involving a character or inventing new actions for herself to perform while being that character. This latter end of the spectrum presents us with behavior that has to do with Anna's embryonic grasp of plot as well, since the incidents which Anna elects to replay may fairly be considered, by the same principle of interpretation we have employed all along, of some significance to her. That portion of Anna's response where imitation of some aspect of a book inspires original play and creative verbal explorations will be the subject of the next chapter.

The areas covered by Anna's explicit comment are not random but reflect interaction between the underlying processes she uses to organize her experience and, specifically, her memories of key images, which she uses to assimilate new things to the model of old experience. On our way through the detailed material, we have already noted examples of this: when Anna asked of the unfamiliar word "breakers" in chap. 3 of Finn Family Moomintroll "did it break?" she was presumably hearing in the word the possibility of hurt and loss--the same association which led her to ask "Was all their things gone?" after the shipwreck in The Story of Doctor Dolittle, an association that apparently had its origin in the crash of the fat black tug in The Little Red Lighthouse. Similarly in Rapunzel, questions or statements about houses, or the difference between houses and towers, may well reflect Anna's much earlier, but long-preserved anxieties about shut doors and children being locked in their rooms because of naughtiness, as happened in Where the Wild Things Are (globally, they may mark latent fear of the witch).

The same motivation which drove Anna to search for, almost to demand, consistency on a literal level--that wall-less

houses have walls "like ours," that a character should be the
same size on each page instead of suddenly swelling and
diminishing--must also have been responsible for her preoccupation with change. "Now the lighthouse can turn itself on!"--
why have not other components of its state altered? Max's hat
is on--now it is off--now it has apparently been replaced by a
crown; Doctor Dolittle used to be a people doctor but he
became an animal doctor; the Hobgoblin's hat can change
Moomintroll's appearance so drastically that we need to
reestablish his identity by asking about the new picture of
him. Change, a concept that brings the category of familiar
things into a direct relationship with the category of
unfamiliar things, is a key area for Anna. And apart from
change as such, any incongruous juxtaposition of elements not
normally found together is subject to question and comment.
Why does Rapunzel wear leaves in her hair? Why does a man
Hemulen wear a dress?

We have already worked backward from Anna's wish to establish
the meaning of "breaker" to her larger concern with hurt and
loss. But, as we have seen when examining the immediate context of that remark in Finn Family Moomintroll, we can also
work laterally within the text itself, discovering that it is
not fortuitous that a lexical question should be asked of this
particular passage, since Anna went on to ask about the Hattifatteners, a subject of emotional as well as intellectual
concern. As we said in that chapter, Anna can extend her
explicit comment backward and forward around nodal points of
initial reaction. Some of the commonest of these nodes we've
already examined: the characters (particularly those who by
strange appearance or menacing behavior call for special
attention); exclamations, of a dramatic or humorous nature. It
seems as if having established some sure ground by way of such
points, Anna can then turn her attention to other features of
the narrative surrounding them; concern for the Hemulen's
sadness comes only after she has worried about the impropriety
of his wearing a dress; realization that Sniff is not being
let in on the secret of the origin of the raspberry juice
follows play with the simple and appealing notion that the
juice is magically transformed seawater.

The "grid" of initial response to a new book remains remarkably constant from age 2.0 to age 5.0: apart from the early
memorizing of exclamations, such focal points as clothing and
food and facial expressions noted in responses to Where the
Wild Things Are crop up again in Rapunzel and yet again in
Finn Family Moomintroll. This grid depends heavily on

previously set associations; is it possible to see, in the overall pattern of responses to the six books, changes over time? The answer is yes, but only a qualified yes, since the extremely limited resources of Anna's vocabulary and syntax in the period before age 3.0 make it difficult for us to be sure that she did not intend as much by her early comments as by later ones which seem to have the same thrust, though far more specific wording. Moreover, it is difficult to measure a variable like "proportion of comment relating to the text" when we are comparing a 200-word full-color picture book like A Lion in the Meadow with a 170-page novel illustrated every few pages in black and white. What we can say is that over the span covered by our selections, Anna's ability to verbalize evaluations of individual pictures or characters increases, and more of her statements refer not simply to one illustration or to a single feature of one illustration but to the picture or the story as a whole. The number of such statements remains tiny, but they are there, in Rapunzel, in Finn Family Moomintroll, in the later response to The Little Red Lighthouse: "This is a pretty page." "This is a frightening story." "That was good." "I like this one--but at the end I'm frightened."

The conventions of adult-created fiction intended for an audience of young children are limited in number. It isn't surprising, then, that the six books we have chosen for this part of our study should present their listeners and viewers with much similarity in structure and theme. To the adult reader, for example, one such unifying theme is the presentation of the adult/child relationship: four of the books-- A Lion in the Meadow, Where the Wild Things Are, The Little Red Lighthouse, and Rapunzel--present the child/adult relationship in terms of some degree of conflict or anxiety. True, the Wild Things and the Great Gray Bridge are not literally adults, but their status as symbols of adult size and power is fairly obvious. At the expense of his doubting mother, the little boy in A Lion in the Meadow proves he told the truth, so that the text ends: "The mother never made up a story again"; mischievous Max, shut in his room by his mother, who is offstage throughout, meets and subdues a whole countryside of massive Wild Things and on his return finds that he has been given supper after all. The Little Red Lighthouse, shamed by the powerful light of the Great Gray Bridge, discovers that it can still perform an independent and valued function. And Rapunzel, who is torn from her real parents as a baby by the grim witch, is able eventually to escape her and start a new life with her Prince.

(In fact, both Rapunzel and Where the Wild Things Are split
the parent figure into two--familiar/accepting and unfamiliar/
menacing--which serves to ease the problem of portraying
children's ambivalent feelings toward their real parents.)

Earlier, when discussing Anna's reactions to The Little Red
Lighthouse, we guessed that the child/adult theme in that
story was not grasped by her; at all events her almost total
lack of explicit verbal reaction to the bridge paralleled her
apparent ignoring of the little boy's mother in A Lion in
the Meadow. Of course, lack of verbal response does not
necessarily mean that Anna failed to perceive the theme in
these two books. In the remaining stories, Anna not only
recognized but commented persistently on the parent figures.

The child/adult theme which we have been discussing enables us
to view Anna's response pattern in relation to one of the
fields of potential involvement offered by the books. But in
itself, the possible conflict between adult and child can be
subsumed beneath a wider theme, most obviously exemplified in
The Story of Doctor Dolittle, where the hero journeys out of
a familiar domestic setting into strange lands inhabited by
exotic (and potentially menacing) creatures, to return safely
at the end. In its broadest form, this pattern presents first
a familiar element, then an unfamiliar element, with a final
return to the familiar; the unfamiliar element may be simply
encountered, or it may be conquered (as in Wild Things and
Doctor Dolittle), or it may remain in antagonistic indepen-
dence (like the Witch and the Groke) or prove unexpectedly
friendly (like the Gray Bridge or the Hobgoblin). In fact,
some narratives present a very commonly used refinement on the
basic binary structure in which the first-presented unfamiliar
character or creature is subsequently incorporated within the
ambit of the hero, becomes his companion or helper, and aids
him against the true antagonist who remains unfamiliar. This
happens in A Lion in the Meadow. One of the things that
can thus be said to happen in many narratives based on this
pattern is that the familiar expands its territory at the
expense of the unfamiliar. What was once unknown becomes known
(even if still feared). The appropriateness to childhood of
this expansion of "me" into the world of "not me" is obvious,
and equally clear is the way Anna's own explicit responses
either outline the map of familiar and unfamiliar already
offered by the book or, failing to follow the contour lines
provided, nevertheless indicate the presence of a new
familiar/unfamiliar structure abstracted by Anna from the
elements provided.

Ignoring the dragon, which Margaret Mahy offers as the real
source of menace and the true unfamiliar, Anna calls A Lion
in the Meadow "lion, boy" or "naughty boy"; the latter indicates her linking of the boy with her own domestic world; the
apple-eating scene seems to provide some element of the
strange or puzzling, though we cannot say in what the exotic
element consists. Things are clearer in Where the Wild Things
Are, where relative densities of comment neatly delimit the
book's own "domestic" and "exotic" foci. In The Little Red
Lighthouse Anna establishes herself on the side of the lighthouse, as the text intends. The text offers her the bridge as
representative of the unfamiliar/menacing category, but for
Anna the tug's wreck is a stronger center and her responses
cluster around it. In Rapunzel Anna's concentration on the
details of the first opening, and in particular on the resemblances between the house and her own image of a dwelling,
strikingly balances her absorption in the latter part of the
tale with the witch and her tower; the familiar/safe vs.
unfamiliar/menacing structure is clear, and Anna has relatively little interest in the Prince and the scenes of
restoration at the end. Finn Family Moomintroll, an episodic
narrative, contains one or two ventures into the unfamiliar,
like the voyage to Hattifatteners' Lonely Island, but its
basic theme is of the transformation of the familiar into the
exotic, so that it presents a special case. Yet here again,
Anna's thrust was to establish firm identification of the
recurring familiar characters, balanced by a concentration in
play on those transformations she could cope with using her
own resources. For clearer concentration on the Groke as a
perceived exotic danger, see chap. 14, "Heroes and Villains,"
for Anna's reaction to Jansson's Who Will Comfort Toffle?

If Finn Family Moomintroll by its provision of numerous
unfamiliars and several potential sources of menace (Groke,
Hobgoblin, Hattifatteners, transmogrified false teeth) does
not enable us to see Anna's pattern clearly, this is not the
case with Doctor Dolittle. Here, the very sparseness of her
comments facilitates our perception that Anna once again con-
centrates her attention first on the domestic initial chapters
and then, of the several possible exotic foci, selects the
Barbary Pirates as her symbol of the unfamiliar/menacing
(the Barbary Pirates themselves being both familiar, insofar
as they are pirates, and unfamiliar, insofar as they are
"Barbary").

The strength of this pattern is further indicated by Anna's
paucity of remarks on time- and space-filling interludes

(usually journeys) that most of the fictions interpose between
the initial presentation of the familiar and the later introduction of the unfamiliar. It is as if she knows that these
are conventional fillers, as if she has from very early developed a sense of story shape that tells her what is important
and what is not. As we said at the outset when beginning our
analysis of the Lion in the Meadow record, Anna's response
is nothing if not selective, and in that selectivity lies the
germ of what adults call aesthetic appreciation. To describe
and understand Anna's aesthetic more fully than has been possible here will be our business in part 3.

Part 2
The Maker

Introduction

So far we have been primarily concerned with Anna's recorded
responses to stories while still in the presence of the stimulus; but especially in the case of Finn Family Moomintroll we
have had a glimpse of how frequently she alluded to her books
outside the reading sessions themselves. Such allusion ranges
all the way from verbatim quotation of phrases, lines, or
whole stories, through extensive incorporation of literary
language into her own conversation, to games and role-playing
inspired by fictional characters and incidents, and, at the
furthest extreme, wholly improvised monologues and stories
that owe relatively little to their book sources. We have
chosen to restrict ourselves in this part primarily to the
games and the monologues, which seem richer in possibilities
for analysis than the relatively predictable process of vocabulary extension or the way she became proficient at verbatim
quotation and then allowed the skill to fall into relative
disuse. In the acting of book scenes Anna sticks relatively
closely to her sources, and we can often learn something of
value about her attitude to them from a study of the games
alone; in the case of the monologues, the situation is
reversed--Anna's compositions say little about the specific
material that inspires them but a great deal about her concept
of narrative in the abstract.

8

Fiction Re-created:
Conversation and Play

To read our recorded accounts of Anna's games is to be struck
by the wholeness of her experience: the stimulus she received
from her reading was no different in kind from any other stimulus. Anna's play drew on whatever was available, words and
pictures as much as objects and people, and she used them all
in ways that were meaningful to her. But in talking about the
specific relationships that existed between Anna's play and
her experience of books, it does seem necessary to begin with
a brief description of the overall pattern of her play activities. Little need be said about the very early period: Anna
was a normal, healthy baby who seemed to ask, and was certainly given, a high stimulus input. She went through the
stages of crawling, running (rather than walking), and intent
exploration of her home and garden in ways that all parents
are familiar with. We should repeat here that her play patterns were influenced by the fact that most of the time she
and Maureen were alone in the house, and that she did not
often have another child to play with. As will be evident in
the course of this chapter, we took part in Anna's imaginative
play where we could or encouraged her verbally when we could
not join in. We also modeled fantasy play, particularly with a
witch puppet and dolls that talked in voices suspiciously like
Maureen's, or with the annual firewood pile from which Hugh
and Anna made forts.

When she was 1.2 we gave her a toy lawnmower, which made an
astounding racket, and which she delighted in pushing outside.
At 2.0 she was recorded as playing with her stuffed giraffe

Ken Kenyek, who was being "naughty" and "eating" various things: <u>Kenyek</u> <u>eating</u> <u>Anna</u> <u>ear</u>!--<u>Kenyek</u> <u>eating</u> <u>Anna</u> <u>nose</u>!

At 2.1 she was chastising her dolls and accusing them of wrong-doing, role-playing the parent with her dolls in the child role. At 2.2, when looking at a library book, she put it down stating her intention: <u>Get</u> <u>Ken</u> <u>Kenyek</u>. <u>Show</u> <u>Ken</u> <u>Kenyek</u> <u>sheeps</u>, <u>hens</u>!

All that year, 2.0-2.11, the descriptions of Anna's play have frequent reference to her doll family: pushed in a stroller, taken on train and ship "journeys" in clothes baskets and car-tons, talking and being made to mimic book characters. When she was 2.9, we noted her "look out" game, in which her dolls were made to look out through windows or over veranda rails, a simple ritual which Anna managed to invest with much joyous-ness. "Children who show consistent make-believe play also manifest a good deal of positive emotion--much smiling and indications of liveliness and elation. Further, they are somewhat more inclined to be able to concentrate" (Singer, 1975, p. 136). Singer's judgment certainly describes Anna accurately.

At 3.2 there is a diary entry recording Anna's play for one day of varied activity, both physical and verbal. The events are recollected in rather desperate tranquillity at night, without any attempt to note the sequence. On that day, Anna was superhumanly full of energy and ideas and patter: making "grass salad" (magnetized plastic letters, grass clippings, and stones in our best stainless steel saucepan); baking (wax crayons and felt pens and Play-Doh in a glass mortar); tell-ing us about the nasty ogre who lived in Hugh's bedside cabi-net and who ate "fish and salads--and slugs." We refused to go to see him because Anna emphasized how nasty he was, and she immediately declared that he was nice. Unconvinced, we re-mained drinking coffee. There was time left for jumping rope, not with a rope, but with two draft-excluding "sausages" from the living room.

At one point, Anna came to Maureen saying "a rhyme." It changed a little as she was questioned, but remained nearly fixed as:
"<u>Tippitty</u> <u>Toppetty</u>" (yes, she named it!).
<u>Tippitty</u> <u>Toppetty</u> <u>made</u> <u>a</u> <u>nest</u> <u>in</u> <u>his</u> <u>screw</u>.
<u>The</u> <u>magnificent</u> <u>thing</u> <u>made</u> <u>a</u> <u>nest</u> <u>in</u> <u>his</u> <u>screw</u>.
<u>The</u> <u>magnificent</u> <u>thing</u> <u>made</u> <u>a</u> <u>girl</u> <u>in</u> <u>his</u> <u>screw</u>.

> A lady came out and gave him a shot.
> And when he was gone,
> Tippitty Top was gone.

Provenance was elusive at first, although we thought of Beatrix Potter's "at the tippitty top of the hill" from Squirrel Nutkin (Potter, 1907, p. 38). But Anna was reciting in an exaggeratedly rhythmic way that suggested someone had taught it to her. "Made a nest in his screw" (made a nest in his shoe?) reminded us of On the Day Peter Stuyvesant Sailed into Town: "While some chickens and ducks made a nest in his hat" (Lobel, 1971, stanza 8). "A lady came out and gave him a shot" recalls "The baker came out and gave him a clout," which we'd read in Fee Fi Fo Fum (Briggs, 1964).

But the meter itself we recognized as like A. A. Milne's "Hoppity" from When We Were Very Young. One of the rare mornings when we were listening to "Kindergarten of the Air" (a radio program for preschoolers which subsequently became a regular feature of our Monday to Friday routine) we heard this poem recited in an extravagantly rhythmic manner and so on occasion Maureen had parodied it. Our detective work was validated a couple of hours later when Anna added:

> Tippitty Top made a nest in his screw,
> And the geese in his path made a squawking,

quoting verbatim a later line from the same stanza of Peter Stuyvesant.

Outside, tidying up the yard after her manifold (and manifest) activities, she steadied the "gangplank" for her "ship," "so the cats won't sleep on it", and said:

> Up the gangplank we go
> To where the engines puff and blow.

This is a variant of a couplet in "Rupert and Ozzie" in the 1960 Rupert Annual (p. 70):

> "Right through the tunnel tracks they go
> To where the engines puff and blow."

Then as Hugh was chopping up ingredients for the evening meal, Anna listed those of which she wanted a piece:

A: Yes, garlic, and onions and--little men--
H: And what, Anna?
A: Little men--and superballs!

Anna owned her own superball, a small ball of some kind of synthetic which bounced extraordinarily high, but the "little men" seemed to come straight from her fertile brain. The game of substituting incongruous elements among a list of familiar things is one that many parents will recognize.

And at the evening meal, Hugh said "Once upon a time . . ."; straightway Anna took over: There was a lonely little baby. It had dark little teeth and golden hair, and the ogre ate him, and he died. This owes something to Zeralda's Ogre, but the loneliness of the baby was borrowed from Maureen's remark a few minutes before about how lonely new babies are when they are left in little beds by themselves after they are born.

The picture that emerges from such a day is true to Anna, energetically using all that came to hand and mind as part of her games. Specifically, we notice the blend of verbal and physical play, improvised rhyme and story alongside role-playing games, skipping and "cooking." The ease with which Anna slots her own phrases into a metrical scheme derived from an A. A. Milne poem is no different from the way she mixes plastic letters and grass instead of regular food in a sauce-pan.

From then on until 4.6, much of Anna's play involved setting up an imaginary situation and casting herself in a particular role within it:
3.9: We'll be gardeners, and I'll be the gardener's little
      girl.
3.11: I'm a robber--a bad robber who hurts people in hospi-
      tals.
4.0: With bared teeth, and growling, Anna claimed to be
      Tyrannosaurus Rex.

From 4.0 on, Anna devoted a higher proportion of her time to riding her two-wheeled bike, painting, drawing, coloring in, playing her toy organ, and making constructions with blocks; with the advent of school and the increased presence of other children, it becomes more difficult to discuss her "spontane-ous" play, and so we end our account here.

The few published records of young children's book experiences make much of the way stories influenced the child's games and language use, seeing such influence as an exciting proof of the relevance of the book to the child and an index of his comprehension (see White, 1954; Butler, 1979). But there is a great deal more to be learned from book-inspired play and talk. In our case, we can treat Anna's choice of incidents or phrases to reproduce as an indication of their significance

for her; we can ask to what degree she elaborated upon the
original; how many scenes or incidents she seemed prepared to
cope with in a single period of play or conversation; whether
a story had only a single crux as far as she was concerned;
whether, in role-playing games Anna took more than one role
herself, and which roles she chose.

In one of Anna's earliest book-based games (1.9) she is recorded as standing on top of a small heap of stones in our
back garden, exclaiming the words "sea serpent" and then
rushing off to her room to fetch the 1964 Rupert Annual: in
several frames of the story "Rupert and the Rock Pool," Rupert
confronts the Serpent from a rocky rise of some sort (pp.
105-8). Anna's words showed that she perceived a resemblance
between her own stance and Rupert's, and we notice that she
has selected for this primitive role playing a picture that
shows two characters in confrontation, a pattern that will
recur in later games of literary provenance.

At 2.0 there began a game based on Gunilla Wolde's Thomas
Goes Out which depended on assistance from an adult--an
early instance of later fully developed improvisations in
which Anna assigned roles to any available bystanders as well
as to herself. Thomas depicts a small boy's amusingly incom-
petent attempts to dress himself in full winter gear, and the
text for Op. 9 reads: "Is he ready now?/No--he's forgotten his
long, green trousers." Pointing to this page Anna said to
Maureen "ready now?" to which Maureen was obviously expected
to reply with the second text line. One day we counted and
found that Anna had asked seven times in a row, requiring the
ritual response on each occasion. The game would disappear and
reemerge now and then (2.6, 2.11, 3.3) but by 2.8 had lost
ground to a second Thomas-derived game which Anna had now
acquired enough dexterity to embark upon. She enjoyed putting
her clothes on when she could; finding her pajamas dumped on
the bathroom floor in readiness for her bath, she usually sat
down to put her pajama trousers on over her daytime pants.
Giggling, she would put both feet in one trouser leg, repeating the words of the book (Op. 5): "'That can't be right,'
says Thomas, as ten pink toes peep out of one trouser leg."
Sometimes at 2.10 she would say the words but omit the actions.
At 2.11 she shortened the utterance to "ten pink toes"; at
3.2, she abandoned giggles and chuckles and simply attempted
to put both feet in one trouser leg and then asked how Thomas
could dress himself. Notice that the "Is he ready now?" game
remained unaltered until its disappearance, because its very
existence depended upon its antiphonal nature. The "ten pink

toes" game on the other hand, engaging Anna only, became increasingly truncated, ending in a serious attempt to puzzle out how Thomas could cope with something she could not.

Probably the continuation of the "Is he ready now?" game depended altogether on a parent's initial willingness to enter into it as if each repetition was a fresh beginning. The strength of the trouser game resided in the ready availability of pants for bed and winter wear, coinciding with the still novel achievement of putting them on. These were the factors in Anna's own life which supported the Thomas games and made possible their endurance over time; but what can the games tell us about Anna's responses to Thomas itself? The first game involves no action. Anna simply selected from the book a question-and-reply segment which was easy for her to master and derived satisfaction from obtaining a predictable adult response. But we can see again the two-element pattern of the Rupert game, with Anna's question complementing the adult's reply, just as Rupert on his rock confronts the Serpent. The second Thomas game is more firmly dependent on Anna's own activities: living in a warm climate, she possessed little of Thomas's wardrobe of winter clothes, but she could easily imitate, and see the fun in, putting both feet into one trouser leg. In this case, then, she seems to have selected an incident that was possible for her to replay exactly and relevant to her own life.

In some of the cases we have looked at so far, what seems to have occurred is that Anna found herself with a prop that triggered off a memory of a fictional scene.[1] In the example that follows, the prop was unwittingly provided by Maureen, whose laudatory ambition it was to instruct Anna about buoyancy. Accordingly she gave Anna (2.11) a cup three parts full of water, with a cork afloat. Anna announced that she was "starching." Her sole model for this household activity was Mrs. Tiggy-Winkle, who on p. 40 of The Tale of Mrs. Tiggy-Winkle uses for starching a vessel very similar in shape to the cup Anna had. There seems little likelihood that Anna would have recalled Mrs. Tiggy's action without the bowl. Similarly we guess that Anna at 3.0, holding a treasured Rupert doll which had been Hugh's, sensed the possibilities offered by her window ledge. Seeing Maureen just outside, pegging out the washing, she showed her Rupert "lying in his manger" on the windowsill. She draped a blanket over him, and when Maureen entered the room, again showed "Rupert in his manger." In a quiet reflective tone (which Maureen recognized as her own), Anna then began to speak:

> Rupert lies in his manger beside the sea.
> Rupert lies in his manger beside the sea.
> Gently the waves rock him to sleep.
> But no one sings him a lullaby.

Then as if she realized her source (Trude Alberti's The Animals' Lullaby), she began again from the beginning:

> Where does the baby seal sleep?
> He lives with his mother beside the sea.
> Gently the waves rock him to sleep
> But no one sings him a lullaby.

She differs from the published text (Op. 1) only in using "lives with" for "lies near"; "no one" for "nobody." It would seem that the pattern "mother beside the sea" generated the phonetically similar "manger beside the sea."

Again, we learn little about Anna's attitude to Rupert or The Animals' Lullaby or the story of Jesus from these references. Her "Snow White" games have much more to tell us about the way she saw the story itself. Anna encountered "Snow White" in five versions, and over the period 3.0-4.6 it had a great deal of impact on her; accordingly we shall give in full the record of Anna's re-creation of the story, bearing in mind that no other tale stimulated Anna to refer to it or reenact it so often.

First came a storytelling of "Snow White" in the night watches when Anna was 3.0, which Anna showed no particular interest in at the time. Two days later, Anna was looking at Spier's To Market, to Market, for the third time, and came to the final scene. She forsook the bedward-wending farmer, whose glowing lantern had earlier caught her eye in this opening. Instead, she concentrated on the apple tree at the extreme right and the fruit at its roots: Are they all right? We said that the wind had blown them off. Anna's next statement seemed staggeringly inconsequential: They are red. By putting the two utterances together, we realized that this distrust for red apples stemmed from the story of "Snow White." We assured Anna that if we ate a red apple, we should be all right.

At 3.6 there was an unidentified television version of "Snow White" which Anna watched with her grandmother for company. At 3.7 her attention was drawn to Bernadette Watts's (1971) picture book and this became the basic text. Her reactions to it when it was being read to her were strong (they can be found in chap. 14, "Heroes and Villains"); we shall look here only

at Anna's allusions to "Snow White" outside the reading
sessions.

11 March '76. Maureen was busy all day preparing for dinner
guests and did not make time to record verbatim the game that
Anna tried to impose on her in the morning. She had to be
"Winnie Bear's wicked stepmother," but since Anna was so
involved in the game, Maureen really felt she was playing
Anna's wicked stepmother. Maureen was told to speak in a
"convenient voice" which Anna defined as "bad-tempered" when
asked for elucidation. Maureen cooperated for a few exchanges,
but at length refused to continue.

The Watts version was then returned to the library, and no
more was said till 13 March '76 when Anna (now 3.8) caught
Hugh in the act of cleaning up rat poison pellets, knocked
over by an enterprising mouse which had led the autumn incur-
sion into our hall closet. Up till then we had hypocritically
concealed from Anna the way we bait mice. Hugh explained to
Anna what he was doing, and that she should not touch the rat
bait because it was poisonous: Anna's response was: We mustn't
put that poison on any apples.

22 March '76. Anna, observing Hugh with disfavor, declared that
he had some prickles (i.e., hair from his moustache) in his
mouth. Then with loud confidence she asserted: And I think they
are bad poison ones, and they will go down into your stomach.

23 March '76. Anna, recalling a word from her current library book, asked what a "hobby" was, and for examples. But
even after an extended discussion about hobbies as they ate
their evening meal alone, she tried to rouse Maureen from the
book she was reading silently, by describing a fierce bad
hobby [that] is coming through the door. It's a bad poison
one and it's going to hurt us!

The same day, Anna looked distastefully at a small apple that
was brought her and made some largely indecipherable comment
about poison. Hastily, she was assured that it was not poisoned. Anna remarked: We should poison an apple for the snails
and slugs. I don't like them. Later that day she said: I am
glad I don't have a stepmother. This helps to explain her
earlier reluctance to have Maureen play her stepmother without
a toy bear as an intermediary.

The following day Anna was offered an apple, but she settled
for a passion fruit and between spoonfuls said: Snow White was

a silly girl because she didn't know what the poisoned apple
was. She stoutly maintained that she wouldn't be taken in
that way.

23 April '76. (Anna 3.9). We went to a stage production of
Snow White and the Seven Dwarfs which featured real dwarfs.
Anna talked about it, selecting inconsequential details, but
particularly she spoke about a rabbit (obviously a well-
disguised dwarf) that she had most desperately wanted to go up
on stage to pat. The Jarrell-Burkert version of the story was
brought out to reinforce the memories, but not surprisingly it
resulted in Anna's observation that the dwarfs looked different.

11 May '76. Anna (3.10) asked for the second time (earlier
instance not dated) why Snow White's stepmother should want to
kill her. The first, lengthy explanation was inadequate, but
the second, briefer version Anna accepted straightway: "Because she wanted to be the most beautiful person in the world."
A: I would never do that.
We were so stunned by what Anna next said that even as we listened we wondered if we were hearing aright; Anna was perfectly serious:
A: I AM the most beautiful person in the world. (!)

6 June '76. Anna (3.10) initiated a sequence of Snow White
games: I'll be Snow White and you be the wicked stepmother--
Father, you be one of the seven dwarfs and I'll be Snow
White. . . . "I wish I was back at the castle . . ." More
was said, but escaped recording. It was not always possible to
start our battery-powered tape recorder without inhibiting
Anna. On those occasions when we had to make do with mains
power, it was sometimes impossible to take the recorder to the
room Anna was in, and plug it in, without arousing Anna's
annoyance. Once roles were allotted to us, Anna expected our
immediate participation and regarded with disfavor parents
scribbling notes.

1 August '76. (Anna 4.0). Hugh recorded a conversation with
her:
A: Do we die when we eat poisoned apples?
H: Yes.
A: Go to sleep and never wake up again? (Our habitual manner
of explaining death to Anna at this stage.)

30 December '76. (Anna 4.5). Her grandparents were visiting,
and Anna put on a "play" for them on her "stage"--the lower

section of our split-level living-room floor. She assigned
parts--Grandpa was to be one of the dwarfs, and Grandma to be
the Wicked Queen. They looked rather disturbed, confiding in
us afterward that they had forgotten the exact outlines of the
story and were afraid that if they took initiatives, they
would prove to be enacting an episode from another fairy tale.
Undaunted, Anna proceeded, directing and starring with equal
vigor, but in order to avoid damping her grandparents' enthusiasm altogether, the tape recorder was left unheeded on its
shelf.

20 January '77. (Anna 4.6).
A: The wicked queen is dead.
H: How did she die?
A: I gave her a poisoned apple.
H: But that was the sort of thing the queen did!
Two minutes later, Anna explained that her doll Samantha, tem-
porarily the Princess Samantha, was ill and asleep.
A:The queen gave her a poisoned apple.

This completes the account of Anna's allusions to Bernadette
Watts's Snow White, but there remain two references which
were inspired by other sources. The first is traceable to the
Jarrell/Burkert version: six days after hearing this Anna
(4.4) said conversationally:
  I'm going to have--a girl as black as ebony and white as
  snow--and as pink as blood.
M: And will you call her Snow White?
A: Yes. I HOPE I can have her.

Exactly a week later, 29 November '76, when out shopping, Anna
saw a 3-D book, which she identified (correctly) as being
about Snow White. Later she said: Mother, I'm going to play
the Snow White game. I'm going to prick myself with my clothes
on. While Anna needs to report that she is going to pretend to
be Snow White's mother sewing, she is able to play the game
alone, without a complementary role being taken by another.

In the Snow White material we can see the full range of
Anna's mature book-based behavior; there are a few questions
and comments similar to those that would regularly be asked
during reading sessions; but for the most part, Anna's allusions re-created some aspect of the story rather than merely
referring to it or querying it. Whether she was coming to
grips with the meaning of poison by inventing "poisoned"
things that might behave the same way as poisoned apples or
involving herself and others in a role-playing game, Anna was

attempting to make some element from <u>Snow</u> <u>White</u> actually happen in her own life. In doing so, she both explored cognitive puzzles and discharged tension caused by emotionally laden incidents. Central to both of these was the image of the queen using a poisoned apple to dispose of Snow White, an incident which powerfully unites the harmless and familiar (apples) with threat and death. The poisoned apple separated into its two constituents on the occasion when Anna accepted our word that our own red apple was not poisoned, and some of her references show Anna simply working out the new concept "poison" in her thinking and in her vocabulary. But the poisoned apple as such continued to recur, and was central to the role-playing games as well.

Dwarfs seemed to be an optional extra, a part to hand out to tall males only, and until she saw the stage play, the story as she re-created it did not include dwarfs. Similarly the re-created story did not include Snow White's real mother until Anna met Nancy Ekholm Burkert's representation of her, sewing at her window. Anna had made reference to the real mother when we first <u>looked</u> at the Bernadette Watts version, but in her talk afterward, and in her own role playing, the king's first wife did not exist till Anna was 4.4. Then Anna had a baby sister aged two months and allotted to herself the role of mother of a baby girl. Anna's second venture into the mother role was ambiguous; seemingly it was to stop at the point where she pricks her finger, but it is unlikely that Anna intended to inflict pain on herself and then consider the game over. Maybe Anna saw the act of pricking her finger as necessary before the queen could become a mother.

Quite clearly, as far as Anna was concerned, the most powerful person in the drama was the wicked stepmother queen, who was the first <u>person</u> she referred to, at 3.7: <u>I</u> <u>am</u> <u>glad</u> <u>I</u> <u>don't</u> <u>have</u> <u>a</u> <u>stepmother</u>, and the <u>last</u> at 4.6 when she was cast as responsible for the unhappy Princess Samantha's illness: <u>The</u> <u>queen</u> <u>gave</u> <u>her</u> <u>a</u> <u>poisoned</u> <u>apple</u>.

Anna was never prepared to try herself in the role of wicked stepmother, and her first approach was to give it to Maureen, but to make Maureen Winnie Bear's wicked stepmother. Anna herself took the safe role of producer, but in a real sense she was testing out the feel of having a bad-tempered stepmother, by allowing a favorite toy to take the role of the abused child. The motivation for the behavior of Snow White, the prince, and the dwarfs went unquestioned. But it was the queen's motivation that puzzled Anna. After months of toying

with the idea of poisoned apples, at 3.10 she attempted to get
to the bottom of why the queen acted thus. The queen is the
agent of evil, without whose action there would be no story,
and once she acts, the behavior of all the other characters is
predictable. Jealousy of someone else's appearance was outside
Anna's experience.

To reenact the scene of the poisoning again and again was, if
we guess correctly, one way Anna could try to render acceptable to herself such unprecedented, perplexing, and frightening behavior, just as she played the roles of several of
Jansson's characters in Finn Family Moomintroll in order to
get a firmer grip on these unfamiliar and confusingly pictured
creatures. And, in focusing on the two-character confrontation
between Snow White and the queen, Anna continues the binary
pattern we have observed in some of the earlier examples of
book-based play.

The "Snow White" record shows Anna's play to be little influenced by the actual words of the text she knew best. By comparison, the following episode owes a great deal to the original
wording. The Upstairs Witch and the Downstairs Witch was
borrowed for Anna and read to her four times when she was 4.6.
Eighteen days after the final reading, she saw Hugh starting
to sweep the floor, fetched her own small broom, and initiated
a game. Some minutes later Hugh thought to switch on the tape
recorder, and minus its beginning, here is Anna's play:

A: [vrum], [vrum] Now I be the Downstairs Witch and you be
the Upstairs Witch.
H: Right then.
A: And right now you have to call "Come here you silly old
witch!"
H: Come here you silly old witch. It's all your fault!
A: Why's all your fault?
H: It's all your fault that that man has come back! [Anna had
earlier spoken this line to Hugh; after a pause he con-
tinued.] It's all your fault that that man has come back!
Now get to work and start sweeping the downstairs properly.
A: All right. Good! That's the best thing I've heard all day
(uttered forcefully)!
H: That's the best thing you've heard all day!
A: Now you have to march upstairs like this (clumps heavily
off).
H (murmurs): All right. [Pause] The Upstairs Witch marched
upstairs clumping loudly.
A: Here we go. Again ("Whee!" noises).

H: You silly old witch [using Anna's own line from earlier]!
A: No. We have to start--dirty the house now.
H: Do we have to start dirtying the house now?
A: Yes.
H: What do we have to do?
A: We have to dirty the windows.
H: Bang the windows and hit the bricks [describing what Anna had begun to do]?
A: Yes.
H: Bash the floor. And what do we do that for? [Unfamiliar with the plot!]
A: That's--so the man won't come back.
H: Why should the man come back?
A: Mmm. [Pause; bangs] I've bashed the floor. Now hurt the bricks. [Bangs] Now hurt the window. [Bangs] There! Now we've done it. [Pause] Come here you silly old witch. What you're doing here?--You're not supposed to be in the room-- And I am going out! [Clomps off. Long pause. Anna returns and the recorder is switched off.]

Briefly, the original story runs this way: two witches live in a shabby house which a potential buyer comes to inspect. The witches have just had a cleaning spree and the man is favorably impressed. Dismayed, the witches who stay hidden, damage the house so that when he returns with his family, he wonders how he could ever have thought the house habitable. They depart leaving the witches in delighted occupation.

Why did Anna select this incident for reenactment? Hugh provided the stimulus by sweeping the lower level of our living room, where she most frequently performed her plays. And the proximity of the step from one level to another served to reinforce the broom stimulus, so that she recalled The Upstairs Witch and the Downstairs Witch. The specific reference to bricks rather than walls in Anna's dialogue is because our "stage" has walls of natural brick.

To judge from Anna's play, she did not grasp the entire plot; she was not able to make a convincing transition from the early sweeping to the consequent destruction. Evidently it was the latter that impressed her most of all. Her dialogue borrows from Susan Terris's (1970) text: "'That's the best thing I've heard all day!'" (Text: ". . . the very best thing," Op. 3). Note that this exclamation, while remembered almost word for word, sits awkwardly in Anna's dialogue. She also recalled: "Come here, you silly old witch. . . . It's all your fault." This is an exact quotation, apart from an omission of

a sentence from Wanda's speech (Op. 10). As well as these two
quotations, there are several echoes, which are recast syntactically as instructions to Hugh, the auxiliary actor, e.g.
A: <u>Now</u> <u>you</u> <u>have</u> <u>to</u> <u>march</u> <u>upstairs</u> <u>like</u> <u>this</u>.
Text: "Wanda marched upstairs" (Op. 3).

While Anna reproduces the order of events and captures the
spirit of the destruction, the conclusion of her play is en-
tirely her own: <u>What're</u> <u>you</u> <u>doing</u> <u>here</u>?--<u>You're</u> <u>not</u> <u>supposed</u>
<u>to</u> <u>be</u> <u>in</u> <u>the</u> <u>room</u>--<u>and</u> <u>I</u> <u>am</u> <u>going</u> <u>out</u>. This seems to be a way
of coping with the fact that after finishing the play with
"There! Now we've done it!" (Text, Op. 12: "That about does
it.") she is disconcerted to find Hugh still on stage. She
produces another line of dialogue which makes it plain to Hugh
(who was unacquainted with the story) that the play is over.
This is the only elaboration Anna makes on the original, and
it is of a minor nature, since it bears the marks of an <u>ad</u> <u>hoc</u>
solution to an extra-fictional problem.

Notice that Anna gave the familiar two-part structure to her
play; cleaning the house is followed by breaking it up, and
only two characters appear. She allotted to herself and Hugh
the roles of the two protagonists, telescoping the other
characters into one man. The destruction is undertaken to
thwart him, but in Anna's play he does not come on stage;
having foreknowledge of the effectiveness of the witches'
planning, she is content to conclude once it is carried out.
In all the examples of her recorded play that we have studied,
she never did encompass three incidents at a time.

To exemplify a type of play which began with a clearly visual
rather than a narrative stimulus, let us look at Anna's behav-
ior on the day that Michael Ende's <u>Jim</u> <u>Button</u> <u>and</u> <u>Luke</u> <u>the</u>
<u>Engine</u> <u>Driver</u> was borrowed for her. Anna was then 4.9. See-
ing the book, worn and lacking a dust jacket, she exclaimed:
<u>Not</u> <u>that</u> <u>green</u> <u>book</u>! Hugh picked it up and began to read at
the title page. Anna obsessively traced round and round the
winding railway track drawn on the title page, and as she did
so, she made a repeated [m] noise.

The next night after dinner, she organized us into playing
"The Three Bears," a story which had been chosen for improvised drama one day at school. A teeth-brushing expedition proceeded to the bathroom, while Anna was asking for suggestions
for another story she knew which we could play. No answer was
given, but Anna put down her toothbrush and rushed out saying:
<u>I</u> <u>know</u>! <u>Jim</u> <u>Button</u> <u>and</u> <u>Luke</u> <u>the</u> <u>Engine</u> <u>Driver</u>! Hugh was

instructed in how to form a house--she demonstrated by making
herself into an inverted U. Anna allotted the roles: she was
to be the engine Emma, Hugh to be the track, and Maureen to be
a house. For Hugh lying full length on the floor as Anna-Emma
shunted back and forth along his body, the game was painful;
the track persuaded the engine that two journeys each way were
enough. The game was not repeated; once Jim and Luke reached
China and encountered (fake) Chinese script, Anna's play began
to follow the route mapped out by Thingumy and Bob and Polynesia, save that this time, the language was written rather
than oral.

This game was clearly an extension, and concretization, of her
earlier "tracing" of the engine's path on the picture--tracing
was a fairly frequent response, but one which was rarely elaborated in this way. Anna seems to be wishing to re-create the
picture in three dimensions. With the available players, she
cannot re-create it in full, and chooses to omit Emma's
driver, Luke, thus giving Emma (played by herself) a more
independent and central status than she has in the book. (She
has also picked for herself the only female figure). Two
earlier engine games (3.11 and 4.0) had involved her in the
engine role but employed no other actors. Perhaps our relative
lack of enthusiasm for the game had something to do with its
never recurring, but it seems more likely that, unlike Snow
White, the picture that was Anna's original stimulus contained no emotional center; after she had played the scene
once, Anna's urge was satisfied.

We would expect to find that Anna's drawings would now and
then take themes from stories, and this was in fact the case.
The most interesting and detailed were the latest, when she
drew her own interpretation of what she understood. But when
she had drawn the Groke at 4.7--the same character that she
met originally in Finn Family Moomintroll and had just
reencountered in Who Will Comfort Toffle?--she added a gay-
patterned dress, explaining: I have given her that sort of
dress because she's going to get married today. She's going to
marry another Groke. A father Groke, and have a baby Groke.
This happened just a week after she had during a reading session made it clear that she disliked the Groke and found her
frightening. It was also five months after the birth of her
new sister Morwenna. During the reading, she had said: The
Groke is fairly frightening. I could do anything I liked with
the Groke. [Embarrassed] I could push [ə] over--Isn't this a
dark story? The Groke has fierce yellow eyes. Yuk! I don't
like the Groke. [ə] was uttered in a sort of giggle, in place

of the anticipated pronoun, and suggests that Anna had failed
to remember the Groke's sex.

We can see Anna's drawing as a way of negating the Groke's
menace--dressing her gaily and granting her a family life
instead of the mournful isolation in which the Groke apparently resides. She was probably partly reconciled to the idea
of the Groke's awfulness by the time she began her drawing and
worked more of it out as she drew and soliloquized.

This addition of new detail to the original stimulus is rare
in Anna's play proper--indeed the first thing to be said in
looking back on the examples collected in this chapter is that
they imitate rather than elaborate. There are seven examples
(in the period 3.7-4.6) which we considered to show some elaboration of the original idea, and these have mostly been quoted
in our text for one reason or another. Such a one is the 12
February '76 entry for Finn Family Moomintroll, where the
Hemulen turned up to play with Anna and behaved unlike his
usual self. Another is Anna's expressed intention to make a
food giant and a Play-Doh witch, as discussed in chap. 13,
"The Limits of Reality."

In the period prior to 4.6 Anna's games simply echoed the
characters and events of their sources; of course when she set
out to re-create a story in her own surroundings, setting and
costume necessarily deviated from the original, but these
changes were unimportant; the characters and incidents themselves remained as she heard them--minus much of their detail.
This contrasts markedly with some of the fanciful speculative
responses during reading sessions, where it was clear that
Anna was prepared to supply, guess at, or at least ask hope-
fully about all manner of details not vouchsafed by text or
pictures. Between 4.6 and 4.7 Anna began school and was absent
from home often from eight in the morning till five or later
in the evening. For a brief space she had a five-year-old
companion, but it was not until she was 5.7 that the strug-
gling little alternative school attracted others of her own
age. At that juncture her teacher reported that Anna was
participating in imaginative play and realized that she hadn't
seen this happen before. It may well be that "mothers and
fathers," "horsies," and "circuses" with the girl across the
street and "wars" at school filled most of Anna's play time in
the 4.6-5.6 period, and that solitary book-based play was no
longer as attractive. We do have a taped play session after
5.0 when Anna improvised very freely around a literary stimulus.

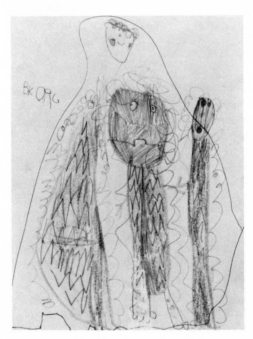

The Groke. Above, Jansson's original (Finn Family
Moomintroll, p. 131). Reproduced by permission of
Ernest Benn. Below, Anna's pencil drawing of the
Groke, complete with the label "EKORG" (i.e., "GROKE"
spelled right-left). "The Groke is fairly frightening.
I could do anything I liked with the Groke. . . . I have
given her that sort of dress because she's going to get
married today."

Secondly, Anna is rarely recorded as having reenacted a plot
in its entirety. She selected individual scenes, and there
seemed to be a definite limit to the number of these that she
would handle in any one session. From "Snow White"--the most
fully developed example of an acted text considered here--she
could play the giving of the poisoned apple and the heroine's
subsequent death, but never (to our knowledge) Snow White's
return to life. Her preoccupation with the "Sleeping Beauty"
led her by her fifth year to numerous improvisations around
the theme of a girl being wakened from enchanted sleep by a
prince's kiss--but in these plays she never acted or even
referred to the preceding stage of the narrative in which the
princess enters upon the charmed sleep. The limits of Anna's
capacity for plot reproduction were especially evident to us
when playing the roles she apportioned to us; left to herself,
she would simply ask us to repeat the same actions or dialogue
over and over; it was normally on our initiative that the
story would move forward a step, and then Anna seemed to
prefer to return to the earlier, more compelling scene.

There are exceptions to this, as the case of The Upstairs
Witch and the Downstairs Witch makes clear. The other recorded exception was inspired by Johnny Lion's Rubber Boots
in which Johnny's wet-day boredom clashes with his mother's
need to carry on with the chores. At 2.11 Anna got as far into
a tall kitchen closet as she could and said "Boo!" several
times.
M (right on cue): "But Mother Lion was too busy."
A: Go upstairs and play, Johnny Lion!
M: Go upstairs and play, Johnny Lion!
But this was unacceptable; what Anna expected was "Go upstairs
and play, Anna!" It was only at that point that it was clear
that it was Anna, rather than Johnny Lion, who had just
erupted from the closet. However, while Anna was able to show
how to take the action further, she rested content with the
one line of dialogue from each actor. Maureen's first contribution, "But Mother Lion was too busy," comes from the narrator rather than either actor. The binary nature of the
interchange becomes obvious, despite Anna's greater-than-usual
participation.

She never, incidentally, moved from the child role to that of
the adult, Johnny's mother. The text (pp. 14-15) reads:
"'BOO!' said Johnny Lion. But Mother Lion was very, very busy.
'Don't be silly, Johnny Lion,' said Mother Lion. 'Go upstairs
and play.' So Johnny Lion went upstairs to play." We notice
that the incident Anna chose to re-create opens with the

exclamation "Boo!" and its concomitant dramatic jump. On four later occasions (3.0 and three times in one day at 3.10) Anna jumped out from behind the same cupboard door with a "Boo!" While she is not recorded as ever having laughed at this particular "Boo!" (see chap. 12, "Funny Ha-Ha and Funny Peculiar," for discussion of Anna's amused appreciation of exclamations), we see again the power exclamations had for her.

It would seem reasonable to say that Anna selected for replay incidents which were striking or dramatic, and which yet contained a familiar element. In the case of Thomas, the latter is to the fore; in the case of Snow White, the former. Moreover, the incident had to be within Anna's capacity to act--if not always within her comprehension (as with the Wicked Queen's poisoning of Snow White). Just as there seemed a limit to the number of incidents that could be played consec- utively in a single staging, so Anna preferred to cast either a single character or (more usually) two. Her nonbook-derived role-playing scenarios almost invariably required two: cat and mouse, nurse and doctor, gardener and gardener's daughter; (king, queen, and princess was a compelling exception). For herself, Anna chose the heroine/victim role and assigned the aggressor/antagonist role to a parent--sometimes with elabo- rate safeguards to distance that character from herself. The binary pattern--two characters, two scenes, or (at its most rudimentary) two complementary lines of dialogue--was not invariably present. Some of her imitative acting seemed to serve the pragmatic function of familiarizing her with a new word, concept, or character. But the binary element occurs too often to be ignored: in the next chapter we will further explore Anna's tendency to create complementary pairs.

9

The Singer of Tales:
Anna as Storyteller

Like many other children Anna engaged in "monologue":[1] without the necessity for any audience other than herself, she would chatter away, producing a stream of words and phrases which might well sound like nonsense to an adult overhearing her. Anna regularly created monologues in bed before sleep, on waking, while playing; and being from very early in her life aware that adults spoke while turning the pages of books, she produced monologues most frequently of all while looking through a pile of volumes on her own. It took us some time to learn to treat these monologues seriously; as we explained in the Prologue, we began to tape and transcribe whole monologues only from Anna's second birthday, and even then only rarely until eighteen months later. Fortunately, our diary does contain enough information for us to reconstruct the period of their genesis. When we come to do this, we find that paradoxically the monologues--which would seem the most original of Anna's responses to books--in fact have their origin in recognizable attempts to imitate our own behavior.

From as early as 1.6, Anna was trying to duplicate what adults did while scanning a page of a book or letter: she would pick up one of our books, or one of her own, and "read" in jargon-- a series of repeated syllables, e.g.[dædædædæd]. Later, she was to use her own surname as material for such "reading," chanting "Gago, gago, gago" (her version of "Crago"). At the same time as Anna was making these imitations of reading, we were supplying her with two very different models of book-related language. The first of these we call the "outside" model, since in it the adult reader consciously explains,

107

identifies, or interprets the content of a book without necessarily using the language of the text at all, and in doing so
stands outside the experience. Such talk would have been
discontinuous and conversational, characterized by fairly
short sentences and by references to ourselves and Anna. No
examples of it survive in the diary, but it can be confidently
reconstructed as follows, using pp. 2-3 of A Lion in the
Meadow:

M: Look--there's a little boy. He's running inside his house.
And there's his mother standing in the doorway. And look,
Anna, I can see a lion in this picture! Where's the lion,
Anna? You see if you can find him. That's right, there he
is, behind the grass.

The alternative "inside" model is provided when the actual
text of the book is read: now the reader no longer comments
but enters into whatever illusion the words create, borne
along by their flow. Less discontinuous, more consciously
rhythmical, the written narrative spoken aloud must have
sounded quite different to Anna from the book talk of the
"outside" model: here is the actual text of the same pages of
A Lion in the Meadow: "The little boy said, 'Mother, there
is a lion in the meadow.' The mother said, 'Nonsense, little
boy.'"

At the stage when most of Anna's utterances were only single
words or two-word combinations, it was not easy to establish
whether she was reproducing the text of a book or a parental
gloss. However by 1.9 we were recording clear examples of memorized glosses or paraphrases. We noted that she would turn to
a page in her Rupert Annual (1964) where an illustration
showed Algy hugging a sprained ankle. This we had glossed for
her previously along the lines of "he's hurt his foot." At 2.0
she leafed through the volume in search of this picture, saying: Find picture Algy hurt foot. There 'tis. All right?
This sequence of statements is notably self-conscious: Anna is
prescribing her own behavior in ways suggested by earlier
adult talk in the "outside" mode. The same mode characterizes
her frequent questions, "any pictures?" (= "are there any
pictures in this new book?") which also occurred in early
monologue fragments. Thus at 2.0 we find a record of Anna's
picking up a paperback belonging to us: Any pictures?--
picture Natasha--picture Mulga Bill--picture Huckle['s]
mother. This particular paperback was unillustrated: the
entire sequence was a fantasy, in which Anna drew on her
memories of characters well known to her through her own
picture books: Natasha's New Doll, Mulga Bill's Bicycle,
Richard Scarry's Please and Thank You Book. It is also one

of our earliest examples of <u>transferred</u> behavior, in which Anna recited the text of one book while looking through another or referred to the pictures of a book not open in front of her. There is no shadow of doubt that Anna was consciously altering the original rather than remembering texts or pictures incorrectly. She was thoroughly acquainted with all her own books and could fetch each of her established favorites off the shelf when we asked for them by name. Often, we can see the associative link: the similarity in format and style between all of the Beatrix Potter books, as originally published by Warne, was probably responsible for her repeating part of the text of <u>Tom Kitten</u> while turning the pages of <u>Two Bad Mice</u>, for example (at 2.4); the sight of a hen in <u>I Can Keep a Secret</u> prompted her (2.3) to recite part of a familiar rhyme ("Higglety, pigglety, my black hen . . .").

Anna did not evolve transferred responses in a vacuum. We were accustomed to interpolate phrases or sentences from familiar books into our conversation, so that Anna quickly learned to do the same; moreover, one of our standard practices when teaching Anna to recognize pictured objects was to compare illustrations of the same subject in different books. So far as we can now recall, we provided no direct model for the speaking of text from one book while looking at another, but Anna's evolution of this is easily explained. An orally oriented child--unlike a literate adult--perceives no necessary link between text and illustration in a picture book. For the child, the words do not come from the book but from the mediating adult. While Anna knew, from multiple readings of all her own books, that certain words officially accompanied a given picture, and demonstrated this in her increasing ability to recite texts word for word, the nexus was weaker for her than it would be for us; not <u>only</u> the official text need be regarded as appropriate.

At the same time as she was learning the official texts, Anna was also displaying her awareness that certain words or phrases occurred in the predictable places in many stories. "End story" (i.e., "end of the story"), her own version of "the end," was acquired at 1.10. At 2.0, she acquired "then . . . ," which joined the already established "One morning . . ." in her repertoire of generalizable narrative markers, and with the ability to deploy both memorized text and explanatory paraphrase or description quite independently of the official wording accompanying a given picture, Anna was ready to create her own "flow." So far as we can tell, her aim was to duplicate the intonation, authority, and (to a lesser extent) the content of an adult reading in the inside mode: it was not, or at least not consciously, to tell a story or stories, though the later monologues depended for much of their length on recognizable narrative sequences.

The earliest complete monologue we possess, and the first of those we will reproduce below, is still at the stage in which the outside mode of the self-conscious, explanatory voice predominates.

"GOOD PLACES--MORWENNA" (4 AUGUST '74, ANNA 2.0)

Characteristically, Anna was seated on the floor with a pile of books (some of her own and some library borrowings); the earlier part of her monologue, recorded at too low a volume to be audible, had covered several Beatrix Potter books and a library book, A Brother for Momoko, from which she had reproduced portions of the text. The transcript begins when she is engaged with her own 1960 Rupert Annual. We were present in the room but, apart from one or two interventions as noted in the transcript, took no part other than to nod or smile when Anna addressed us. As she usually did, Anna turned backward and forward through the Rupert Annual looking for "good places"--i.e., pictures which had particular meaning for her. Though the Annual contains four separate stories in modified strip-cartoon format, Anna's turning of pages was random and made no attempt to stay within the compass of a single story (we suspect that these boundaries were not real for her in any case). We reproduce the transcript in sections which, as we shall see, contain certain structural regularities.

Transcript

1. Algy--not Rupert!
   Algy Pug!

2. Mmm! (Giggle.)
3. Mmm! Morwenna does--
   (Anna places a hand
   over her mouth in imi-
   tation of Morwenna's
   gesture, p. 47d.[2]
   This gesture repeated,
   4 and 5.)
4. Mmm! Morwenna does--
5. Mmm! Morwenna does--

Explanatory Notes

1. This could refer to any
   of a large number of
   pictures showing Algy,
   drawn from pp. 7-27.

3. Morwenna, Anna's sister,
   was named after this
   character.

H: Mm--what's she [i.e.,
     Morwenna] doing?

A: (Giggles.)

6. Dark <u>place--over here</u>

6. Black area of same pic-
    ture, p. 47d.

7. Dark <u>place--yes</u>
8. Dark <u>place--bad temper</u>
9. Bad <u>temper</u>
10. Bad <u>temper</u>
11. <u>Anna</u> <u>read</u> <u>Rupert</u>

8. Cf. <u>Zeralda's</u> <u>Ogre</u>,
    Op. 1. The Ogre is pic-
    tured in a red skullcap
    against a black back-
    ground.
    Text: "Like most ogres
    he had . . . a bad
    temper . . ."

12. <u>Oh</u> <u>Anna!</u>
13. <u>Oh</u> <u>Anna!</u>

12, 13. She is reproducing
     the chiding phrase we
     customarily used to her.

"Dark place--bad temper": the source--<u>Zeralda's</u> <u>Ogre</u>
(Op. 1). Reproduced by permission of Harper & Row,
Publishers, Inc.

Anna begins this section by identifying Algy and then states
the identification negatively ("not Rupert--Algy Pug!"). It
seems highly unlikely that Anna found any difficulty telling
Algy and Rupert apart at this stage, when she'd had the book
for months: what we are witnessing seems a deliberate filling
of space with words: an attempt to create a flow. In the remainder of the monologue we will find several devices used to
the same purpose--most obviously, repetition of a whole phrase
as in 3, 4, 5. And in passing, we note the prevalence of three-
fold repetition and of an incremental tendency whereby one
word or phrase remains constant while the others change,
leading to a new "base word." Turning now to p. 47, Anna
begins afresh by making another identification (Morwenna),
this time naming and imitating the character's gesture. She
giggles at Hugh's interruption but remains intent on the same
picture, repeating the identification "dark place," as if to
give her time to remember the fragment of text ("bad temper")
that went with a similar "dark place" in Zeralda's Ogre--a
nice example of the transferred behavior we mentioned earlier.
Having repeated "bad temper," however, she can go no farther
and shifts to a description of her behavior (11). Her own name
suggests the next statement, also repeated, which similarly
belongs to the world outside rather than to Rupert and its
characters. Temporarily she seems to have run out of steam and
keeps up the flow only by altering the subject to herself.

14. Mmm--
15. Mmm--
16. Mmm--
17. Good places--Morwenna.

17. I.e., "I've found pic-
    tures with Morwenna in
    them."

18. Mmm! Morwenna does--

18. Repeats gesture, as in
    3-5.

19. Sitting floor

19. I.e., "I'm sitting on
    the floor."

20. Piskie man--red boots

20. See pp. 45-49. In fact
    the Piskie does not have
    red boots, though he
    does have a red hat
    (like Zeralda's Ogre).

21. (Inaudible.)
22. Good place!
23. Ozzie Kangaroo--hand--
    camera

23. I.e., "Ozzie Kangaroo
    has a camera in his
    hand." See p. 58.

24. Ozzie Kangaroo--hand--
    camera

25. <u>Ozzie</u> <u>Kangaroo</u>--hand--
    camera
26. <u>Morwenna</u> <u>does</u>--
27. <u>Morwenna</u> <u>does</u>--
28. <u>Good place</u>--<u>that</u>
    <u>good place</u>

28. Cf. <u>Peter's Chair</u>,
    Op. 8: "'This is a good
    place,' said Peter."
    (She owned a copy of
    this from 1.1.)

29. <u>There</u>--<u>a</u> <u>good</u> <u>place</u>
30. <u>Good place</u>
31. <u>Good place</u>
32. Anna reading "Rupert
    Crystal Ball."

32. I.e., "Rupert and the
    Crystal," title of one
    of the stories.

33. Not "Crystal Ball--
    yes?"

33. Cf. 1.

34. <u>Not table</u>

34. I.e., "I'm not sitting
    at the table"(?)

We notice immediately how much of the matter in this section
is akin to that used in the first, yet it has its own theme in
the recurring "good place." Some of these repetitions of "good
place" almost certainly refer to different pictures of significance to Anna, but she does not talk about them more explicitly; she singles out only two for actual description: "Piskie
man--red boots" refers either to the "Morwenna does" picture
or one nearby; "Ozzie Kangaroo" is pages away in another part
of the book. In 19, Anna comes temporarily "out" into allusion
to her own behavior, but 32-34 seems a clearer end to the
cycle. "Anna reading 'Rupert Crystal Ball'" parallels 11 in
form and content. Anna then corrects the false identification;
the negative marker carries through into "not table," another
reference to herself. This time there is a considerable bridge
passage in which Anna stays almost wholly outside the book
world:

35. <u>Ah? Nice place</u>
36. [<u>Giggle</u>] <u>Dear old</u>
    <u>bear</u>

36. Endearment used between
    Hugh and Maureen.

37. <u>Anna lying down</u>
38. <u>Rupert dear</u>
39. <u>Anna sit</u>
40. <u>Tired floor</u>

40. I.e., "Tired on the
    floor." Cf. her phrase
    "Tired in chair" used

41. <u>Anna</u>
42. <u>Anna sit</u>--
43. <u>Sitting down</u>

    to describe Mrs. Tittle-
    mouse. The phrase is
    a telescoping of the
    text's "She was too
    tired to do any more.

First she fell asleep
in her chair . . ."
(Potter, 1910, p. 53).

44. <u>Finish</u> "<u>Morwenna</u>"   44. I.e., "I've finished
reading 'Rupert and
Morwenna.'"

45. <u>Anna</u> <u>finish</u> "<u>Morwenna</u>"

The context of 37-39 is that Anna lay down on the floor,
briefly putting aside her books, and pretended to be asleep,
and to wake up. Even during this game, though, she reworks the
phrase "dear old bear" into an allusion to <u>Rupert</u> (38) and
may well be creating "tired floor" by analogy with "tired in
chair" from <u>Mrs. Tittlemouse</u>. Finally she resumes her book
and announces her intention to "finish Morwenna," an aim only
briefly sustained.

46.
47. ⟩ Indecipherable,
48. repeated.
49. <u>Two</u> <u>pictures</u> <u>Ruperts</u>   49. I.e., "Here are two
pictures of Rupert."

50. <u>Everything</u> <u>all</u> <u>right</u>
51. <u>Everything</u> <u>all</u> <u>right</u>

We were not able to see or to deduce later which picture Anna
is referring to in 50-51; it may well be the scene in which
Algy's hurt foot is restored to health (p. 20a). More important than precise identification is the fact that this reassuring statement with its flavor of finality comes before another
departure from the fictional frame:

52. <u>Anna</u> <u>moved</u>
53. <u>Table</u>
54. <u>Anna</u>--
55. <u>Not</u> <u>now</u>--   55. Parental phrase.
56. <u>Anna</u> <u>moved</u> <u>yesterday</u>
57. <u>Anna</u> <u>table</u>
58. <u>Get</u> <u>shoes</u> <u>off</u> <u>chair</u>   58. Parental phrase.
59. <u>Anna</u> <u>read</u>--<u>reading</u>
<u>Rupert</u>

As can be readily guessed, Anna has now moved to sit at the
table. It is not clear what "not now" refers to, but it is
almost certainly an internalized parental phrase, as is 58,
when Anna realizes that she is not supposed to put her shoes
on the chair. "Anna move," the theme of 52 and 56, now recurs
in the middle of a book-related passage:

60. <u>Good</u> <u>place</u>
61. <u>Anna</u> <u>move</u>
62. <u>Anna</u> <u>find</u> good place
63. <u>Good</u> <u>place</u>! (Excited.)
64. <u>Ah</u>!
65. <u>Oh</u>!
66. <u>Oh</u> <u>Rupert</u>!
67. <u>Poor</u> <u>Rupert</u>!
68. <u>Morwenna</u>--
69. <u>Momoko</u> <u>hurt</u>   69. <u>Momoko</u>'s cover had
70. <u>Don't</u> <u>want</u> <u>Momoko</u>   been torn by a
                                         previous borrower.
71. <u>There</u> <u>Momoko</u>   71. I.e., "There is <u>Momoko</u>"
                                         (on the table).

We notice that Anna has managed the fullest statement yet of
her own search for key pictures (62), actually using the word
"find." This time the "good place" on which she lights appears
to be one which moves her to sympathy; scenes in which characters are hurt had from very early drawn her attention; see
chap. 14, "Heroes and Villains." Her abortive mention of
Morwenna leads by sound association to another girl's name
starting with [m]: Momoko. And of course <u>A</u> <u>Brother</u> <u>for</u> <u>Momoko</u>
is within her field of vision, too. Having "read" it earlier
in the monologue, she now makes it clear that she has done her
duty by it.

This is virtually the end of the portion of the monologue
dealing with <u>Rupert</u> and close to the end of the monologue
itself; we have chosen not to reproduce the final section,
which contains perfunctory reference to other books.

Though we have commented on the books to which Anna is referring in some of her statements, it would be misleading to
analyze the monologue as a whole in this way. Only by accepting it as a creation independent both of particular pictures
and of Anna's own activities in the room can we begin to see
that its seemingly random repetitions and juxtapositions mask
a definite order. Overall, as we have already seen, that order
consists in a series of moves "into" and "out of" the world of
the <u>Rupert</u> Annual. In the first two sections of the monologue, the divisions are clearly marked; thereafter absorption
within the book world becomes harder and harder for Anna to
sustain. If her search for "good places" is temporarily
fruitless, the pressure to keep up the flow by describing her
own behavior becomes greater. The word "hurt," applied first
to some disaster Anna sees pictured in the book, then serves
her for a description of a battered library volume.

On several occasions, moreover, we notice that Anna's move "outside" is preceded by similar <u>types</u> of "inside" statements: thus we see:

   ⎰10. <u>Bad</u> <u>temper</u>
   ⎱11. <u>Anna</u> <u>read</u> Rupert
   ⎰31. <u>Good</u> <u>place</u>
   ⎱32. <u>Anna</u> <u>reading</u> "Crystal Ball"
   ⎰51. <u>Everything</u> <u>all</u> <u>right</u>
   ⎱52. <u>Anna</u> <u>moved</u>

In each case, it is a statement with some sort of emotional coloring that precedes the shift to self-consciousness, as if Anna is aware that emotionally toned language marks a high point or a climax. It seems that she begins each section of the "inside" parts of the monologue with an identification of some character or situation, and ends each with a statement that possesses affective content. What comes between beginning and end of each cycle is less predictable, but all the indications are that Anna has already established a way of starting and finishing a sequence of phrases uttered over a book. In this particular monologue she employs none of the "one morning" or "end story" tags on which we commented earlier. Nevertheless there remains a kind of shape, beginning with the identification of a character, leading to accounts of actions by (usually) different characters, further identifications, and finally, a summarizing affective statement. Readers may have noticed how the tendency of the book-related cycles is to identification/description, whereas the "outside" sections are heavily action-based. Perhaps Anna is in this unconsciously echoing the way we concentrated on pointing out and describing, rather than relating actions, when we first shared books with her.

Between the stage represented by "Good places—Morwenna" and the period from which our final examples are drawn, Anna's verbal resources broadened enormously, and her monologues became much more sophisticated. At 3.9 we noted that the most fruitful time for monologues was during Anna's daytime rest: "When she is alone, her monologues seem likely to be longer and less self-conscious than when she is in a room with us." Another characteristic of solo monologues was the predominance of partially formed or slurred words: "There is a 'pressure-off' atmosphere which allows Anna's speech to regress to a much earlier phase of jargoning and free experimentation with individual syllables and their combination." We noted in the same entry "monologues consist at least half of dialogue,

complete with dramatic voices, and appropriate tags at the end
of each segment of direct speech: 'she said,' 'said the fox,'
'they cried,' etc. Typically, dialogue features dramatic exclamations of the sort which she has always tended to select from
book texts and reproduce in conversations." It seemed that
dialogue very often served Anna as a compositional resource
when she had momentarily run out of inspiration; likewise she
would make use of that standard tool of the oral composer, the
"catalogue," to continue the flow while working out where to
go next. Catalogue sequences were wont to include enumeration
of colors, seasons, members of a family, and actual counting
of objects or persons. Features of this kind confirm our view
that Anna's fundamental aim was less to tell a story as such
than to sustain at all costs a fluency comparable with that of
an adult reader.

Such compositions contrast markedly with the "paraphrase,"
which flourished from about 3.8. The period when Anna had rote
memorized passed by about 3.0, and in its place there came a
growing ability to retell in her own words a book she knew,
usually an Easy Reader with a relatively short, simple text.

An extract from her paraphrase of The Bears' Picnic by Stan
and Jan Berenstain will sufficiently represent this class of
monologue: we have reproduced the book's actual wording parallel with Anna's for ease of comparison.

Anna	Berenstain
Mother Bear, Mother Bear, take off your apron! We are going for a picnic today! "Where are we going today, Papa?"	Mother Bear, put your apron away We are going to go on a picnic today! "Where are we going on our picnic, Dad?"
"To the bestest place-- in far	"To the very best place in the world,
This is the place that we went to	my lad!
when we were young,	Now you remember this spot, my dear.
when we were young."	When we were young We picnicked here."

Anna's composition rhymes only once (Papa/in far), but it was chanted in a strongly rhythmical manner. Paraphrases of this type might easily form part of a multibook monologue, where Anna "read" through several volumes, using some for textual reproduction or paraphrase and others (normally those with longer or less coherent texts) for monologues of the type we will be mainly concerned with in this chapter.

While Anna continued to use illustrations to suggest new content, so that at times her turning of a page would signal the end of whatever coherent snippet of narrative she had been engaged upon, she had become relatively independent of pictures to maintain a theme, as our next example shows.

"Lars and the Robber" is one of the great flood of monologues generated by Anna between 3.6 and 4.0. The character Lars, together with the domestic detail, derives from Astrid Lindgren's realistic stories; Anna was turning the pages of The Six Bullerby Children, a sparsely illustrated story book, as she composed her tale. The robber is probably inspired by Anna's recent acquaintance with The Good Robber Willibald, but as we shall shortly see, even a close study of Anna's sources has as little light to shed on "Lars and the Robber" as it has in the case of "Good places--Morwenna." And though Anna's fluent phrasemaking seems vastly more mature than the compact, discontinuous phrases of the earlier monologue, we will see that the two productions still have a surprising amount in common.

As usual, we failed to move the tape recording equipment quickly enough to catch the beginning of "Lars and the Robber," and the transcript starts abruptly, with what is to be one of the motifs of the monologue, the discovery by the hero/es (as yet unnamed) of a robber inside a house.

"LARS AND THE ROBBER" (17 JUNE '76, ANNA 3.11)

Transcript   Explanatory Notes

1. He thought he was all   [grɛd]: We are unable to
   [grɛd] But then he   determine what this word
   thought: 'Oh! A   is intended to be.
   robber inside!'
   [Inaudible.]
   But it was too late.
   The robber had catched

them and took them
inside.
They gave him--
They gave us some dolls,   Cf. The Six Bullerby Chil-
and we started out the   dren illustrations, pp. 11,
way back to our own   16, 40; all show dolls.
house.

The finality of "it was too late--the robber had catched them
and took them inside" seems difficult for Anna to handle.
Clearly, this is the end of a cycle, for now she changes the
subject from "them" to "he" to "us." Who "gave us some
dolls"?--the robber? Hardly, but it doesn't matter. What
matters is that reassurance has been provided in the form of a
parting gift, enabling Anna to move smoothly into relating a
return home. Now the whole uncomfortable episode can be reworked by being "told" to Mum and Dad, and the improbable
present-giving which owes its provenance to Bullerby, rather
than to a world of robbers, can be more firmly linked with the
previously established antagonist:

2. "Where did you get these   Presents are referred to
   presents?"   on several occasions in
   asked Mum and Dad when   The Six Bullerby Children.
   we arrived.
   "The robber eventually   It seems likely that Anna
   took us inside   is unaware of the meaning of
   and locked the door on   "eventually," though she
   us and gave us these   does know how to place it
   presents and opened the   correctly in a sentence.
   door and he started on
   the lane way home."
   Lars laughed. "We   Cf. Pig Tale (see below).
   couldn't go back the
   lane way because we
   remembered it wasn't
   our closest way so we
   went the close way and
   found it was our own
   home. So we goed and
   knocked on the door
   and you opened it."
   "Oh" said Mum, "I didn't
   notice that."

From p. 13 (frame 1) in Helen Oxenbury's Pig Tale, a book
which made a considerable impact on Anna between 2.8 and 3.10,

she had memorized and often quoted the couplet where Briggs the pig realizes he is unable to fix his car: "Briggs put down the spanner and uttered a moan:/He'd just have to start on the long walk back home." This is the likely source of ". . . he started the lane way home." What seems to happen then is that Anna senses that "lane way" and "he" don't fit the present context, refers obliquely to their ludicrous sound in "Lars laughed" (i.e., Anna laughs at the mistake she has made), and then proceeds to correct the wrong elements in the next few lines: "we couldn't get back the lane way" is a covert expression of "I was wrong about the lane way" without denying the lane way the existence it has already acquired. Mum's statement is prompted more by sound ([o] in "open" and "notice") than meaning, and Anna, as if realizing this, comes to a halt. A cycle of capture, escape, and return to domestic certainties has been completed, and suddenly we are "outside" again, with Anna identifying a character in the volume open in front of her (the identification is another consciously false one).

That one's Lars, the one with the spotted dress.	Lisa wears the spotted dress, as Anna well knows; she also knows that Lars is a boy!

Now she casts around for new content and finds it in going by sound association from "Lars" to "lies," and by semantic association from "lies" to the "making up stories" passage of A Lion in the Meadow:

3. "My what lies," I said, "You are making up stories so I will make up one too. Take out that matchbox," said the robber. "Inside will be a terrible big dragon. The dragon will eat up all the robbers in the house and then come back to us." So Lars took the matchbox and went out to the robbers' house.	("Lies" could also be "liars.") Text: "The mother said, 'Little boy, you are making up stories—so I will make up a story, too. . . . Do you see this matchbox? Take it out into the meadow and open it. In it will be a tiny dragon. The tiny dragon will grow into a big dragon. It will chase the lion away.' The little boy took the matchbox and went away" (p. 11).

There is a further, compelling reason why Anna should draw on a memory of A Lion in the Meadow in this monologue: Margaret Mahy's little boy runs inside to escape a danger (the lion) and is told by his mother to go back outside with the match box, which will contain a second threat (the dragon) to dispose of the original menace. Later the lion, now perceived as friendly, comes inside with the boy. In its basic structure of inside/outside-threat/no threat, A Lion in the Meadow's plot bears more than a casual resemblance to that of "Lars and the Robber." Out of the somewhat confusing welding of Anna's two characters with the syntax and content of the Margaret Mahy text, one thing is certain: Anna is still preoccupied with the idea of a house containing robbers; a new cycle is about to start, with a journey to that house as its opening motif.

4. The door was shut
Everyone--everything
was quiet.
The sailor broke one leg,
which was their Dad
They were sorry for him,
which was their doggie,
and then they started
back up the lane way
to the robbers' house.

The apparently nonsensical material about the sailor, the doggie, and the broken leg derives in part from The Six Bullerby Children, chap. 5, "How Ollie Got His Dog." The dog, Svipp, belongs originally to a bad-tempered cobbler called Mr. Good. "Then one day the shoemaker fell and broke his leg." Olaf tends the dog while his master lies ill, and eventually his father buys Svipp from Mr. Good. Lindgren's shoemaker becomes Anna's sailor; Dad suggests doggie (repeating the initial [d]); sailor suggests sorry (initial [s]).[3] Notice, though, that Anna's narrative does not use the incident as a coherent whole but employs its events and characters in a structure of her own: door-house-quiet-a hurt occurs-return. This sequence is soon to be repeated.

5. The door was open
Everything was quiet
and all the people
were out.
Lars and Pip and I

"Lars and Pip and I" is an

[inaudible]
other people came to the
party
but Lars and Pip and I
weren't allowed in.
The robbers shut the
door as closed as
it could be, when
about one of Lars's
arms
was stuck in the door.

entire phrase from The Six
Bullerby Children.

Quickly opened the door
and let out the arm
but then the arm dropped
off

Perhaps the subject of
"opened" is still "the
robbers."

The loss of Lars's arm, perhaps a development of the idea of a
broken leg in the preceding section, is the most explicit violence yet encountered in the monologue. That it is linked
clearly with the established antagonist, the robber--whether
one or several--shows that Anna intended robbers to be harm-
ful. Previously the harm has been potential; now it is actual.
Anna dwells for some three sentences on the amputation:

Lars just cried.
He was very sad.
He couldn't have any more
arm
for a long, long time.

It could be that Anna is deliberately deluding herself when
she implies that arms are not lost forever, only for a "long,
long time," but in fact the sentence most likely represents
her belief at this stage.

6. When he goed home, Mum
said:
"Quickly you get that
arm of yours.
You better put that on,
because I can't.
I'm too late and lazy
You forgot your [stɪlmz]
and then I quite forgot
my [vɪlmz]
You can't go anywhere
else

"Late" produces "lazy" via
phonetic association.

You been so naughty."
Lars cried after that.

Though play with sound patterns dominates the middle, the
general import of this passage is clear enough. Lars is being
reproved for the loss of his arm, and his mother's phrases are
almost the same as those we have ourselves used in chiding
Anna ("You'd better put that on, because I'm not going to.")

7. And nothing was--every-
   thing was quiet.
   Lars and Pip and I said
   to all of the [inaudi-
   ble] "How could I go
   and sing

"Lars" produces (last) minute. This is the second
time an inaudible section
has followed the formula
"Lars and Pip and I." If
Anna found it an embarrassment to be dealing with an
"I" that was not herself,
she could well have lowered
her voice--hence inaudibil-
ity. See further chap. 15,
"What Makes a Story?"

   in just a minute?
   And dance in just a
   [kpɪnɪt]?"
   said Lars when his arm
   was fixed on again.
   "Have a Lars [pɪnɪt]
   Have a Lars [pɪnɪt]"
   chirped Dad.
   His leg was fixed back
   again.

Singing and dancing are
happy activities. Is it
this which suggests to Anna
that the arm must now be
restored?

In this section Anna uses quite a lot of material that occurred earlier, in section 4. The phrase "Lars and Pip and I"
recurs, as does "everything was quiet," and Dad pops up again.
The only development is that Lars's arm is "fixed back again"
and it seems to be this which prompts Anna to remember that
Dad's leg is in need of like treatment. (For "When his arm was
fixed back again," see Madeline and the Bad Hat, read four
months previously.) Of Pepito, who had his arms in plaster,
she said: "He has two new arms now. I said he has two new arms
because he has not any plasters on but this bit of plaster.
And this is his new arm." We explained that the plaster cast
was not a new arm, but Anna rejoined: "But can people get new
arms when they die?--Sometimes people do, when they die."

Behind all this may lie Anna's early experience with Arnold Lobel's Mouse Tales in which a mouse "wears his feet out" while traveling and buys a pair of "new feet." Apparently Anna firmly believed in the truth of this at 3.3. On the other hand, the tendency of preschool children to understand a broken limb as broken off (on the analogy of broken objects which they have seen) may be sufficient in itself to explain the leg's being "fixed back again."

Having repaired the first real damage she has allowed into her narrative, Anna now moves into yet another cycle of approaching threat; we are back at the house with its all-important door, but this time it is the robber who is outside seeking entrance, and the somewhat shadowy heroes who are inside abed, a detail probably derived from chap. 7 of The Six Bullerby Children where the three girls spend the night in the barn, apprehensive of a possible intruder, and are surprised by the boys as a joke.

> They were all cheerful
> when one of the boys came
> to the house,
> and knocked on the door
> so loud
> that we had to pull the
> covers over our heads again.
> "Let me in!" he shrieked.
> The people awoke,
> went to the front door,
> and opened it.
> No one was there.
> They rushed to the back
> door
> and there was the robber.
> "Let me in.
> I'm going to kill your
> [inaudible] boys and
> girls."
> [inaudible] back to our
> beds,
> and jumped in and shut
> our eyes.
> The robber came into our
> bedroom now
> to eat them up?
> But it didn't work!

"To eat them up": the questioning tone was present in Anna's voice, hence the punctuation.

Though there are several changes of roles and persons here
("the boy" becomes "the robber"; "the people" become "we" and
then "they" again as Anna veers between Bullerby's first-
person and her own third-person narrative), it is the longest
passage so far in which Anna has maintained a consistent
thread without material introduced via some kind of semantic
or phonetic association. But Anna's wish to ward off unhappy
outcomes prevents the robber's threat from being fulfilled.
And after the laconic "but it didn't work!" the coherence she
has so far preserved in this cycle goes abruptly to pieces.
Can we see in this disintegration a consciousness that she has
deliberately evaded something?

There was such a [strɔ:g]
straight away.
He tried to open their   "He": presumably the robber?
eyes
by shouting, talking,   A short "catalogue."
walking and taking.
The back door was now open.
He pushed and pushed and
pushed until he had opened
it.

It seems that having said "the back door was now open" she
feels a need to explain how this had happened and so adds the
next line.

We had tried to take the   Note that she maintains
tears (?) away   the pluperfect tense.
but the robber had hanged
on to them long enough
and then he had rang home
one two four two bells   The "one two four two" is
                                perhaps influenced by our
                                telephone number (25 42 75)
                                which Anna memorized and
                                quoted. She also fabricated
                                other "phone numbers" at
                                this time.

and then he ran back home
to his own house.
That's the part!   An "outside" comment; per-
                                haps meaning "That's the
                                part of the story I was
                                looking for."

He seemed pleased to see
their son.

And so from now on the
racket (?) had gone.
She cut back to the
beginning

"She" = Anna herself? turning back to the beginning
of the book? Winnie = Anna's
teddy bear.

When Winnie (?) stayed

and so we all goed back
to . . .

Monologue modulates into sequence of chanted syllables.

What can we learn from our close look at "Lars and the Robber"? First and foremost, that the monologue consists of a
series of cycles containing broadly similar material; that
each cycle embodies variants on the themes of approach, encounter with menace, return to house and security; that the final
cycle is the most elaborate and also the most consistent in
maintaining a single recognizable narrative thread. Perhaps
"narrative thread" is not the correct phrase: we have been
discovering that Anna can keep up a coherent sequence of
actions even though the characters performing those actions
may change. It was on this same basis that Vladimir Propp
(1928) developed his celebrated analysis of Russian folktales
in terms of functions--i.e., actions--rather than of
characters. It will be seen from the analysis of "Lars" in
the following pages that there are also resemblances between
Anna's recurrent motifs and some of those that Propp lists,
which is hardly surprising in view of the prevalence in her
literary diet of traditional narrative patterns.

It is the (apparently) arbitrary changes in characters ("he"
to "us," "a boy" to "the robber"), derived in part from Anna's
juggling of a third-person narrative and first-person phrases
derived from The Six Bullerby Children, that render her monologue superficially playful or nonsensical; if we simply set
down the incidents in generalized terms, the result is rarely
incoherent. And the digressions can be seen to be structurally
and thematically as apposite as the Lion in the Meadow
borrowing if we are in a position to know where they came
from. So Anna tells roughly the same story three or four
times: let us now examine in more detail the components of
this story.

1. The approach. Anna does not waste much time on describing
journeys to the house which is the scene of the action; usually a single sentence suffices; and the home from which the
protagonists start is implied rather than stated:
  "So Lars took the matchbox and went out to the robber's
  house."

"And then they started back up the lane way to the robber's
house."

2. The threat. As we have seen, the threat motif does not
always materialize after a door has been opened. Nevertheless
the presence of two major threat scenes--the loss of Lars's
arm and the intrusion of the robber into the bedroom--and two
minor ones ("the robber locked the door on us" and the loss of
Dad's leg) is sufficient for us to consider threat as basic to
Anna's prototype story in this monologue. As a rule, the
threat is rapidly glossed over, but there is a notable exception, the arm episode, where the loss is dwelt on at length.
It seems that for Anna in this monologue, the presence of a
threatening person is a clearer narrative idea than what such
a person might do. This is hardly surprising if we consider
that the great majority of the books Anna has been read present either slight threats or rapid restitution of any harm
done. Indeed, many modern stories deliberately disarm their
villains, creating "bad" robbers who are really good, as in
The Good Robber Willibald, a source for this monologue.

3. The harm is righted. If a threat has been offered or
actual damage has been done, Anna seems to feel obliged to
rectify the situation as soon as possible. This can be done by
proceeding as if the threatful situation has not happened, or
by a more specific reversing of harm:
  "The robber . . . gave us these presents and opened the
  door."
  "Quickly opened the door, and let out the arm."
  ". . . said Lars, when his arm was fixed back again."
  "His leg was fixed back again."

4. Someone returns home. Anna seems to have a firm notion
that going back home is a proper recourse after a frightening
episode--indeed, it would be odd if she did not, since so many
of the stories she knows end in this way. In fact, study of
the monologue reveals that the homecoming motif is one of
Anna's most consistent compositional resources, and she seems
to resort to it when other ideas fail her. It seems important
to emphasize that Anna's indebtedness to literary sources is
of a general order, not often at the level of specific incidents. Likewise, we note the relatively low proportion of
statements in the monologue that can be traced to a particular
pictorial source in the book Anna had before her at that time:
contrast with this the greater indebtedness in the Rupert
monologue we analyzed earlier. Far less, too, than in the
earlier monologue, does Anna come out of the storyteller's
illusion into the outside world. Only one or two statements

can be definitely classed as in the "outside" mode. However, the less coherent transitional passages may fulfill the same function as the self-conscious description of Anna's behavior in "Good places--Morwenna": that of carrying on the essential flow of words when no immediate narrative resource suggests itself. In the singing with which "Lars and the Robber" ends, we have an early example of the later development of such transitional passages into a kind of recitative in which sound matters far more than sense.

"Lars" is a good example of Anna's mature composition, if atypical in its clear articulation and relative coherence of theme; however a truer picture of the structure of thought that governs Anna's monologue making emerges only when we analyze another, slightly later sample, one in which the book Anna had open plays scarcely any part at all, and which thus reveals her thought patterns operating without interference from specific pictures or textual memories. "Another Girl Called Anna" was told while Anna leafed through C. E. V. Nixon's Penguin Handbook Childbirth, one of our books which had never been read to her, and whose only pictures are a few monochrome plates showing clay models of fetuses in utero.

"ANOTHER GIRL CALLED ANNA" (31 JULY '76, ANNA 4.0)

Childbirth was on the table. Picking it up while Hugh was in the same room, Anna began a monologue. As usual, our taping missed the first couple of sentences, but it was noted that both of them were conventional openings of the "once there were . . ." type. Then Anna observed the cassette recorder: "Oh, I don't want that tape recorder to hear me." She improvized: Every cake in the world of hers [inaudible] to eat, which probably owes its provenance to Haakon Bjørklid's version of the folktale The Very Hungry Cat, returned to the library a few weeks before. Still self-conscious because of the recording she then said defensively: It's another girl called Anna, not me--another girl called Anna. Then, resuming her narrator's voice (a high-pitched singsong):

And she--
the girl called Anna--   Another catalogue.
had no mother or father
grandma or grandpa,
aunt or uncle
to look after her.
She was alone and a big

<u>girl</u>.
<u>She</u>--
<u>Her</u> <u>mother</u> <u>and</u> <u>father</u> <u>had</u>
<u>died</u>--
<u>seven</u> <u>years</u> <u>ago</u>--
<u>so</u> <u>that</u> <u>wasn't</u> <u>very</u> <u>much</u>
<u>help</u>.
<u>She</u> <u>always</u> <u>didn't</u> <u>help</u> <u>it</u>.

This section of the monologue, on the theme of Anna's loneliness, falls into two parts, each ending with a summarizing, emotionally charged statement: the first is "She was alone and a big girl," where the potentially threatening implications of "alone" are in part balanced by the reassuring note of "a big girl," a phrase which for Anna signifies adultlike competence she doesn't now possess. When she is "a big girl" she will be able to do up her own shoelaces, go to school, have proper birthday parties, travel to Africa, etc. The second summarizing statement is "So that wasn't very much help" (falteringly restated in "She always didn't help it"). Here we have a vastly more articulate equivalent of the final utterances of each cycle in "Good places--Morwenna."

"So that wasn't very much help" leaves Anna with a negative which, by what seems to be her normal rules of story construction, needs to be countered by a positive. To supply it, she draws on the topic of hospitalization. Maureen was currently in hospital while pregnant with Morwenna, an event which had revived Anna's longstanding interest in nurses:

<u>So</u>, <u>they</u> <u>just</u> <u>went</u>
<u>and</u> <u>got</u> <u>her</u> <u>out</u> <u>of</u> <u>hospital</u>
<u>and</u> <u>took</u> <u>her</u> <u>home</u>
<u>She</u> <u>was</u> <u>the</u> <u>nurses</u> <u>a</u> <u>good</u>   = She was a good girl for
<u>girl</u>   the nurses.
<u>and</u> <u>she</u> <u>had</u> <u>to</u> <u>go</u>!
"<u>Goodbye</u>!" <u>she</u> <u>had</u> <u>said</u>
<u>long</u> <u>ago</u>, <u>because</u> <u>she</u>--
<u>a</u> <u>long</u> <u>ago</u> <u>her</u>--

It seems as if "had" in "had to go" has suggested the pluperfect of the next line, "she had said," and that Anna has felt compelled to continue in the past, since "long ago" is rhythmically and phonetically similar to "had to go." However, this move has led Anna to a dead end, and after two false starts she apparently splits her initial protagonist, "another girl called Anna" into two: "Anna" and "the other girl."

The other girl
that had lived with her
mother and father--
when the other girl died,
the mother and father were
all--
dead--
as well.
But anyway, there was that
girl
and pooh pan and the cookie
and the other girl to look
after her
so she was not learning
at all.

Anna's voice loses conviction.
(A garbled version of "Pooh pong! and the Chinese cookie factory!" an exclamation of disgust which Maureen claims to have uttered spontaneously and then employed again several times.)
"Learning" = "lonely"?

Despite her adoption of "the other girl" as heroine, Anna seems to remain bound by her previous subject matter--death and loneliness--but having killed off her protagonist, revives her immediately to become a nurturing figure. "Pooh pan and the cookie" seems to register Anna's frustration that things are going wrong with the story, and this frustration increases as her next development also fizzles out.

Anyway, one day she put
poor cages
on her thing(?)
and was lonely.
She wanted to be lonely
that day--
she had to.
Anyway, I think she
thought--
nothing!

"Poor cages" = "four pages(?) (Has Anna just turned several pages of Childbirth?)
Another negative-into-positive. "Lonely" isn't bad if you want loneliness.

"Nothing" was Anna's way of expressing anger and refusal to cooperate when asked to perform by overzealous or pressuring adults. Here it most likely means "I don't want to go on with this any more!" and she promptly asked Hugh about a detail in one of the volume's few illustrations: Hugh, what is this bit between this baby's legs? This? Apparently satisfied with the explanation that it was part of the baby's umbilical cord, she went straight back into monologue.

"Oh" said Anna,
"I wish I had a mother
and father!"
But many years went past   Anna's voice deeply senti-
and she didn't get a   mental.
mother and father.
When she was a lady
she got a mother and
father,
but she [the] baby [?] was
no use--   (Partly inaudible.)
She was dead in seconds.

The overall structure of this section is of a piece with the
rest: negative is followed by positive, upon which negative
reasserts itself ("She was dead in seconds"). We could view
this section as a restatement of the opening one: where the
girl initially lost her parents through death, she is now
stated to have grown up, given birth to her parents, but still
lost them. We cannot insist on the parallel because of the
uncertain transcription of what seems a confused thought to
begin with. Most likely the sentence reflects an internal revision of the type Anna is wont to employ and would thus read:
   But she was--
   The baby was no use--
   She was dead in seconds.

The low mutter in which Anna pronounced these words suggests
embarrassment at an unacceptable sentiment--quite possibly a
wish for her unborn sister to die. Now Anna begins to exploit
her earlier references to nurses and hospital, exploring the
topic of what nurses do, a frequent subject of conversation
with us in the past.

She didn't
hostess--   "Hostess" has been misunder-
the mother's abdomen,   stood by Anna, but the exact
because she was a nurse   sense in which she uses it
when she grew up   here is not clear. Perhaps
and she didn't do any-   = "palpate."
thing like--
give--
the ladies any test blood,   I.e., "blood test." Anna
pints,   accompanied Maureen to her
or any milk bottles for   blood test and on regular
the babies   visits to the gynecologist.

She just didn't do
anything at all,
'cept help sick people
and people who had babies
that's--
all she did

Then, abruptly, she starts to develop the theme of a child-
Anna going home from the hospital, last mentioned some considerable time before.

When she went home
[the next day]   Bracketed words unclear.
she could hear their lark   Cf. Péronnique (on loan
singing outside   that week), whose hero has
and she thought that was a   "learned to whistle the
lovely song,   song of the skylark."
so she thought she would--
go out and pick some
apples.
It was a lovely day--
next morning,
and she--
thought that she would--
do something outside,
so [she] tried
to pick up the grass or--
the husband
that she was going to have.
But she had to do that in-
side--
pick out the husband
that she was going to have.
So--

We realize in examining this section that Anna's mode of composition does not depend simply on countering a negative with a
positive. Instead, we find a different kind of opposition, between inside and outside. This was a key distinction in Anna's
own play, since there were times when she was restricted to
the house and desperately wished to go into the garden (or
vice versa).

At this point Anna again paused in her narrative (perhaps
realizing that "picking out husbands" was going to create
problems if she was going to persist with a child heroine in a
domestic setting) and asked whether a page had been torn from

Childbirth. Asked if she had finished her story, she replied
"No--this's a very long chapter--goes right to the end of the
book" and continued her earlier train of thought:

She didn't [see] anything as she chupped through the grass.	"See" unclear; the word could also be "eat."
Chapter Two: "Anna in the Rain."	
Anna was not in a happy [mood?] that day.	
It was all miserable-- and cold--	
from the rain outside that day.	Cf. Finn Family Moomintroll, chap. 2: "One warm summer
So she decided to take a sun-bath inside.	day it was raining softly in the Val-
There was lots of sun in- side,	ley of the Moomins, so they all decided
and outside,	to play hide-and-
but she got tired of that,	seek indoors"
so she bathed in the rain,	(p. 33)
and then she felt much better, and drank some of	"Sun bath" from Lois Lenski, Davy's Day.
the drops. The drops were not very much but she	"Not very much" = a great deal, a large quantity.
drank them in ONE FULL GULP	Anna normally reversed quantities at this time, saying "a lot" when she meant "a little."

Here we can see Anna adding rain/sun to inside/outside so that
a giddy sequence of statements and opposites ensues. But the
dominant themes of the monologue are about to recur.

Then she gulped and gulped it up	
and was--	
dead in a few [minutes?]	
She was dead that morning.	
And all the next day.	
She couldn't see anything as she mumbled through the rain	
[. . . .]	This phrase indecipherable.
at the next rake.	"Rain" produces "rake"?
So she COULDN'T LEAVE	Anna's voice emphatic.

when the nurse was lying
on the cushion,
waiting for--
Anna
to test out her gloves--
The nurse's gloves
[sickness?]
the nurse was sick all
the [sickness?]
Anna had to take the nurse
to the doctor.
The doctor tested out the
nurse,
then put her in a sick--
person's bed--
it was Anna's bed,
which she used to lie in
when she was sick--
and then the nurse came
better,
in the nice June morning--
in the next morning.

"Blood-test" produces "to test out her gloves" [blʌ] produces [glʌ].

It is difficult to be sure whether Anna's concept of time and being at this stage enabled her to understand the finality of death, just as we could not be sure about the extent of her understanding of lost limbs in "Lars and the Robber." When she says that her heroine was "dead that morning and all the next day," she may be reflecting her belief that death is transitory, or while admitting privately that it is not, she may prefer to assert publicly that it is (like sickness) merely a passing phase. We cannot know the answer, but we can look at what transpires directly afterward in Anna's composition.

It seems, when we do this, as if Anna is substituting for the massive negative of death a number of lesser negatives: first, the clauses "she couldn't see anything" and "so she couldn't leave," then the reintroduction of the sickness theme. Having thus modified the greater into the smaller evil, Anna works toward a restitution: "And then the nurse came better." At the same time, she juggles roles, transferring the role of sufferer to the nurse. However, once the nurse recovers, the recovered person is no longer a nurse, but the heroine (based on Anna herself). From all these maneuvers, it seems that Anna is aware that death is a great calamity but bends her compositional resources to the task of denying this, first diminishing the extent of the calamity and then arranging that it should not happen to her heroine but to someone else.

The next section, a reworking of the earlier one dealing with play inside and outside, is more explicitly drawn from Anna's own everyday experience than anything in the monologue so far.

It was a beautiful day
next day,
so--
she just went out
and picked apples,
and played in the grass,
and picked up the grass
to make a hat,
and made the cushions
outside,
and picked up [inaudi-
ble]
and took--
all the house away
to another house,
and ate the plants
in her mother's garden
and did so many naughty
and nasty and nice
things
that she couldn't bear
it.
Then she went back inside
and telled her mother all
the damage.

Péronnique has to fetch an apple from its dwarf guardian. Our climate is unsuitable for apple trees. Anna often put grass clippings on her head, perhaps as "hats."

Anna customarily made "houses" from piles of grass clippings and lifted the piles from one place to another. The "houses" might well be furnished with cushions or gear from inside our house.

"The" pronounced [ði], unusually for Anna: the effect is to heighten the rhythmical, chanting quality of the phrase.

Here the opposition has been good behavior/bad behavior, and the next step is to modulate back from bad to good:

Then, next morning,
she did not do any damage,
just picked up the apples,
combed all her hair,
dressed herself,
and went out to ride on her

big, big bike
to look at the world
outside
and give it a [sprinkle?]   Word barely audible.

Time for another modulation, and the hospital theme recurs:

But next day,
she was not very well.
She had to go into her bed
in the hospital.
The--
doctor was not glad to
see her--
he was--
turning [into?] a--
patient of his   Is Anna toying with a
"Don't go--   "patient"/"impatient"
don't come here again!"   dichotomy, "into a patient"
he said.   perhaps garbled for
He was annoyed that morn-   "impatient"?
ing.
All the day,
and all of the other days.
But it was a lovely day
next day
and she--
Anna wasn't well yet,
So he took all the sun-   Anna has been told that
light--   sunlight may help you get
there was and then--   better if you are ill.
took it into her room.
Then it was lovely.
So she--
had to get covered from   "Covered" = "recovered."
the sickness straight away
and go out.
When she was going to test
out her bike,
she was--
nearly over it.
"So"--
she said
[Anna laughed at this point]   Anna is beginning to come
and laughed,   "out"; perhaps "nearly over
so hard they nearly cried,   it" describes her own

and then he went outside
and laughed and laughed
and laughed and laughed.
He didn't--
do--
anything
except do out the blood
of his,
but, in the next few
seconds
he was fixed.
Then, he went--

position in relation to her
composition? Notice how
she abandons the feminine
singular pronoun, substi-
tuting first "they" and
then "he."
"Do out" = "take out."

"Outside" would be the predictable complement to this phrase
had Anna intended to continue, but the signs we saw a few
lines ago were true indications of her desire to finish, and
she ends on a firmly positive note:

to us.
There--I've read all the
book.
It was about BABIES!

In analyzing "Lars and the Robber" we observed that Anna told
the same basic story several times over in the course of the
monologue. This is a possible way of analyzing "Another Girl
Called Anna," but more precisely, we can see its structure as
a succession of opposites. If death and loneliness are the
theme of the initial segment, then hospital and recovery are
the theme of the second: death reappears in the third and
(after a brief interval in which the heroine grows up) fourth.
Hospital and recovery recur in the fifth section, and this
leads to a play theme, after which death rears his ugly head
again. Then predictably, we have "hospital," "play" ("good,"
"bad," and "good" again), "hospital," and a conclusion on a
note of recovery. There is a dropping away of the initial negativity associated with death and loneliness; the intervals between their recurrences widen as the composition progresses,
and Anna chooses to end on an optimistic note. In the mean-
time, the theme of sickness has largely replaced death, giving
way in the domestic play segments to bad behavior. As we noted
earlier, Anna's basically binary thought structure seems to
take priority over any concept of a linear, logical plot. If
something good happens, something bad must follow it, which
means that the narrative spirals rather than progresses as an
adult would expect.

A word on the sources of "Another Girl Called Anna." As we saw earlier, they owe little to Anna's book experience except, perhaps, for the notion of death as a temporary state. Anna's knowledge of the Christian story of the resurrection and of a number of folktales (e.g., "Snow White") in which a character appears dead but is revived by a kiss from the right person may have influenced her thinking on this matter, since her fictional encounters with death far outweigh her experience of it (so far confined to dead birds and cats and knowledge of the deaths of persons relatively distant from her world). It is surely significant, though, that death appears as a key topic in a monologue which also deals with babies, growing up, getting husbands, and being a nurse. Anna has been exploring the whole area of adult life which is as yet known to her only at secondhand--all the things which make adults mysteriously different from children. There is no doubt that Maureen's being in hospital and the impending birth of Morwenna were on her mind and helped to prompt the emphasis. But she could have dealt solely with babies and the process of birth rather than ranging through maturity, sickness, and death as well. Less influenced by literary models than "Lars," "Another Girl" reads as if Anna has seized an opportunity to express the current state of her knowledge on "the matter of adulthood."

Though Hugh was in the room throughout, Anna appeared little influenced by his presence after the early break in continuity near the beginning of the monologue. As in "Lars and the Robber," she is able to maintain flow with only occasional lapses in the fictional illusion; in some of those breaks she seems to be drawing on her own behavior but putting it inside the fictional frame and ascribing the relevant actions to her established characters rather than to herself (e.g., "and laughed" in the final segment). Consistency of characters is still not strong, but Anna changes protagonists less often than in "Lars" and (when muddled by such changes) makes more attempts to rationalize them.

It is appropriate to end this chapter with "Another Girl Called Anna" because soon after we recorded it, Anna's monologue making began to decrease. During the period 4.0-4.6, paraphrases, and combinations of paraphrases and rote-memorized text, became more frequent and free monologues less so. The last recorded specimens of the latter were taken at 4.6 and 4.7; Anna commenced school at 4.7, but the decline had set in before this, and well before she began to learn to read (which in itself might be expected to divert energy from old skills to new ones). Now, at 6.0 Anna will tell a story if

pressed, but the resulting compositions are brief and self-
conscious, a far cry from the fluent, spontaneous compositions
of two years before.

CONCLUSIONS

In choosing to spend many pages following three monologues in
minute detail, we have had perforce to sacrifice the possibility of giving a real sampling of the entire range of recorded
monologues—a range that stretches from apparently incoherent
sprechstimme to highly self-conscious short narratives told
to us as deliberate parodies of the whole idea of a story. As
we have already hinted, both "Lars" and "Another Girl Called
Anna" are probably atypical in the clarity of their articulation, and the presence of an adult in the room with Anna may
have influenced both this and their greater degree of
conscious narrative purpose. Nevertheless, it has become clear
in the course of our study of the three examples that certain
fundamental qualities of Anna's compositional method are
instanced in them, and these qualities hold good for much of
the material we have excluded from analysis here.

We saw at the outset that Anna's book talk had its genesis in
the attempt to imitate adult book talk in both the inside and
outside modes, and that "Good places—Morwenna" seems to
indicate that the outside mode was the more compelling model
for Anna at 2.0. Nevertheless this monologue does exhibit a
recognizable structure based on the alternation of "fictional"
sections with sections referring to Anna's own behavior in the
here and now. Within each "inside" cycle, we were able to
observe a pattern leading from identification of a picture or
character to statements about that, or other characters
(including actions performed by them), and finally to some
sort of conclusive, emotionally toned statement which completed the cycle. By the time Anna had reached the stage represented by "Lars and the Robber," her linguistic competence
enabled her to express this pattern in a much more specific
form, within a recognizable narrative mode, best expressed as
"introduction-threat-restitution-return." In "Another Girl,"
we were able to see a pattern of binary oppositions,[4]
perhaps so fully developed here because of the deeply ambivalent feelings that form the content of this particular
monologue. Anna composes, then, by a succession of incidents
or cycles, each normally containing statement and antithesis,
the material of each proposition leading by sound or sense
association to the next. To this structure is subordinated

the immediate content, whether derived from pictures in the book open in front of Anna, or from descriptions of her own behavior, or from some other source. Though details may change with apparently random suddenness, though characters or narrative personas may vary widely from one sentence to the next as a new picture suggests fresh associations, these changes make little difference to the basic underlying structure in which good things follow bad, doors open follow doors shut, sickness follows health quite inexorably. Though our sample is somewhat biased in this regard, it does seem as if Anna became decreasingly dependent on specific pictorial stimulus and increasingly able to convert outside process to inside content as she composed, while still remaining within the fundamental binary structure.

The examples we have reproduced here demonstrate that Anna conceived of story in terms of <u>characters acting</u>: description is rare[5] and confined to a handful of conventional adjectives ("it was a beautiful day next day"); there are no extended descriptions of objects, people, or places, nor any introspection, though there are occasional descriptions of feelings ("Lars just cried. He was very sad."). In this, Anna's practice is closer to that of the traditional folktale than to the style of most contemporary fiction for young children. Anna does not compose like an oral-formulaic singer, but there are points of similarity--her repeated variants of a single basic phrase (the homecoming sentences, e.g., in "Lars and the Robber");[6] and she makes considerable use of incremental repetition (seen in its primitive form in statements 6-8 of "Good places--Morwenna").

Composing monologues was a very significant complement to Anna's experience as a listener. A monologue must have functioned for her as a linguistic and artistic laboratory in which words, phrases, syntactic structures, characters, incidents, introductions, conclusions, and climaxes could be tried out, revised, recombined, or abandoned as the composition progressed. In particular, we have seen how Anna faced the problem of dealing with threatening or frightening material in her monologue. Composing at her own pace, having to please only herself, she must have felt secure enough to experience some aspects of stories on which she rarely or never commented directly during reading sessions. Becoming her own singer of tales gave her complete control over a fiction in a way not possible when she was a listener.

Part 3
Learning the Language of Art

10

Order from Chaos:
Learning to Read Pictures

Learning to read pictures is as complex as learning to read print, and in the process children will pass through barriers some of which will never impede them again; others will go on posing problems of a minor nature all their lives. To accept these statements adults have to be sensitive to the momentary unverbalized difficulties they themselves have when looking at pictures. If an adult can be brought to articulate such difficulties, or if he has read picture books to children, admitting that he is not sure what that funny green mushroom shape is, then he can begin to see the continuity between the child's way of confronting illustrations and his own.

Again and again in this chapter we will see how Anna's "naïve" questions are in fact reasonable, logical responses to such difficulties. And in considering a record of requests for explanation, we must remember that what Anna understood or thought she understood she mostly passed over in silence; the analysis of her difficulties in picture reading can cast much light on the rules of interpretation she herself had formulated, but they cannot give a complete picture of the unspoken triumphs of her progress.

Basic to picture reading is a knowledge of which way is <u>up</u>. After an initial period when she was apparently untroubled by looking at books upside down, Anna began at 75 weeks to orient volumes correctly,[1] once she came to a recognizable illustration. Thereafter she reversed the book to "right" a figure that an artist had deliberately depicted upside down (e.g., a character standing on his head or falling) until 3.6; since then there have been three occasions, at 3.6, 4.0, and 4.3, on which she moved her head rather than the book in order to view the character in a pose closer to the normal. We ourselves feel a tension on seeing something depicted upside down and wonder if Anna felt this tension too. Was it released when she attempted to restore the pictured object to its rightful orientation? Her behavior in this sort of situation can be attributed to a tension set up by "something wrong" in the material.

There is a similar tension when an artist has drawn something which is not consonant with Anna's preconceptions. A passion for princesses and the extravagant dress that is customarily theirs made it hard for Anna to interpret, at 3.4, Maurice Sendak's King Grisly-Beard, in which a princess is forced to leave her palace and dress like a servant girl. On the second reading of the book, Anna pointed to a supernumerary girl wearing a coronet of white flowers and asked "is that her [the princess]?" at the same time rejecting the drab princess inside the house. When the princess is restored to her old status at the end and once more wears her crown, Anna said "Look, there's that lovely princess again!" A concentration on the signs of wealth and position that she has come to associate with princesses closed Anna's eyes to the evidence that is plain for a detached observer to see, that the princess's white dog present in every opening is here shown beside the princess-servant; that her short black hair is peeping from beneath her headdress; that she displays as well those large, sturdy bare feet we have come to recognize as the princess's. In this case the text would have glossed the illustrations for Anna, but from the beginning of her picture book experience, she had tended to treat pictures independently of text. Sometimes (as with King Grisly-Beard) it would be clear that the text was linguistically or conceptually beyond her, but there were many times when Anna was thoroughly familiar with a book and yet asked what a character was doing, particularly one coming or going, climbing or descending (e.g., The Pirates' Tale at 3.3, where she mistook the descent of the rope ladder for ascent--the pirate has reached the last rung in Op. 14. These are stage pirates who always face the audience, and this complicated matters for a child accustomed to seeing people climb up and down a ladder while turned to face it). In every case, there is a reason for Anna's questioning, and yet it requires adults to look before we can see as she does. We have so thoroughly learned the way to interpret illustrations that it is hard for us to entertain another interpretation. Less sure of the rules to apply, Anna verbalizes some of the alternatives which we would regularly suppress.

FIGURE AND GROUND: "GESTALTS"

Actively participating in each reading session, Anna did not
want to depend entirely on an adult's superior knowledge when
faced with a visual puzzle, nor did we encourage her to do so.
If the text mentioned something unknown she would eagerly seek
it in the corresponding illustration, regularly choosing an
object that was unfamiliar, though not necessarily the right
one.

At 4.0, Anna was listening to Carol Barker's How the World
Beg
an, a picture-book summary of the evolution of life on
earth. On Op. 6 the text reads: "First there were sea weeds,
sponges and corals. Then came tiny animals like jelly-fish and
worms. Shell-fish developed next."

The highly stylized illustrations show some of these objects,
in orange, white, and plum color. Anna, not having seen a real
jellyfish, looked for one on the first reading, but we were
unable to comprehend what she thought was the jellyfish and
settled the question by saying: "I can't see any there." Two
days later, Anna tried again:
A: This must be jellyfish (pointing to plum-colored background on the right between sponges and corals).
H: Which bit--that red bit there? I don't think it's a
   jellyfish.
A: No, some of it. All jellyfish must be in it.
Does she mean that jellyfish must be depicted because the text
mentions them? Or that this is a mass of tiny jellyfish?

The plum color draws the eye so strongly that it is hard to
say which is figure and which is ground; furthermore, the plum
color is textured, encouraging the viewer to see it as
figure.[2] There is nothing by which the eye can judge sizes,
and while the stylization has gone so far that the illustration verges on pattern rather than representation, the text
sets up an expectation that we can locate the objects in it,
and this to Anna is the overriding consideration.

Sometimes we were amused or startled momentarily by what Anna
said she saw in illustrations. Some interpretations were easy
for us to understand, like her seeing a snail with extended
horns as a long-eared rabbit at 2.5.[3] However a visual conun-
drum was posed for us when Anna at 2.8 pointed to Maureen's
apron saying: That's like Mickey. The apron had a repeating
pattern with yellow roundels in the center of which was a quad-
ripartite shape which had always seemed to us to be ground. It
was brown, like most of the pattern, and to our eyes, the

yellow roundel always leaped out as figure. Looking with fresh
eyes, we knew which Mickey Anna meant--she was referring not
just to Maurice Sendak's Mickey in In the Night Kitchen but
to one particular illustration, the second from the left on p.
30, where Mickey dives to the bottom of the milk bottle.
Facing the reader, he is spread-eagled like a flattened x in
his suit of dough. The figure on the apron fabric is more like
an uppercase H with a tear-shaped serif at each of its extrem-
ities. The lower two of the tear-shaped appendages look like
Mickey's dough shoes; the upper two look less like the gloves.
To look too closely is to destroy the illusion, but for us it
is now impossible to see the pattern without immediately
seeing the Mickey shape and even a shadowy head where Mickey's
should be. Anna had imposed on the apron pattern a Mickey
"gestalt"--a mental picture based on a familiar figure, its
details simplified to gross features like splayed arms and
legs. A gestalt, by interpreting visual evidence in the simplest way, is a tool for speedy processing of novel visual
data, but one which may lead to incorrect identifications.

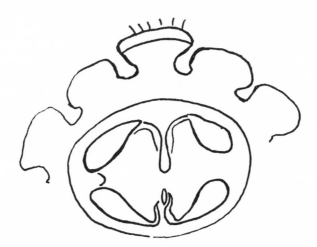

"Mickey" recognized in a fabric design. Note the "head"
with its "hair"--the topmost semicircle of the outer
border of the motif. Compare Sendak's In the Night
Kitchen, p. 30.

Over the period studied, Anna identified a wide range of
things where no meaningful figure was intended by the artist,
but our records show that she was more likely to see faces (or

parts thereof), animals, birds, or insects than flowers,
trees, grass, landscape forms, or man-made objects of any
kind. In other words, Anna's pattern-making vision was geared
to some shapes more than others; she identified a "rabbit" six
times, and an "elephant" and a "giraffe" four times each. In
the case of both rabbit and giraffe, it emerged that she
worked from a single form cue; anything with a long neck was a
giraffe, a creature with long ears was a rabbit; other features of the animals in question seemed superfluous, and we
are given an insight into the rules by which Anna must earlier
have learned to distinguish these particular animals when
intentionally portrayed as part of a picture. In examining
Anna's "mistakes" then, we have a chance to see what, for her,
constituted the essentials of a given pictured thing. Let us
look in detail at the four "elephants" that she distinguished,
where an adult viewer would see only unimportant background
shapes and colors, bearing in mind that the thirteen-month
period they cover (2.1-3.3) represents only the central portion of the time when similar visual miscues were being recorded (1.0-4.6).

The first of the elephants was seen in Ezra Jack Keats's Over
in the Meadow, given to Anna at 1.10 and never a favorite.
For the sixth opening, Keats has set his crows and their nest
against one of his characteristic marbled backgrounds. On the
left-hand page where the marbling is subordinated to the large
figure of the mother crow, it is more obviously "ground" than
on the right-hand page, where it occupies the entire space and
separates into maplike seas, islands, and coastlines and thus
contains its own figures and grounds. At 2.1 Anna turned the
book upside down at this crow opening and identified a portion
of the marbled background as an elephant. She repeated this
about a week later. It has been claimed that young children
find less difficulty in viewing a figure depicted upside down
than an adult would (Arnheim, 1964, p. 69) but we notice that
Anna felt the need to orient the elephant correctly when
talking about it to us.

The elephant shape that Anna saw consisted of a trunk, eye,
and head only. In itself the head is an undistinguished blob;
the eye is one of the blue "lakes" mentioned above. This
leaves us with the inescapable conclusion that it was the
"trunk" that signaled "elephant" to her.

Old MacDonald Had Some Flats never became a favorite of
Anna's (her preference for color over black and white, which
we shall discuss in the next chapter, probably played some

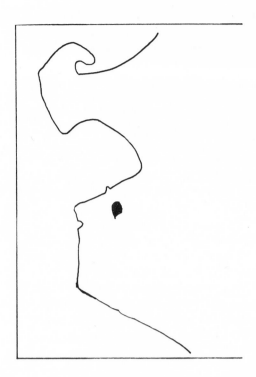

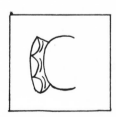

Two "elephants." <u>Above</u>, the outline of the shadowy
"head" and "trunk," redrawn from <u>Over in the Meadow</u>
(Op. 6). <u>Below</u>, the elephant-foot lamp base, redrawn
from <u>Old MacDonald</u> (Op. 4).

part in this). Old MacDonald starts with a drooping tomato
plant in his basement flat and ends with a full-blown inner-
city farm occupying the quarters of the tenants, who have
left. When Mrs. Katz departs, the removalist stands holding a
table lamp in the crook of his arm, so that the bottom third
of the base is divided from the rest. The bulb-shaped base
flares out to a pedestal decorated at its lower edge with
half-circles; a second row of the design consists of arcs
concentric with each of these semicircles. Anna at 2.9 pointed
to the lamp: "That is like an elephant's foot," she said. Just
two months later, 21 June '74, she saw in the diary the sketch
of this lamp base and said it was an "elephant." Specifying
"foot" on the earlier occasion, Anna gave a clear indication
that she was not claiming to see a whole elephant, and there
is no doubt at all that she knew there was no actual animal
intended. Despite its unlikely position, she picked up the cue
that an elephant's foot has crescent toes. What assisted in
the division of the "foot" from the rest of the lamp base is
that the unfamiliar object is not differentiated into parts by
colors and is further disguised by the overlapping arm.[4]

At 3.2 Anna borrowed Mrs. Beggs and the Wizard, describing
it as a "lovely book," enjoying, it would seem, the Mayer
parade of monsters in strange places. One in particular, a
peculiar hybrid in shades of pink and gray, has wrapped himself around a bedroom scene (Op. 3), with coils of tail creating an upward curve to the left, balanced on the extreme
right by the downward movement of the creature's head, its
hand leeringly held to its nose. The overlapping of the coils
has resulted in a seemingly separate section--the last taper-
ing end of the tail--and this Anna saw as the tail. Moving
down from that, the next coil has an apparent central seam;
the gray, the lines to indicate wrinkling and curving, and the
sinuous form of the whole coil all add up to make an acceptable trunk.
A: That's a funny elephant.
M: Why do you think it's an elephant?
A: There's its nose--and there's its tail.
M: Isn't this its nose here? (At the other end.)
A: Yes. And here (sticking to her initial statement).

A "funny elephant," she said. It consists of nothing but tail
and trunk, and Mercer Mayer has compounded the problem, since
a gap which would logically reveal part of the monster's body
shows only the moon in a cloudy sky outside the bedroom
window. Again, as in Old MacDonald, an object overlapping
another seems to have reduced a figure to the sum of its

parts, and Anna has sought to discover meaning in the parts. The head at the other end of the creature caused no confusion because a head and face do carry meaning. (Questioned at 4.9 she was clearly reading the picture as the artist intended.)

When at 3.3 she next found part of a nonexistent elephant in Me and My Flying Machine it was again the trunk that was the cue. Coming across wood, a hammer, and nails in an old barn, an enterprising small boy builds himself a flying machine in which his dreamed flights enable him to "see everything. So I'd always know where everything was and I'd never get lost." Mercer Mayer has illustrated the text at this point with a landscape stretching across the opening, and the boy looking down at the panorama. Anna pointed to where the boy's shirt sleeve is filled with air, and his earflap and strap are hanging down: Look! he has a trunk there! The top half of the flying helmet has to be ignored, but not the creased bottom half from the ear-circle backward; this is the "elephant's" large and floppy ear, the strap is its trunk. On this occasion, she is again aware that there is no full representation of an elephant; or, since she has said "he has a trunk," she is too conscious of the boy's presence to be lured into seeing that there is an elephant there as well.

By the time we reach this final example, it is obvious that Anna is not so much making visual blunders as simply searching for possibly meaningful details in otherwise puzzling segments of a picture. But in the process she is prepared to neglect some of the evidence of the whole picture and concentrate on a small part independently of the rest; she has not learned that the interpretation of such portions is generally governed by the interpretation of the main, foreground subject; even though she could identify that subject easily, it does not yet (as it might do for an adult) reduce the remainder to insignificance or pretty accompaniment.

SHAPE AND SIZE: PERSPECTIVE

The way an object was oriented on the page had a bearing on how easily Anna could recognize it, partly through unfamiliarity with the objects themselves and partly because on the whole her early books had presented objects from conventional angles. An extreme case of this is Dick Bruna's Polly, who sits on her page in The School, eyes front, as if posing for a passport photograph. From books in which characters and objects had mostly been depicted from child's or adult's eye level, Anna at 2.11 had not built up sufficient experience to make sense of a picture of a horse seen, foreshortened, from above and behind. Hence her puzzlement at Op. 8 of Charles Keeping's Black Dolly (1966). Her confusion was resolved when she was shown the ways Dolly's appearance varied when viewed from different angles, and there was no further comment after the first two readings. Tested at 4.8, she unhesitatingly and correctly identified horse and action (pulling a cart).

At 4.5, almost two years later, she looked at the mole in Hosie's Alphabet (Baskin, 1972, "M" page). The mole is seen as if from a cricket's viewpoint, emerging from a hole which conceals half his body. Anna's reaction: Does a mole really look like that? Had she possessed similar experience and language skill at 2.11, she might well have asked of Black Dolly: "Does a horse and cart really look like that?" The essential shape of objects can be dramatically altered by foreshortening and by overlapping; in the case of Baskin's mole, cut off halfway down his body, the adult eye expects that the remainder of the body is concealed below ground. The child has to learn this.

From shape distortions due to viewing angle we pass on to size differences that result from other classical perspective conventions. There were two occasions on which Anna verbalized her perception that there was a size difference between a near object and one in the background, which would have been the same size if drawn side by side. At 3.2 she suggested that the garment Mrs. Badger is knitting was "too big for Frances." A tiny Frances consuming a cookie under the table is in real terms only half as long as the sleeve Mrs. Badger is holding in the foreground. But the sleeve is intended for Frances after all (Hoban, 1964, Op. 11.).

The other example comes from the fifth reading of Uncle Timothy's Traviata when Anna was 3.5. Uncle Timothy is a splendid visitor with a car named Traviata, in which the boy and his mother are borne off on a series of picnics and outings. The book is basically black and white, and the economical addition of color does not distract from the line work; this may have had a bearing on Anna's focus on a distant telegraph pole: Look, there's a little one! Anna's exclamation revealed no sense that it is inappropriate to have a little telegraph pole, only that it is worth remarking on; a small pole in the distance is inconsistent with the larger pole in the foreground. (Asked at 5.0 if the distant pole were small,

Anna said: It's only that it's far away, having learned the convention in the interim.) What does seem possible is that she was quite unaware of the existence of a "perspective problem" in picture books, and that only the differences arbitrarily produced by altering sizes for effect, from opening to opening, and the ordinary size differences between things at the same distance gave her pause.

In fact, one of the first rules a child must learn as she looks at picture books is that a character who appears on more than one page is likely to alter in size. The adult who reads the text is clearly not put out when a character shrinks or expands and thus reinforces the lesson that size differences are meaningless. A quick glance at A Lion in the Meadow shows, for example, one view of the mother standing upright using all the vertical space (p. 5), but another on p. 2, roughly one eighth the size! While this particular variation never caused Anna to comment, she did remark on the last page in Little Hedgehog at 2.10. Little Hedgehog is captured by a small girl, is taken home and petted, until it becomes apparent that he is sickening for his home in the woods. Then the girl lets him go. Little Hedgehog is seen in different perspectives throughout the book, varying from tiny to half-page size. When he bulked large, Anna responded: I want him to be tiny. This is unlikely to be a plea for consistency, as it is the only time that Anna demanded a change in size for a pictured object. Could it be that the beast's triumphant sidelong glance once he is liberated is threatening, since he is now suddenly grown large? Or is the near view of a hedgehog, with solid sharp quills, so dismaying that she found herself wishing, on the fifth day of her acquaintance with the book, that he would become small and manageable again?

By 3.7 the lesson that what is big on one page may be little on the next was so well internalized, thanks to parental explanations of the convention, that Anna could volunteer a demonstration; in The Selfish Giant, borrowed and treasured soon after she had seen the film version of it, she said: You see how a big [sic] wall it is in that picture--in the next picture--you see in that picture it's small (Ops. 7 and 10). Here she does not venture to give a reason, but she accepts the variation in size without confusion.[5]

THE DEMAND FOR CONSISTENCY

When she was 1.11 we observed Anna's new ability to compare, using "like" ("Anna has hat like big boys" in discussing

Goggles), and at 2.0 she is recorded as having pointed out things that were the "same"--endpapers, jacket illustrations repeated within the covers, and so on. Starting with consistency, she was set to go on to inconsistency and to notice subtle differences from picture to picture. Such subtleties she picked up when reading Zeralda's Ogre (we didn't). Two days running (at 2.2) she talked about Zeralda's face in the scene where she is cooking food for the unconscious ogre and is flushed with exertion and the heat from the fire. Anna remarked, Face pink, despite the fact that the difference between this and earlier renderings of Zeralda's face is minute.

Anna was 2.4 when she borrowed The Wonderful Ball. She had had previous acquaintance with Dick Bruna's The School (at 1.9) but with nothing else as stylized as this. Despite (or perhaps because of) her understandable confusion arising from the obvious inconsistencies in the drawing and in the use of color, The Wonderful Ball made a strong impact on her. On the thirteenth day after borrowing, she first mentioned the fact that in Op. 6 (the night scene) Bob the dog is all black and white, whereas on other pages his body is yellow and his ears and tail are blue inside the black outline. This differs from the Zeralda instance in that Anna now makes the comparison explicit: her focus on the changing colors of Bob the dog is unambiguous. This example of a concern for consistency in color use from illustration to illustration is the earliest verbalized in the record.

Fears expressed that "small children . . . may be confused by blue elephants and lilac swans"[6] do not seem to be justified by Anna's experience. Since Anna's introduction to a lion came not in the tawny beast of A Lion in the Meadow but in her "lions and tigers" pajamas, which boast an orange lion, a bug-eyed elephant with green-fringed ears, an orange- and green-striped tiger, and an orange moose spotted in green, any alternative color scheming in books was already building on an eccentric foundation. Color changes from book to book passed unnoticed. But at 2.10 she made her first protest that while the text of a book spoke of an object of a certain color, the illustrations showed it in another. After four readings of Johnny Lion's Rubber Boots it suddenly struck her with a gurgle of amusement that in the pictures Johnny Lion's boots were orange rather than the red mentioned in the text.

When Anna was 2.11, her wish for consistency of color (in the characters of a book) and accuracy of color (when the text laid down what to expect) was balanced by a sudden awareness

of alternating page colors, as in for example the Noggin
books. Her first perception of this came in a simple remark,
Now he's yellow, when she realized that the Moon Mouse's
color changed. This was in Noggin and the Moon Mouse, which
recounts a space age incident at the court of Noggin the Nog.
We showed her how the colors changed throughout the book, and
she seemed to enjoy the accuracy with which we could predict
the color in the next opening. And since Noggin books enjoyed
great popularity with her from then until 3.3, she had plenty
of opportunity, which she seized, to anticipate the color of
the next page. Although there have been many times since when
Anna could have chosen to comment on this particular feature
of book design, after its vigorous birth and flourishing in
that period, her concern mainly lay dormant. It surfaced as
late as 4.8, when she drew our attention matter-of-factly to
alternating pages of black and brown line drawings (Stuff
and Nonsense, p. 56).

At 3.6 she objected to a lolly-pink Keeping bird (Black Dolly,
Op. 6): Birds aren't colored that color, thus verbalizing for
the first time a comparison between the color of a pictured
object and its real life equivalent. She was 3.9 when she commented on the eyes in The Pirates' Tale, drawn as blue circles
or ovals containing black pupils and ringed with black:
A: Are these animal pirates?
M: No, why?
A: Because they have pink, blue eyes. We don't have blue
   eyes, do we?
While Maureen replied accurately that some people do have blue
eyes, she omitted to add that, nevertheless, they don't look
like the eyes of these pirates. Anna, sensing something not
right, had identified the problem by using the word "animal"
to mean "not normal in the human being." See the next chapter
for more on the development of realism as a criterion for
assessing the merit of a picture.

Color was the touchstone for measuring consistency until 2.11
but in the period 2.8-3.6 Anna broadened her concerns for
evaluating text-picture matching to include whether a character was doing what the text said he was. Most frequent was
her perception that someone said to be speaking was shown with
his mouth closed. This is the case in Father Bear Comes Home,
p. 49, which we borrowed for the second time when she was
2.11. On the third day of our second borrowing period, we were
reading "Hiccupping" (which remained Anna's favorite story in
the volume) when she said emphatically, pointing to Father
Bear: His mouth is closed. He can't roar like that! The text
opposite begins: "Father Bear roared . . ." Twice further down

the page, he is said to "look at" the others. We pointed this out to Anna and said that the picture showed him looking rather than roaring, and she seemed perfectly ready to accept this. Since the visual cue for speaking is a much stronger one than for watching, which is particularly hard to convey, it was speaking that she expected to see portrayed.

OBJECTS INCOMPLETELY SHOWN

It has been stated a number of times that small children may interpret figures cut off by the page edge or overlapped by other objects as in some way hurt or broken and feel distress as a result.[7] In fact the Newsons's evidence (1970, p. 211) suggests that such a problem may be only part of a wider phenomenon: a particular form of heightened sensibility which in some children manifests itself in a horror of broken or distorted objects in life must be seen as extending into the picture book experience rather than arising out of it. Nevertheless, the problem has been widely enough aired for reviewers to have chided artists for failing to show pictures complete in a book intended for preschool audiences,[8] and we were interested to see whether our own daughter manifested the kind of concern that had been reported of some other children.

Until Anna was 1.9 she had never shown distress at figures overlapped by others or cut in two by the page edge. The second book she owned, The Pirates' Tale at 1.0, is full of figures cut off by the page edges. However, in no instance did we record a question about "missing parts" in this book between 1.0 and 4.8 when she last asked for it to be read to her. For Anna the moment of insight came at 1.9, sitting on a visitor's knee as they shared Old MacDonald had Some Flats. Worriedly, she kept saying as they studied Op. 8: Wheel gone, wheel gone. Significantly enough, the first incomplete object which arrested her eye was a circle, that simplest of shapes, which more than all others demands completion (Arnheim, 1954, pp. 80-81). An object that is cut off at the frame or at the page edge is normally completed by the mature viewer's eye, unless it is cut off at a natural joint when "visual amputation rather than overlapping is the result, because the visible part looks complete in itself" (ibid.) After this, Anna commented a number of times on incomplete objects, but never again with any semblance of distress.

At 2.4 we found that she could cope with the questions "What do you think?" or "Where do you think?" as a device for reaching her own understanding, and we used these responses

constantly as a counter for her questions during a reading
session, except where adult knowledge was obviously required.
Moreover, when appropriate we answered her questions about,
e.g., missing feet by explaining that there was no room for
them on the page, but that they'd really be "down there" if
the drawing could extend beyond the page. She internalized
this to the extent that she took it upon herself to teach it
to a visiting child: when Anna and Lisel were being read to
(Anna was then 2.11, and Lisel 2.8) the latter wanted to know
where a missing head was. Anna, with wild exaggeration of the
distance involved, explained "out there."

She began at 2.9 to show an ability to elaborate reasons of
her own for the nonappearance of something. When listening to
Wish Again, Big Bear at 2.9, she interrupted to say about Big
Bear on p. 2: We can't see the rest of him--maybe he's fallen
into a car. This was followed a moment later, while we were
reading p. 3, with Maybe he's run into a donkey. She was gain-
ing control over the convention; her thinking still ran to
concrete possibilities, but she seemed to be quite happy to
speculate about why we couldn't see the missing part. At 3.2
Anna looked at Wildsmith's small boy in A Child's Garden of
Verses, p. [9] and asked: Is there a hole there? From the page
opposite, we can see that the boy has (sometimes) white socks
and black shoes, which seem to be concealed by grasses. Anna's
understanding is that we cannot see his feet because they are
in a hole.[9] In Anna's case, incomplete objects caused little
distress and were tackled simply as problems of comprehension.

To summarize the stages that she passed through:
1. No awareness (apparently) of anything out of place or
   missing (up till 1.9).
2. Awareness of part missing from object depicted (with distress on first occasion only).
3. Question: "Where's his (the)-----?"
4. Speculation about possible location of missing part (from
   2.9).

The first three stages in this chronological progression seem
likely to be universal; with the last we feel some reserve
because we are unsure to what extent speculation is a learned
strategy, particularly in a child as young as Anna was when
she learned to employ it habitually. Maybe children whose
parents readily supply answers to all their questions come to
speculate later than Anna did.[10]

There is a pattern in the times that Anna talked about something missing until at 3.7 the problem apparently ceased to

exist. We have already spoken of The Pirates' Tale; her subsequent books provided multiple instances of incompletely shown objects on which no comment was made, including a famous "missing part" crux in The Tale of Peter Rabbit, where Peter takes refuge in a watering can and somewhat unwisely lets his ears protrude.

In fact Anna was most likely to ask questions about missing objects when the page contained relatively little (e.g., one or two figures against a plain ground), or when the artwork was stylized against a plain ground (e.g., Bruna). In both these instances Anna's eye is focused on the missing part by the absence of other, potentially distracting material. And, we found, she was more likely to notice disappearing parts when the figure in question is portrayed going off the extreme right-hand edge.[11]

In just two instances among the twenty-eight recorded accounts of her questions concerning this phenomenon in the period 1.9-3.7 did she focus on an inanimate object; people and animals, as was consistently the case with her, mattered more than things. Roughly half of these examples feature bit players, like a monkey who is making his exit off the top right hand corner of the "toesy-woesy" page of A Very Special House.

One other element that many of these examples have in common is that there is on the same page or opening a similar character who has whatever feature is lacked by the figure to whom Anna calls attention. Close by the vanishing monkey in A Very Special House is a monkey shown entire; Wildsmith's boy with feet lost in herbage is pictured opposite a larger, complete version of the same boy contemplating his shadow.

The object overlapped by another or hidden by the angle from which it is viewed is a visual problem we have to interpret in our daily lives. The object chopped off by the page edge is an artistic convention, corresponding to the way that our field of vision is limited, until we move our heads. For the sake of keeping this section of the discussion within bounds, we have represented our abundant material on Anna's understanding of other artistic conventions by an analysis of her comprehension of the ways of depicting water and of showing movement.

REPRESENTATION OF WATER

We first paid attention to Anna's possible understanding of conventional representations of water when she was 2.9; she

pointed to Old Mother Hubbard's dog on p. 17 of Galdone's Old
Mother Hubbard and her Dog and said: He's standing in the
water. The dog is standing on his head upon a ground of aqua
blue laid on in horizontal lines, which in fact represent
grass. Compare this grass with water in The Story About Ping,
which is largely shown in a turquoise blue, horizontally stri-
ated, like the Galdone grass; Anna's Grandmother had given her
Ping when Anna was 1.4, and we believe that it helped to
form her concept of water-as-illustrated, along with The Cow
Who Fell in the Canal, which she owned from 2.3. In the latter, the lines on the water are always horizontal whether
across the stream or along it (except, of course, for ripples
and wash). Spier uses corrugated lines, blue on blue. It is
notable that Anna made her statement about the dog standing in
the water, not about a page where there is a solid block of
color beneath the feet of the Dame and the dog (p. 32), but
only where there are horizontal lines beneath the figure. At
2.9 then, Anna's rule for pictured water was that it should be
in some shade of blue (or black and white), and that it should
not be solid but show either horizontal striation (blue and
white) or horizontal corrugation. We did not read the book
together again until three weeks later, when Anna was 2.10.
Instead of stating "He's in the water", she asked: Is he in
the water? which suggests that our explanation had been
partly, but by no means wholly, absorbed.

Just three days after the first time she confused the Galdone
grass with water, she glimpsed our art book Lyonel Feininger:
City at the Edge of the World. Although she had seen illustrations of sailing vessels in Hurrah, We're Outward Bound and
steamboats in The Little Red Lighthouse and the Great Gray
Bridge she was unable to marshal any memories of them to help
her recognize Feininger's wooden models, which rest upon a
plane surface. Anna described this shiny plane (ranging from
gray to ink blue) as a road--presumably thinking of bitumen.
Once more it seemed that Anna expected some striation or wavy
lines in a representation of the sea, or any body of water.
Two months later when Anna was 2.11, she interpreted Carol
Barker's stylized river, represented by blue corrugations on
white ground in King Midas, pp. [44]-45 as being "like
little houses." We reread the text aloud several times and
prompted her to compare the river with the drops that Midas is
sprinkling. She finally guessed correctly, seemingly working
from the turquoise color of the drops to the turquoise river.[12]

The examples we have quoted indicate that Anna's ability to
recognize pictorial representations of water rested on her

abstraction of two or three key elements from the pictured
water in her early books. Striation, either horizontal or
wavy, combined with color (blue) to form a "water" gestalt
similar in many respects to the gestalts we discussed earlier
in this chapter. Where separate lines were replaced by a solid
block of color, she was unable to identify the result as water
even when the color was blue, so that striation seemed to take
precedence over hue. When corrugations were altered in the
direction of squarer forms (as in King Midas) she could no
longer connect them with water. In the examples cited, contextual clues were less important than would be the case with an
older viewer. Anna seemed often to see a given section in
isolation from the remainder of the picture, and as we have
observed previously in this chapter, to expect it to be meaningful in itself. Since the latest of the cited examples,
however, we have recorded no occasions on which she failed to
identify pictured water correctly.

REPRESENTATION OF MOVEMENT

In Mulga Bill's Bicycle, a lively interpretation of a poem
familiar to generations of Australians, Ops. 6 and 13 feature
a mode of drawing (multiple image) which, following the medi-
eval tradition, shows a figure in the various stages of one
action within the one frame. Op. 6 also depicts a boy up a
tree watching Mulga Bill, and this boy drew Anna's eye at 2.0
rather than the four views of Mulga Bill attempting to mount
and ride his new penny farthing. In Op. 13, however, there is
no small boy to attract the attention, and the right-hand page
has, as well, a plain black backdrop. This opening, and especially the right-hand page on which "three Mulga Bills" are
falling, puzzled her.[13] At 2.11 she again showed confusion
when confronted by this technique, but she did not comment on
later examples until an ambiguous instance at 4.0, when looking at Op. 11 in In the Night Kitchen (heard many times from
2.1). She traced out the plane flight from left to right (saying "sshh," etc.), treating each frame as a new beginning.
Questioned at 4.8 about both of these cases, it seemed sure
that she understood the use of multiple images seen in Mulga
Bill's Bicycle, but it was unclear whether she understood
the four frames of In the Night Kitchen.

At 3.1 Anna asked specifically for an explanation of lines
denoting pressure that is applied to a yielding surface, in
this case a whale being prodded (Noggin and the Whale, p. 28);
at 3.5 she misinterpreted the direction in which a bone was

being thrown, confusing the person throwing with the one being thrown to, missing the cues given by the pose of each and by the dotted flight path of the bone (Uncle Timothy's Traviata, p. [14]); at 4.2 she confused a smoothly revolving robot with one untidily disintegrating (that is, she was not familiar with the multiple circular or elliptical lines which signal a revolving object [Clanky the Mechanical Boy Op. 5]. In all these cases the artist's attempt to convey movement had to be explained to Anna. Had she had extensive contact with comics, she would have perhaps been more practiced in reading conventions of certain types, particularly stylization, speech balloons, and the methods of indicating all kinds of violence and movement. In fact, her acquaintance with strips has been minimal--odd Sunday comics and three volumes of Tintin.

Much of what we have seen to date in this chapter shows a dynamic interaction between Anna's own self-deduced rules and the laws of conventional pictorial representation. In considering her understanding of the convention of lines to show movement, however, we have seen that the interaction is less equal: rather a case of Anna's coming up against an unfamiliar convention, failing to understand it, and then internalizing the adult's explanation. More interesting are the few examples where she puts her newly acquired rules into practice.

Richard Scarry gets himself into real trouble in creating Lowly Worm, the worm who can't wriggle but instead wears one shoe on his "foot." In the Please and Thank You Book Lowly is seen (Op. 14) bounding away from the Horrid Pests he has just introduced to the reader. Lowly is at the bottom of the curve described by his bound, and the distance he has already covered is indicated by a single black line. Anna said at 3.0, after owning the book from 1.9: Look at Lowly's big zoom! As a noun, "zoom" seemed to be an invention of Anna's to use when talking about movement lines. Two days later as she rode up and down the cement path on her tricycle, leaving wet marks behind, she called out: Look at my zooms, mother. We have always thought how difficult it must be to understand the convention of lines of movement, because they make visible on the page something which has no visible equivalent in nature. It is likely that because Anna found the visible lines made by her tricycle tires, she was able to interpret for herself the line of Lowly's bound.

She was given for Christmas at 3.5 the Dr. Seuss Marvin K. Mooney Will You Please Go Now, and in the fifth reading she commented on Op. 4 where Marvin is departing in a hat: He's

<u>going</u> <u>a</u> <u>zoom</u> . . . <u>yes</u>, <u>that's</u> <u>because</u> <u>the</u> <u>hat</u> <u>made</u> <u>a</u> <u>zoom</u>--
<u>made</u> <u>a</u> <u>line</u> <u>like</u> <u>that</u>. In Op. 11 the text reads "Get yourself
a Ga-Zoom. You can go with a.........BOOM." The resulting
explosion is supported by seemingly solid columns of white
(zoom lines?). Perhaps the term "Ga-Zoom," combined with the
lines of movement, reminded Anna of the word she had used five
months earlier. Certainly she again uses it as a noun.

CONCLUSIONS

Where published research findings are available for us to
compare with our observations of Anna, we have found that
generally speaking, she was capable of more, earlier, than we
might have expected. This in itself is not surprising, for two
reasons; more work has been done in testing school-age children than preschool children with their attendant language
constraints; and second, Anna's constant high exposure to book
illustrations made her a somewhat exceptional case.

Her ability to read pictures depended to a large extent on her
previous artistic experience. It was not necessary to have
seen a lion in the life to be able to recognize one on the
page and enjoy the reunion. Having seen one in a book in
another art style was no barrier to recognition, except for
the times when Anna had borrowed a highly stylized or nonrepre-
sentational work.

She came to prefer to see pictures correctly oriented on the
page comparatively early. The devices which artists use to
accommodate three-dimensional objects to the two-dimensional
page with finite boundaries all gave Anna a measure of difficulty; such devices as overlapping, foreshortening, and cutting off an object at the page edge are conventions which do
not always make an effective compromise between two- and
three-dimensionality. The conventions which convey sound and
movement on the silent, static page needed to be explained to
her.

There seems a likelihood that to 4.6, Anna had not always
separated pictures reliably into figure and ground. This was
masked by her preference for human or at least humanized characters; these she knew to be figure.

Consistency was important to her. She was alert for textual
statements which contradicted the evidence of the corresponding illustrations. Color differences were the first that she

noted, and she then became aware of poses and actions which did not match up with the text. The text gave rise to other expectations which the illustrations failed at times to fulfill; in attempting to identify something mentioned but not illustrated, Anna would seek to find it in the most likely place. Her behavior seemed to show that she regarded the illustrations as the authority, rather than the text, until she became familiar with "chapter" books, in which there is a preponderance of text. She seemed to expect that everything ought to make sense, and she enjoyed being in control: she liked being able to solve for herself the question of where the rest of something was, if it was obscured. On occasion we could see the way she learned to identify an object by selected cues (e.g., long ears for a rabbit, horizontal blue striations for water) which could allow her to ignore other evidence.

We have at all times been struck by the sensible nature of Anna's questions, bearing in mind the static nature of the medium. She had to learn to interpret poses eternally frozen as part of continuous movements. She had to contend with varieties of style and with all sorts of arbitrary tricks by artists. By the time she was 5.0, she had served an apprenticeship and seldom wanted any explanations of what was happening in an illustration.

11

The Genesis of Taste:
Anna's Picture Preferences

In the previous chapter, we looked at some of the ways in
which Anna learned the language of pictures in her books,
concentrating mainly on the things which she found puzzling or
difficult, and her acquisition of picture-reading skills. Now
it seems appropriate to turn to the broad area of her aesthetic appreciation: what she liked and disliked, the form in
which she cast her evaluations, her dawning awareness of
style.

BLACK AND WHITE OR COLOR?

Anna's two earliest books were both in color: her first (at 11
months) was Thomas Goes Out, which we mentioned in chap. 8,
"Fiction Re-created," in connection with the games it inspired; its clear pictures and white backgrounds are what many
would consider suitable for a very young child--less stylized
than Bruna but similar in their deployment of a single figure
per page. The Pirates' Tale, which she received a month
later, was very different; crowded, brightly colored spreads
and Rouault-like black outlining. It may well be, though we
cannot be sure, that these two volumes were influential in
forming Anna's expectation of what a picture book should be
like.

At the same time as she was poring over Thomas and The Pirates'
Tale, however, she had ample opportunity to look through our
own books, many of them illustrated in black and white. The

first occasion on which we observed what might have been a
preference for color was when Anna (1.9) took advantage of an
open door and our absorption in the washing up to raid our bedroom bookshelves, emerging with Peg's Fairy Book, a vulgarly
pretty volume, which sold thousands of copies in Australia in
the forties and fifties. Anna was extraordinarily excited by
the book, uttering a series of loud high "oooos" until we went
to talk about the book with her. She went through the book's
colored pages three times before she paid any heed to the line
drawings. Her clear preference on this occasion was for color
rather than black and white[1] but she made no verbal statement to this effect.

At 2.3, an unequivocal comment confirmed the preference. Anna
settled into her pram studying her new library books, replying
to a suggestion that she might like to look at our library
books too, as she usually did. This time her words were dispar-
aging: Mother books have three pictures. Mother books have
black pictures. Being interpreted, this reads: "Mother's
books have only black and white pictures, more than two, but
not many."

In all, there are in the record fifteen clear examples of
Anna's preference, verbally or nonverbally expressed, for
color over black and white. After Peg's Fairy Book at 1.9,
four statements came between 2.0 and 3.0, six between 3.0 and
4.0, and three between 4.0 and 5.0, and referred to both line
drawings and b/w photographs. Her comments took such forms as
these:
At 3.5: I do not like the black color (The Bee, 1973). This
remark was made by way of comparison with the two colored
photos she said she liked.

At 3.5: I do not want to look at those nasty black pictures
(Dragons and Other Things, 1973). Anna referred to black and
white photographs, pp. 42-43.

At 3.11: I hate black pictures (Discovering Northumbria,
1975). Anna was looking at the b/w photos.

At 4.0: They should be in color (The Travels of Oggy, 1976).
Talking about the line drawings in this book, which she spontaneously showed a visitor.

Knowing her dislike for b/w, we stopped choosing such books
for her when we had opportunities for solitary selection, with
infrequent exceptions designed to test whether her opinion had

changed. Her last recorded comment was made when she was 4.4.
A visitor had brought along a carton of her children's books
with her, and Anna had selected one when asked to do so:
Excuse me, I chose this book. It hasn't any colored pictures--
but that doesn't matter (The Little Farm, 1942). To the extent
that she felt the need to mention the book's lack of color,
she showed that the deficiency did matter to her. These
instances have all been negative; but she also remarked
positively on the presence of color.

At 3.0 she leafed through a book of alternating full color and
b/w, showing the "pretty pages," which were all colored. At
3.5 she talked about what constituted a "nice book" and said
it would have "colored pages." When she was 4.5, having to
remain at home, she requested the right sort of library books:
Books that look like fun on the cover. These, she said, were
books with bright colors and people and houses. Despite the
apparent strength of her preference for color over b/w, she
was perfectly prepared to accept story books illustrated in
line, as the records for Finn Family Moomintroll and The
Story of Doctor Dolittle make abundantly clear. If the story
exerted a sufficiently strong pull, then lack of color would
be tolerated in silence. Had her earliest books been uncolored, she might have developed an entirely different aesthetic: as it was, her enjoyment of color led her to establish
an order of preference for certain hues, to comment critically
on artists' color use, and to be able to distinguish minute
variations of color.

In Anna's first and second years we were not keenly observant
of her interest in color. We did believe in surrounding her
with brightly colored objects and clothes, which stood out
against the soft creams and dark browns of our interior, and
she spent hours playing with our many-hued plastic pegs. We
taught her color names, and as soon as she could manage them,
she was given thick crayons to draw with--nothing out of the
ordinary in any of this, but it may well have influenced the
importance she was later to place on color in book illustration.

At 2.8 we borrowed for her Yutaka Sugita's One to Eleven, a
counting book in vibrant shades. For Anna the key page was an
opening showing ten pencils, from the points of which there
stretched colored lines. Each time she opened the book there
she listed all the colors. One day after looking at this page
and ignoring all the rest of the book, she got up to find her
crayons and draw, obviously spurred on by the colors.

Though it is clear from these and other early records that Anna derived enjoyment from such color-related activities, her verbal communication was confined to the enumeration and iden- tification of colors until 2.9 when a poster showing Babar was hung in her room: It's lovely--all those colors (in fact only green, blue, black and white). From this time on the flow of remarks about colors never ceased.

Color Preferences

Anna's approval of the lavish use of color in general is strik- ingly exemplified in the record for Wildsmith's The Miller, the Boy, and the Donkey, which we brought home for her when she was 3.5, to give her another chance of liking Wildsmith (for whom she had displayed little enthusiasm). Her response was an unequaled intensification of her color-oriented behav- ior. Having listened to it the first time without any overt reaction, her second hearing of the book proceeded like a mail-order buyer's perusal of a glossy catalogue. Since Wild- smith's consistent predilection is for stripes, multicolored splashes and particolored buildings, we made no consistent attempt to detail in the diary exactly what she was indi- cating.

A (looking at endpapers): Let me tell you what I like--
M (breaking in): Puce.
A (ignoring Maureen and pointing to a color): We could use
    that sort of color in--We could get that sort of color
    paint for me--And we could make that sort of [i.e., "that
    color"] cushion for our chair. [Half-title floral background
    to donkey] And we could make--grow--all these sorts of
    trees, and get these nice ones. What are these [flowers on
    the first text page]--nice bits? [Maureen then began reading,
    skipping the title page] There's another color--this color
    that I want for clothes--and this color that I'll have a
    donkey for [clothes and donkey on the third text opening]
    and we could have this sort--these sorts of clothes for
    Father.
M: You really like the colors in this book?
A: Yes--is that a picture for you to read? [Taking Maureen
    back to the skipped title page] Ah--I want all those sorts
    of flowers [Op. 10]. Um--we could have these sorts of
    vegetables--and all these sorts of cities behind us--
    because I like all these colors.

Notice the way Anna characteristically expressed her apprecia- tion for the colors by "taking possession" of them, planning how they could be <u>used</u>, incorporated into her life. This is parallel with her desire to "go to Sweden," etc., on which we have already remarked.

The reactions in this reading are altogether color-cued without reference to the story. In the next reading she asked about the story (three text questions, one objection that the illustrations did not properly match the text). Twice more the book was read to a silent Anna, who then rejected it and took it back to the library. The graph upward from silent introduction to a peak of interest, followed by a lessening of involvement and a rapid descent to the base line, is a pattern repeated many times. What distinguishes this particular record is the single-mindedness of her focus on color in the second reading in a book in which color is a pleasant external to the story rather than integral to it.

She proved to have a fairly consistent pattern of color preferences over the period we studied: pink, purple, and red in that order, with "pink and purple" becoming a ritual choice. This aesthetic carried through into everyday living: her purple trousers were beloved through three winters; she made frequent suggestions that our pale walls would be improved by painting them purple, and purple was the shade she deemed appropriate for carpet tiles in her room.

A broader picture of Anna's color preferences is given in the following table, based on a simple count of recorded verbal and nonverbal references to individual colors over the entire period studied.

Preferred Colors

Color	No. of Times Pointed To	No. of Times Named
1. Purple	14	7
2. Pink	13	4
3. Green	8	3
4. Red	7	4
5. Blue	6	3
6. Yellow	5	2
Orange	5	0
7. White	3	2
Brown	3	1
8. Gray	2	1

Disliked Colors

Color	No. of Times Pointed To	No. of Times Named
1. {Brown	0	4
Black	0	4
2. Yellow	0	3
3. Gray	0	1

As with most of Anna's comments these were unsolicited, rather than systematically required of her. However, over time, they give a true picture: she spoke more often of what she liked than what she disliked; she was always specific about what she disliked, though apt to wave her fingers vaguely at a pre-ferred color or a combination, which at times left us flounder-ing in a flood of "and that and that and that"--colors which were left undifferentiated in the record. A taped session faithfully preserved the words, but not the colors, unless a pedantic parent had had the forethought to say something like "You like the gold and the red and the blue in this picture?"

As we look down the list of books that elicited from Anna some specific response to color, one thing emerges clearly. Not a single Beatrix Potter is included: is it because she was early accustomed to the style (she received one Potter at 1.9, two at 1.10, two at 1.11) and was not later moved to remark on it? Or because the colors were insufficiently strong to appeal? Hardly a book in the list is one in which pale colors predomi-nate, and if the colors are pale, there is another factor involved in Anna's commendation apart from a liking of certain colors. For example, the soft shades in Bunny in the Honey-suckle Patch, which Anna discovered and enjoyed at 3.5, stood out for her because they were used for initial capitals of the title, on cover and title page. Isn't this pretty!-- This and this and this. As she spoke, she was jabbing at the colored initial capitals. An adult who has seen such a device many a time will probably ignore it, but its novelty in Anna's experience made it attractive to her. Similarly in other books which overall were quiet in tone there was an occasional page in which a touch of brighter color drew Anna's eye, even if only by comparison with duller surroundings.

Care must be taken in analyzing unexpected preferences of Anna's for colors which she would normally show no interest in or openly disparage. One such instance occurred when Anna was 3.7 and looking at The Selfish Giant, a story which had great impact on her (she borrowed it at 3.6, 4.0, and 4.9), and because of the story's hold, she made a conciliatory statement about the habitually disliked color--gray. In Op. 6, the text reads: "They tried to play on the road, but the road was very dusty and full of hard stones, and they did not like it." This gave Anna her cue: I like the color of it--of the bricks and of those and these--and the color of these children's clothes and hair and bows and clothes. Illustrations in this book are in gray, black, and white only; Anna is in fact saying that she likes the story, in this oblique way.

It will be noticed from the tables that yellow was both liked and disliked: unlike the other disliked colors (brown, gray, and black), it is not a dull hue but perhaps earned her disfavor because of its associations with babies' excrement!

EVALUATION AND VISUAL MEMORY

Anna's first explicitly commendatory remark about a whole picture concerned Carol Barker's King Midas, borrowed by us when she was 2.11 and which in spite of its length she insisted on having read. To emphasize the famed wealth of Midas, Carol Barker designed an opulent, gilded book, unique in Anna's experience to that date. Bacchus (p. 27) is clad in purple, highlighted in puce, with a swirl of grapes and grape leaves from his bare right shoulder to his left armpit. He wears a circlet of vine leaves in his hair. Anna responded: That's lovely. At 2.11, Anna's attention was on Bacchus rather than on the rest of the opening, and it was keen enough for her to say when she saw the opening again at 4.9: I remember that page.

In this opening the river, a broad band of turquoise blue corrugated in white, runs across the top of the illustration. Bacchus, directly facing the viewer, holds both arms up stagily, palms outward, at shoulder level. Starting from his right hand, we trace the movement down his arm, across a short span of vine-leaf girdle to join Midas's outflung left arm, till we reach Midas's left shoulder. The roses which surround Bacchus and Midas are bright pink, their leaves light and dark green. Midas's robe repeats the turquoise of the river, although much admixed with black.

When Anna was 3.11 we gave her our copy of Fiona French's King Tree to look at. King Tree tells the story of a masque at Versailles when Louis XIV was king; various "trees" boast of

their superiorities, hoping to be declared king of the trees,
and the Orange tree wins. We watched her turning the pages
with scrupulous caution, then running her fingers over an area
of rich color in Op. 10. The entire opening, apart from white
slivers down each side for text, is taken up with Vine's oval,
green face, and the huge bunches of blue-purple grapes inter-
spersed with leaves which form his hair. As she turned to Op.
11, she breathed reverently and said: Isn't this lovely.
This opening is in warmer tonings; the grapes are predominantly red-purple. Violet and puce are used for the Vine
tree's elaborately slashed clothing, and red for the wine in
his glass. It was only much later that we realized how similar
in color and form both the King Midas and King Tree pictures
are to pp. 12-13 of A Lion in the Meadow, the opening over
which Anna pored, as we saw in part 2. When we compare the
color in the three books we find:

Color	A Lion in the Meadow	King Tree	King Midas
Red	Dragon flame	Wine	
Pink-purple	Foliage, grass	Grapes, clothing	Clothing
Bright pink	Dragon wing	Clothing	Roses
Turquoise	Foliage, grass	Wineglass, foot	River
Mid-brown	Hair	Vine stems	Hair

Not all the details correspond: the tawny lion color of A Lion
in the Meadow is not repeated in the other two. Greens are
totally lacking from this opening in A Lion in the Meadow,
but the boy's skin tones are ochre, which at least in its
divergence from the standard European pink recalls Vine's skin
color, which varies from yellow green to true green.

Bacchus's pose differs from that of Vine and the little boy,
who share a slanted posture. Vine lounges against a balustrade
and in his left hand holds a wineglass level with the top of
his head. He leans his weight upon his left forearm and his
relaxed hand hangs down from the balustrade edge, at waist
height. The little boy's pose, although different, is equivalent in that one arm is up, the other down. In all three illustrations, the interest on the left-hand page of the opening is
counterbalanced by a movement to the right.

King Tree links elements found separately in A Lion in the
Meadow and King Midas. In King Tree, purple-clad Vine is
inclined to his right (our left), producing a strong downward
purple movement to the right. The corresponding movement in

"That's lovely." Top, <u>A</u> <u>Lion</u> <u>in</u> <u>the</u> <u>Meadow</u> (pp. 12-13);
Reproduced by permission of Franklin Watts, Inc.
<u>Center</u>, <u>King</u> <u>Midas</u> (p. 27); reproduced by permission of
Franklin Watts, Ltd.
<u>Bottom</u>, <u>King</u> <u>Tree</u> (Op. 11); reproduced by permission of
Oxford University Press.

A Lion in the Meadow is contained in a tree to the boy's
right, with varying shades of turquoise, blue, purple, and
pink in its foliage. The movement in _King Midas_ comes, as we
have seen, not from the purple-clad Bacchus but from Midas's
overlapping arm. In _King Tree_, the focus has narrowed,
leading to an intensification of the elements, now conjoined.

What are we to make of all this? First, Anna very rarely commented evaluatively on whole illustrations (as opposed to her
multitude of remarks on details like colors); when we find
that two of these rare statements of appreciation refer to
pictures similar in coloring and composition, we should take
notice. And when it can be demonstrated that both of these
pictures share certain of their common elements with an illustration in one of Anna's early books, we must begin to suspect
that the later responses are being influenced by that early
experience and that an "ideal picture" has formed in her mind
against which later illustrations will be measured. Moreover,
the preferred color tones of this archetypal picture correspond well with Op. 8, Anna's favorite opening in her second
book, _The Pirates' Tale_. It looks more and more as if her
color and composition preferences date from very early; and
that they remain remarkably consistent throughout the period
our records cover.

We have already noted briefly another example of the power of
her visual memory in chap. 9, "The Singer of Tales," when we
saw how Anna recalled the first opening of _Zeralda's Ogre_
while looking at a particular frame in "Rupert and Morwenna."
But we can offer a more extended and hence more exciting
instance. At 3.10 Anna was looking through our volume, Robert
Hughes's _Heaven and Hell in Western Art_, illustrated with
reproductions of paintings and carvings on eschatological subjects. On p. 101 are Poussin's _Et in Arcadia Ego_ in which
four figures are grouped around a tomb, pointing to its in-
scription; and below, Guercino's work on the same theme, two
men with staves contemplating a skull atop a tomb. Pointing to
the Guercino, Anna exclaimed: _Urgghh--a skull! . . . Look! It
shows us the most terrible things_. Pointing now to the Poussin
above, she indicated the shadow of one of the men on the side
of the tomb, explaining that the man "has cut somebody's head
off" (paraphrase only). The shadow does at a quick glance
resemble a head, and in our last chapter we discussed Anna's
tendency to such visual miscues. Why should she leap to the
conclusion that this is a _severed_ head? (Anna had never confused skulls with heads, severed or otherwise.) Hugh recalled
that earlier in her progress through _Heaven and Hell_, Anna

"It shows us the most terrible things." <u>Above</u>, Poussin's
<u>Et</u> <u>in</u> <u>Arcadia</u> <u>Ego</u>.
<u>Below</u>, Guercino's <u>Et</u> <u>in</u> <u>Arcadia</u> <u>Ego</u>.

had stopped at a Temptation in Eden scene by Bosch (p. 81) and observed "we've got that one in the Jesus book." The "Jesus book" was her name for Guy Daniel's The Bible Story, which contains color plates by the old masters. In fact this volume contains not the Bosch but a very similar Cranach Temptation, but what matters is that she, having thought once of the pictures in The Bible Story, might now be carrying its store of images over into her interpretation of the Poussin in Heaven and Hell. It was worth checking. Sure enough, we found plate 14 in The Bible Story to be Cima's picture of David carrying Goliath's severed head. He is accompanied by a companion (Jonathan?) who carries a spear across his shoulder; David carries his sword over his--these two figures thus parallel those in the Guercino (those in the Poussin are differently grouped, though there too the men carry staves). The Cima thus provides a visual antecedent for the figures in the Guercino and for the "severed head" Anna sees in the Poussin--but how is it that the skull provides the link? The answer was soon found: The Bible Story also includes de la Tour's Mary Magdalen, in which Mary sits contemplatively, chin in hand, the other hand resting on a skull she has placed on her knee.

Now we have a parallel for the pose of one of the figures in the Poussin; one hand touches his chin while the other touches the shadow on the tomb which Anna described as the "head." Our guess at the way her memory worked can be represented thus:

Stage 1 (Guercino): 2 figures with staves   contemplate skull
                                ↓
Stage 2 (memory of   2 figures with "staves" skull + figure
    Bible Story):   + head (Cima)   with chin in hand
                                ↓   (de la Tour) ↓
Stage 3 (Poussin):   figures with staves;   "head"; figure with
                                                      chin in hand

It was the skull which acted as the initial focus for Anna-- skulls had always had evil/frightening associations for her; but her quick scanning of the Guercino had also taken in the two figures. Both elements then set off memory associations which resulted in her imposing on the Poussin elements of two pictures she had not seen for a considerable period. She interpreted a roughly circular shadow as a "head cut off" not on wild guess or random association of ideas but as a result of a specific memory of a certain visual configuration. There could be no more suggestive evidence of the ability of key images to carry with them considerable portions of their context.

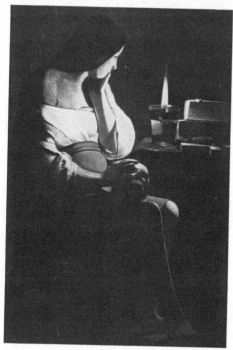

Severed head and skull. <u>Above</u>, Cima's <u>David</u> <u>and</u> <u>Goliath</u>.
<u>Below</u>, de la Tour's <u>Mary</u> <u>Magdalen</u>.

Content Preferences

Occasionally Anna's enjoyment of a picture is derived from its content, as when at 3.10 she observed about the endpaper of The Cabbage Princess: Isn't it lovely--All these people--and these. The endpapers portray courtiers in eighteenth-century costume, with worldly-wise putti, partly framed by willow leaves and heavy wrought ironwork; "and these" refers to the festoons of wrought iron. As we have suggested earlier, land- and seascapes without human or anthropomorphized animal fig- ures did not hold Anna's attention, though such scenes are rare in picture books. Anna evinced lack of interest by turn- ing away, by asking irrelevant questions, or by not stopping to look at the page when spending time alone with the book. An appreciation for landscape has not always been a component of the Western aesthetic, and as landscape is often background to the action of the characters, it may be that such a scene was for her just that.

It is probably true that an emotional involvement in a subject or story will spill over into the attention that any reader gives an illustration. Anna's pleasure in the story of The Selfish Giant led her to attempt to articulate her liking for the story, as distinct from her distaste for the color range of the illustrations: I don't like the text (regularly used by her to mean "illustrations" at this stage) of this book because it has a nasty color in it. But I want the words and the people in it . . . (Anna 3.7). But in view of the commonly held belief that young children respond principally to content rather than to form and presentation, it is worth reiterating that few of her evaluative comments referred to the subject matter pure and simple.

Composition and Page Layout

In our experience, there has never been anything in Anna's comments to indicate an explicit awareness of color balance or of composition, and during the period of this study we made no attempt to teach her such notions. There was however an iso- lated example of a nascent perception of page layout, begin- ning at 3.0 when in four days (six instances)--19, 20, 21, 24 July '75--she spent time searching through three of her books (The Flying Mouse, Noggin the King, and Farmer Barnes at the County Show) to see if a picture was "long enough." This accolade seemed to depend on having the picture spread all the way across the opening for at least part of the height of the page. This search was altogether self-motivated and baffling to us, as we struggled to determine her criteria. The search for pages "long enough" then ceased, never to recur.

One other lone indication of a preference for a particular
page layout cropped up when Anna was 3.3, looking at Frog and
Toad Together; pointing at the illustration and the white
space on p. 38, she said: That's what I like best. And then,
pointing to pp. 40-41: It's not like that. The illustration on
p. 38 is neatly contained in an upright rectangle with rounded
corners framed by generous margins on three sides, with five
lines of text beneath it. On the page opposite, the text
begins one-quarter down the page, allowing a deep margin at
the top. Half of each of the following pages, 40-41, is occupied by an illustration which runs across the opening, framed
by white space on all eight sides (for it is divided into two
down the center). Apart from its orientation on the page and
its twofold nature, what most distinguished this illustration
from that on p. 38 is lack of clear limits. The color stops in
a relatively straight line on six of the eight sides, but on
the top of each half of the diptych, the upper edge of the objects illustrated--flowers, birds, and Frog's house--dictates
the limits of the picture. Lacking further evidence we cannot
generalize beyond this one preference for a neatly framed rectangular picture over an irregularly shaped unframed diptych.
The same two colors are used throughout the book, so that we
are able to rule out color as a factor. These two instances of
Anna's incipient awareness of page layout at 3.0 and 3.3 show
that she was capable of turning her attention to the medium,
but it was a concern rarely verbalized.

Perception of Style

Awareness of artistic style begins, in Anna's case, with her
ability to recognize familiar content in new contexts. Our
records contain multiple examples of this, but we paid special
attention when she made a connection between a known and an
unfamiliar book by the same artist, guessing that this might
underpin style sensitivity proper. Thus, having owned both
Peter's Chair and Goggles she found at 2.2 a library copy of
Whistle for Willie which again features the boy Peter and his
dachshund. Pointing to the boy, she asked: There's Peter? At
3.0 she saw for the first time the nursery-rhyme book To
Market, To Market, illustrated with Peter Spier's usual attention to detail. This Anna seized upon with "Look, Mother."
Since in a library display shelf crowded with colorful picture
books, one volume has little chance of standing out from the
rest unless its jacket is compelling or unless it is familiar,
we wondered what had motivated Anna's exclamation. At the time
we could explain it only as a memory of the jackets of Spier's
Hurrah! We're Outward Bound (read at 2.4) and And So My Garden
Grows (read at 2.3). The same day she asked: Who is that?

pointing to the cow in the dairy in To Market, To Market (Op. 5). Instead of giving the answer "the cow" when we asked her who it was, she asked instead: Is it Hendrika? Hendrika is the Cow Who Fell in the Canal from Spier's book of that name. True it is to say that our reading did not supply us with an over-abundance of named cows, but there were others Anna could have thought of.

The similar layout of the jackets of these three Mother Goose Library books is not in our belief a sufficient stimulus for Anna to connect them. There must as well be some sort of aware-ness that the illustrations with the different-colored frames are similar, even though the content varies. Once we look at the relevant openings of To Market, To Market and The Cow Who Fell in the Canal, the common content is obvious. However, it was Anna who made the leap, connecting one Peter Spier with another, when we had not thought to remind her that this art-ist had also illustrated The Cow Who Fell in the Canal--a book which incidentally she was given at 2.3 but which never engaged her greatly.

At 3.7 Anna was examining the preliminary page in A Very Special House, a list of books by Ruth Krauss, each title illustrated by a small excerpted drawing. Opposite the title The Carrot Seed is a boy drawn by that book's illustrator, Crockett Johnson, and she asked three times if this boy was "Harold and the Purple Crayon." We were puzzled, but a compari-son of the two Johnson boys shows how alike they are. Both are drawn with an economy of line; the little boy from The Carrot Seed faces the right and appears to be holding something in his hand. His pose is similar to that adopted by Harold on several occasions, when the thing he is holding is of course the purple crayon. The Carrot Seed boy is clad in beret, sweater and overalls, not unlike Harold's one-piece suit. His eyes seem like Harold's vertical ovals, his nose equally peaked, and his ears are similar--two-lined--in comparison with Sendak's boy in A Very Special House, which are three-lined. In other words, Anna was responding to a stylistic similarity, though she expressed her perception in terms of a simple identification of the new picture with the familiar one.

We do not advance any of these examples as proof of style sensitivity proper: she has not attained Howard Gardner's "first stage in style detection": "reached when the child's sensitivities to persons and objects combine, leading to aware-ness that a person's way of behaving will leave recognisable

imprints on his creative products" (Gardner, 1972, p. 333).
Though we had often enough explained to Anna about the artists
who had made her books, and pointed out, e.g., that this was
"another book by Maurice Sendak," she has not in the quoted
examples linked an artist's name with her recognition of
similarities.[2] Nor were we ourselves aware at the time that
Crockett Johnson was the artist for The Carrot Seed. But that
she was perceiving a style similarity, though not conscious of
a concept of style, is clear. It seems to us that perceptions
of this type probably predate and form the basis for Gardner's "first stage" (we must recall that his youngest group
of subjects were six or seven years old); see also Machotka
(1966).

Anna's Response to Keeping

Anna seemed to prefer representational art, and we learned to
anticipate fairly well whose style she would respond to, just
as we learned to appreciate what sort of story she would most
enjoy at any age. Mostly we respected her preferences, when
drawing books to her notice, but over the years when we wanted
to see whether her response to more expressionist or nonrepre-
sentational artwork had altered, it was usually a Charles
Keeping title that we offered her. In all, she had six Keeping
titles borrowed for her at ages ranging from 2.11 to 5.3. She
never chose one for herself.

The first of these, Black Dolly, was borrowed when Anna was
2.11, 3.5 and 4.7, a total of a month's stay. It is the
Keeping which has been most available to her. For her at 2.11,
the setting was most unfamiliar and the story as well. Her
evaluative comments about this book were vague, one of the two
being perhaps a statement about a color preference: I like
that (2.11). She was pointing at pink brickwork in Op. 3.
Asked what it was, she replied: Stones I think. At 4.7 she
said before the book was read to her: I like this book. But
the next day while sick in bed she rejected it when it was
offered to her in a pile.

Next came The Nanny Goat and the Fierce Dog, borrowed for
two weeks when Anna was 2.11-3.0. Like Black Dolly, it was
full of perceptual puzzles for her. While looking at the book,
Anna exclaimed: Oh look at this! as she paused to study the
page (Op. 16) in which the rooster and hen have electric blue
comb and wattles. Her interest in this page never reappeared.
The next day she said: This is a frightening story, and it
may well be that her fear was too great for her to want to be
much involved with the book.

The <u>Garden</u> <u>Shed</u> was read at 4.0, and to see what she thought
of it, she was asked questions. For much of the time, she
refused to cooperate. She did volunteer that she saw "lovely
things" in Op. 12, where the flames are leaping. Of Op. 15 she
said: <u>That</u> <u>isn't</u> <u>very</u> <u>nice</u>. We asked "What does it look like?"
expecting her to say that when the grandfather calls Daniel,
his head looks skull-like. Anna's dislike for anything resem-
bling skulls was well established, but she perfunctorily
replied: <u>Naughty</u> <u>nasty</u>. Hugh asked her about the wood-grain
endpapers:
H: What's that?
A: <u>Lovely</u>.

In the second reading, at 4.2, Anna said about the boy hero,
whose still face is depicted in Op. 2: <u>I</u> <u>don't</u> <u>like</u> <u>his</u> <u>face</u>
. . . <u>it's</u> <u>just</u> <u>good</u> <u>he</u> <u>isn't</u> <u>here</u>. Of Op. 6, where the statue
of the lonely lady makes her first appearance, she said: <u>I</u>
<u>don't</u> <u>like</u> <u>the</u> <u>colors</u>, <u>but</u> <u>I</u> <u>like</u> <u>the</u> <u>statue</u>. In Op. 6 she
stagily averted her eyes from the boy Daniel, whom we see full
face again. Of Op. 11, where the colors are becoming warmer as
the fire heats up, Anna said: <u>Hmm</u>, <u>lovely</u> <u>isn't</u> <u>it</u>! And of
Op. 12, with the fire at its height: <u>That</u> <u>looks</u> <u>lovely</u>, <u>doesn't</u>
<u>it</u>. In this reading, she was allowed to respond as she wanted,
and the statement she makes seems less withholding. The preference for Op. 12 remains constant--a range of reds and yellows
against the darker tones of the garden-shed wall. Her dislike
of the grandfather has this time been replaced by her dislike
for the small boy's intent face. Her enjoyment of some of the
visual features of this book was not matched by an engagement
in the story, and she has made no move to seek out the book
since.

She heard <u>The</u> <u>Spider's</u> <u>Web</u> twice at 4.4, but she made no unprompted comment. In the same month she listened to <u>Railway</u>
<u>Passage</u> which she promptly dismissed: <u>That's</u> <u>a</u> <u>brown</u> <u>nasty</u>
<u>book</u>, <u>isn't</u> <u>it</u>. <u>I</u> <u>don't</u> <u>like</u> <u>its</u> <u>dull</u> <u>colors</u>. These strictures
could not be said to apply to the gaily colored <u>Alfie</u> <u>and</u> <u>the</u>
<u>Ferryboat</u>, read to her once at 5.3, but she had nothing to
say.

There was no other illustrator whose work we continued to lay
before Anna despite her comparative failure to respond, so
that we do not have a comparable series of behaviors in response to, say, Adrie Hospes. While it is true that Keeping's
world of inner-city streets and junkyards is altogether
strange to Anna, the same can be said of the peculiar creatures who people Hans Arnold's pictures for <u>My</u> <u>Very</u> <u>Own</u>

Sister, which she adored. The combination of the setting,
frequent use of colors not to her taste, and the strong
emotional tone seems to militate against her liking Keeping.
To judge from her response to The Garden Shed, there are
also features in Keeping's figure drawing which she disliked,
but we have no clear evidence that her distaste stemmed from
Keeping's somewhat expressionistic style in itself.

CONCLUSIONS

Anna had access during the first few years of her life to a
wide range of art styles and formats, but in no sense were her
books selected for the express purpose of exposing her to a
balanced artistic diet. It will be clear to our readers
already that Anna had relatively little exposure to abstract,
semiabstract, or even markedly impressionistic styles; as was
the case with black and white illustrations, her own lack of
enthusiasm for such styles dictated her choice of library
books and (to a lesser extent) our choice for her. We did make
conscious efforts on occasion to borrow something visually
stretching for her. On the other hand, it could equally well
be said that the great majority of children's picture books
today are in full color and in relatively representational
styles, so that her books were in no way atypical of what artists, publishers, and libraries have made available. Because
of the extent of her book experience, it is certain that she
did have access to a greater variety of styles than most children.

In many ways, her preferences seem to confirm much received
doctrine on young children's likes and dislikes: Anna preferred color to black and white; a profusion of bright colors
in itself appealed to her; she seemed to prefer saturated hues
to pale tones and, perhaps, also to prefer neatly framed
pictures to ambiguously bounded ones; as we have seen earlier
in this book, figures of humans or animals held her attention
much more readily than landscapes or inanimate objects. All
the these things have been stated to be typical of her age[3]
range. By contrast, she seemed to have no need for extremely
simplified representations in her early books nor for unclut-
tered pages with few focal points nor for clear outlines--all
of which have also been claimed to be necessary for preschoolers.[4] Moreover, the appeal of a particular book's text
could override her distaste for its style of illustration, or
even lead her to express admiration for that style. Her preferences were not absolute. More significant than any of these

things, we feel, is our evidence for the remarkable <u>consistency</u>
of Anna's preferences and the extent to which some of them, at
least, can be traced to very early exposure to certain key
pictures which then functioned as archetypal scenes against
which the appeal of new pictures could unconsciously be measured. The power of Anna's visual memory, amply demonstrated
above, lends credence to our feeling that she possessed a rudimentary awareness of artistic style, even though her perceptions were largely expressed in contentual terms. These things
have been rarely discussed in relation to children so young
and must go some way toward qualifying the tendency of adults
to see the aesthetics of young children as undeveloped, [5]
requiring only educationally simplified styles of illustration.
For example, Machotka (1966) states that <u>realism</u> is the
earliest formal criterion of artistic worth to appear in young
children, and he sees it emerging about age seven. We have
already seen how Anna used realism of color as an evaluative
criterion as early as 3.6; explicit use of words like "true"
or "real" emerged for the first time at 4.7--still much
earlier than Machotka's material suggests--when she suddenly
observed of the magnetized plastic shapes (owned since age
4.0) which were normally arranged on the refrigerator door:

A: <u>All of the things on the</u> 'frig <u>door are not true--the horse
ought to be either black or brown</u> [it is red], <u>the door
should be brown, the cat and dog</u> don't lo&k like <u>cat and
dog</u> [they are stylized] <u>and the boy and girl aren't wearing
any clothes.</u> [Like the other figures, they are one-color
silhouettes, so it is impossible to know whether they are
clothed or not.]

At 5.7 Anna was examining Jon Chalon's <u>Sir Lance-a-Little and
the Knights of the Kitchen Table</u> which she had not previously
seen; she commented: <u>Sometimes in these pages you can't see
what it really is when it's not colored, and sometimes</u> [she
broke off and started again] <u>and if they wanted to look more
like real, they should have better heads.</u> Here again, realism
is her <u>explicit</u> criterion, as it is in the comment made five
days later about our stylized woolen wall-hanging of a tree
with curling leaves drifting from it: <u>Those aren't very good
pictures of leaves</u>, because there're <u>no leaves like peaches</u>,
and <u>no leaves like sixes and nines.</u>

In a year at school (4.5-5.7) Anna was exposed to a strong
normative influence in the form of other children's drawings
in which houses always have smoke curling from the chimneys,
trees are always green, etc. This may have pushed her in the
direction of these preferences for the conventionally

representational: on the other hand, we have noted other evidence in the same period for Anna's growing tendency to model her response--e.g., to jokes, to statements of surprise or appreciation or fear--on those previously given by us or other persons present. We point to Anna's early development of certain aesthetic responses not to assert her superiority but to indicate the need to look for earlier and less clearly verbalized evidence when assessing young children's perceptions and preferences.

12

Funny Ha-Ha and Funny Peculiar: Perception of Humor

What sorts of things does a young child find amusing? Authors and artists whose work is aimed at preschool audiences think they know: picture books, story collections, and cartoon films are full of slapstick, simple wordplay, nonsense, caricatured figures; there are long catalogues of familiar and unfamiliar objects in incongruous juxtapositions, and there are frequent exclamations, imprecations, and terms of abuse--all avoiding taboo words in favor of nursery equivalents like "pooh!" "ugh!" "yuk!" "beans!" Humor intended for a child audience is characterized by a dense clustering of these and related conventions, at the expense of sophisticated humor like irony, double-entendre, and satire. In other words, there is a consensus of opinion among adults as to what children ought to find funny, and what they will not find funny (Butler, 1975, pp. 12-13; Jones and Buttrey, 1970, pp. 82-84). Our records give us the chance to check this against the actual responses of a single child. What did Anna consider amusing? Did she consistently prefer a certain type of humor? Or did different patterns of response develop as she grew older?

Before we can attempt to answer these questions, we shall need to set down the basis on which we claimed that Anna's response was "amused." It sounds self-evident to say that laughter or smiling is an external sign of amusement, until we remember that a young child's laugh may express many things, of which a perception that something is funny is only one. A laugh may embody sudden, joyful self-affirmation; triumph or satisfaction at some achievement; or even fear transformed into embarrassment that is more socially acceptable. Consequently we

have had to rely on our own judgment when selecting examples
for this chapter to ensure that true amusement was being expressed. We should remind our readers at this point that we
rarely questioned Anna about the causes of her laughter, and
it was only late in the period studied that she was prepared,
on some occasions, to volunteer an explanation. Similarly
there have been problems in the perception and recording of
laughs and smiles--the latter are not easily seen by an adult
whose eyes are on the text being read rather than on the
child's face; the former are of variable length, and it may
not be clear exactly what point in the text an extended giggle
refers to. Moreover, extended laughter becomes a self-perpetu-
ating phenomenon: does a series of giggles at intervals during
the reading of a whole page (as happened in Finn Family Moomintroll, constitute a single response to one stimulus or several responses? Sometimes it was clear that only the initial
cue was humorous to Anna in itself, and that later amusement
was provoked by a recurrent memory of that cue; at other
times, we seemed to be dealing with several cues, though
perhaps Anna would have laughed at none of them had she not
responded to the first.

Despite these difficulties, and the consequent occurrences of
a number of ambiguous or baffling instances of amusement in
our record, we nevertheless have as a basis for this chapter a
multitude of clear-cut examples of laughter where the stimulus
was readily identifiable.

AGE 2.0-3.0

Anna may have laughed at fictional events or characters before
the age of 2.0, but we have no record of definite amusement
before that age: Anna's early responses frequently took the
form of a generalized excitement, often unaccompanied by
actual words and impossible to differentiate into specific
categories. The earliest unambiguous example of her finding
something funny came when hearing Aldous Huxley's The Crows
of Pearblossom, with pictures by Barbara Cooney. Her favorite
illustration was a double-page spread showing the snake in
bed, with a great coil of tail overflowing. In talking about
the book, we compared this picture with one on the final page
of Scarry's Please and Thank You Book, explaining that like
Lowly Worm, the snake was too big for his bed. Anna would
point to the snake with a tiny chuckle: Too big bed! [i.e.,
"too big for the bed!"]. This is a poor example on which to
base any analysis of her unaided concept of the humorous--we

had already provided both the words and the intonation that
connoted excitement. Anna's chuckle could conceivably have
indicated pleasure in having successfully learned a piece of
parental lore, though it seems more likely that she did find
the picture funny as well, having selected it spontaneously to
begin with.

In the second example (Anna 2.0) there is still a chance of
adult behavior having conditioned her response. She brought
our copy of Michael Foreman's Dinosaurs and All that Rubbish
and was read an edited version of the text of Op. 8, thus: "A
dinosaur held his nose. 'Pooh! What a mess!' he said." Anna
went into gales of laughter and wanted Maureen to repeat the
performance, holding her nose, again and again. Once Anna
could control herself she pointed to the dinosaur in question
as a sign for Maureen to repeat the words and action, while
she herself would say: Anna dirty nappy [in the] bucket.
Pooh! What mess! ["nappy" = "diaper"]. In the next phase
of this incident, Anna chanted "Pooh! What mess!" while she
tried to make her doll Snow White hold her nose.

There seems no doubt that the original stimulus here was the
phrase "Pooh! What a mess!" Both words had prior associations
for her, having been used of her excrement; we attempted to
make the changing of soiled diapers into a time of giggles
rather than disgust, so the words had been used lightheartedly. Though both the words and the playacting (holding nose)
were Maureen's, it was Anna who made the link with diapers and
so revealed the cause of the laughter. It was also Anna who
prolonged the game, using the same structure as she was later
to do in the Thomas game discussed in chap. 8, "Fiction Re-
created." There can be no doubt of Anna's amusement this time,
nor of her investment in repeating it. If we list the elements
contributing to the Dinosaurs response we get:
1. two cue words (words with previous humorous associations);
2. the cue words appear as part of a brief, dramatic exclamation;
3. the content of the exclamation was relevant to her own
   experience;
4. mimicking or acting behavior was provided by the adult.

The notion of relevance in point 3 is neatly confirmed by
Anna's behavior at a subsequent reading of the same opening of
Dinosaurs at 2.0 when she identified the two larger creatures as "Mother dinosaur" and "Father dinosaur", the small
one as "Baby dinosaur," thus imposing a domestic grid on the
initially unfamiliar content. In later readings Anna's

amusement seemed forgotten, and her comments moved toward a new focus in the "Father" dinosaur's expression of fear.

Again at 2.1 the cue word "pooh!" stimulated laughter, this time when Anna encountered a friend's copy of a Disney picture version of Winnie the Pooh. Her initial reaction on hearing the title was to giggle and repeat the words "boo, Winnie Pooh!" For her "Pooh" was not the name of a toy bear but a funny word, and she made her own exclamation (on the model of "Pooh! What mess!") by adding to it the similar-sounding and equally exclamatory "boo!"

The next examples, however, seem to have little in common with the Dinosaurs model. At 2.3, Anna went into peals of laughter when, in Frog and Toad are Friends, Toad yells at would-be helpful Frog who is trying to identify his missing button: "'That's not my button! My button is small!'" (p. 33). There is no cue like "pooh!" here, though the element of dramatic exclamation is present. Rather, there is a dramatic denial based on the size discrepancy between the two buttons. But since Anna had owned the book since 2.1, we should consider as well the cumulative effect of several readings.

When 2.4, Anna looked at a page showing large swans in Adrie Hospes's The Six Swans and chuckling, said of the largest, red-beaked one: "marvelous nose!" We remember that she used the same phrase to refer to the beaked and wattled Wild Thing, but what Anna actually found funny is unclear. Presumably such "noses" were unprecedented in her experience, and she is registering a mixture of wonder and amusement at this departure from the norm. In the same month she laughed at the Ogre in Bruna's version of Hop-O'-My-Thumb, commenting "Anna likes he." Is this, as with "marvelous nose" an expression of admiration for something strange and new? Or is she deliberately contradicting the text's message that the Ogre is (mildly) menacing? The second hypothesis seems the stronger, because (Bruna being Bruna) the Ogre differs less from the other characters than one might expect; moreover, it was at this same period that Anna customarily corrected the opening sentence of The Pirates' Tale: "Once upon a time there were some bad pirates . . ." to "Once upon a time there were some good pirates . . ."

The responses we have quoted so far are not always readily interpreted. Nevertheless a number of them have one thing in common--an element of negation, whether explicit or implicit. Thus: "That is not my button." "That is not an ordinary

nose." "That is <u>not</u> a nasty Ogre." (and perhaps) "That snake
is <u>not</u> the right size for the bed." Broadly, we could describe these instances as involving incongruity, or denial of
what would normally be expected. By contrast, the <u>Dinosaurs</u>
and <u>Pooh</u> examples embody cue words and some degree of perceived personal relevance.

So far we have listed all our recorded material to age 2.4; to
a remarkable extent, the remaining examples from 2.4 to 3.0
fall into one of the two broad types we have just identified.
Thus the "hiccup!" noises in Minarik's <u>Father Bear Comes Home</u>
evoked giggles and requests for repeats at 2.6, and the loud
chant of "MORE MORE MORE MORE" in Krauss's <u>A Very Special
House</u> an immediate laughing imitation. In all, there were
six examples which seemed to follow this pattern, either
depending on the presence of a cue word like "mess" or on some
abrupt, dramatic exclamation (where the adult reader's surprised tone of voice would itself serve as a cue). Only two of
the six seemed to contain that element of personal relevance
which characterized the <u>Dinosaurs</u> example, but in a sense
Anna <u>made</u> the stimulus part of her own behavioral repertoire
by repeating the word, phrase or sound over and over again
until the ritual dulled the stimulus quality of the original
cue, and sooner or later, the amusement faded. Thus on pp. 30-
31 of <u>Noggin and the Moon Mouse</u> the extraterrestrial creature
says "ugh!" when offered hot sausage. Naturally, "ugh!" became
the focus of amusement; after a few readings Anna (2.11) began
to giggle <u>before</u> the word, anticipating the ritual response;
then the <u>giggle</u> began to sound more automatic and had died by
the time the book was returned to the library at the end of
the two weeks.

Eight of the fifteen amused responses in this period appeared
to depend on the stimulus of an incongruous element or a denial of expectation. So the statement in <u>Johnny Lion's Rubber
Boots</u> that Johnny lacks boots led Anna at 2.10 to a chuckling
"but he <u>has</u> rubber boots" because she could see them pictured elsewhere in the book. Often perceived incongruity is
linked with that sensitivity to color variations within a
single book which we examined in the context of her visual
orientations. At 2.10, the green-black-and-white illustrations
to Elizabeth Coatsworth's <u>Bob Bodden and the Seagoing Farm</u>
provoked the statement that monkeys pictured on p. 13
"shouldn't be green--they should be white," because on some
pages, they <u>are</u> white. We have classed this among humor
responses because Anna was clearly amused by her perception,
but it is obvious that it also could be considered as a search

for visual consistency. In this case, the fact that the comment was accompanied by laughter points to its being well along a knowledge continuum, at one end of which would be a puzzled question; further along, this would give way to a statement, as Anna's certainty of her own understanding grows; a laughing statement would indicate that she is so sure she is right and the book is wrong that she can triumph over the author or artist. Whether or not she laughs seems a question of the width of the gap between her knowledge and the book's apparent error; by laughing she is in effect saying that something is absurd, as well as wrong. So, at times, her perception of an inconsistency or incongruity led her to speculate with amusement on further absurdities: in the final opening of John Burningham's Trubloff, the mouse hero's face is suddenly green, having earlier been gray. Anna commented laughing: He could be blue--or yellow--or red! She was then 2.9, and several times since being given the book at 2.6 she had commented on the changed color of the faces in this opening.

AGE 3.1-4.0

Between the ages of 3.0 and 4.0, Anna's recorded responses to humorous stimuli were much more frequent than in the preceding year. Undoubtedly the decision to make our record complete rather than selective is the major factor in explaining this, but it also seems feasible to see a real increase in Anna's responsiveness to humor; a real broadening of her knowledge and experience in the same period would in itself have widened the range of incongruities and inconsistencies which she was able to perceive. Because of the amount of material available to us, we have analyzed a sample only: twenty-six books with titles beginning with letters A-F to which amused responses were recorded have been culled from the total. Between them these books evoked fifty-nine separate instances of laughter or amusement, and it is immediately clear that the two major categories of response we have established continue to dominate. Seventeen examples can be described as instances of incongruity humor of some kind, two of them (from Lobel's Frog and Toad titles) also containing an element of slapstick or violent action. Eighteen examples belong to the cue-word/ exclamation type, six of these (each repeated several times) being in response to Finn Family Moomintroll and, hence, printed in full in part 1. Together, then, the established types of humor response account for thirty-five of the fifty-nine examples, with three more readily identifiable as depending on personal relevance. What of the remainder?

At the very end of the twelve-month period we are examining, when Anna was 4.0, Astrid Lindgren's Cherry Time at Bullerby provided something of a new world for Anna as far as humor was concerned, concentrating as it does on low-key comedy in a realistic domestic setting (which was nevertheless exotic to Anna in many of its details). Unfortunately, the complexity of the stimuli it presents makes it difficult for us to be sure exactly what Anna was laughing at. On p. 41, she giggled at the sentence "Olaf . . . giggled as if someone were tickling him." One's first guess would be that she is recognizing the relevance of the situation to her own life--being tickled does make one laugh, especially since this book even contains another girl called Anna! But subsequent examples have led us to speculate on a different cause: on p. 82 she failed to laugh at an obvious cue word, "ubblelibubblelimuck," but instead laughed at the next sentence: "It wasn't a bit funny really, but Anna and Britta and I couldn't keep from laughing." It begins to look as though Anna is interpreting the behavior of the fictional characters as a directive for her to laugh too, and as if "Olaf . . . giggled" had the same effect earlier. With these Bullerby examples we can perhaps class a couple of occasions when she responded with amusement to a book character pulling faces (An Anteater named Arthur, 3.7) or to an illustration showing a laughing expression on a character's face (Albert and Henry, 3.8). In some ways, all of these examples seem best described as a development of the cue-word type, but they are not identical. Though words like "laughed" or "made faces" (or a visual equivalent thereof) function as cues to provoke laughter, there is in these examples an element of self-consciousness that was not present in Anna's early laughing repetitions of "pooh" or "ugh" or "hiccup," perhaps because the new cues are more abstract, being neither onomatopoeic nor exclamatory. In this sense they seem sophisticated, yet they demand less cognitive processing than responses of the incongruity type.

Incongruity humor depends on the listener's setting up a prediction which the book then unexpectedly denies; but there is another type of humor the appeal of which resides in the very predictability of a certain situation. On humor of this kind depend many folktales of the fool or dummkopf variety, where readers rejoice as the dunderhead performs one stupid action after another. Our sample provides few stories of this kind--and Alison Jezard's horse Henry in the Albert series was the only figure whom Anna seemed automatically to expect to be funny regardless of what he did: it may well be argued that she could have displayed a response to predictive humor

earlier than this, had a book which worked so hard for the
effect been available to her between, say, 2.0 and 3.0. (Perhaps "That's not my button!" may be considered as a case.) Our
sample provides only one other instance, and that an unclear
one, of predictive humor, this time referring to the probable
consequences of a character's action. When Anna was 3.4 she
heard <u>The Berenstain Bears' New Baby</u> where in Op. 10 Small
Bear is balancing on a jagged tree stump. Suddenly Anna
laughed and said: <u>He'll hurt his bottom if he sits down there.</u>
There seems little doubt that her ability to predict a cata-
strophic outcome was a key factor.

We come now to a consideration of wordplay, humor that is
purely verbal in conception. Here again, our evidence from
within the sample is slender. During the period Anna listened
once to the Dr. Seuss tongue twister <u>Fox in Sox</u>, but treated
it for the most part quite seriously with straight-faced questions about the nature of the Knox and the activities of the
tweetle beetles (whom she disliked). In the case of <u>An Anteater Named Arthur</u>, however, we have unequivocal evidence
for her appreciation of familiar words uttered in a distorted
form. Our records show that she had spontaneously initiated
such wordplay at 3.1, systematically altering the first consonant of a sequence of words with much giggling; at 3.7 she
laughed heartily at this episode (pp. 6-11):

"'We are called anteaters, right?'
'Right,' I answer.
. . . .
'But the cat is not called a fisheater,
the bird is not called wormeater
and the cow is not called a grasseater.
Right?' Arthur asks.
'Right,' I answer.
'Then I shall be called by another name.'
'What will you be called?' I ask.
'I shall be called a "blion."'
. . . .
'Then I shall be called a "brabbit."'
'But you are not a "brabbit."'
'What shall I be called?' Arthur asks.
'You shall be called an anteater,' I tell him.
'An anteater named Arthur.'"

At 4.6, overhearing our discussing her earlier response to
this passage, she laughed loudly when she heard the word
"brabbit," and we ventured one of our rare questions as to why

she thought something funny. Her reply "because it's not 'rab-bit'" constitutes a nice proof that the negation rule under-lies this sort of verbal humor, and that it should therefore be classed with examples of incongruity.

AGE 4.1-5.0

Between Anna's fourth and fifth birthdays the number of recorded responses to humorous stimuli increased again. To ensure a sample of response roughly comparable with the one for ages 3.0-4.0, we again extracted titles in the alphabeti-cal range A-F, but this time twenty books were sufficient to yield fifty-six separate examples of amusement. It became more difficult to assign these to discrete categories than previ-ously; while we counted seventeen examples that belonged to the incongruity pattern and sixteen to the cue/exclamation pattern, these figures do not give an adequate picture of the overall trends, since most of the remaining instances, when analyzed, contain elements from both categories. When Anna laughed at the sentence "The chair started galumphing about like an enormous toad" (The Boy and the Magic), she may have been reacting primarily to the cue word "galumphing" or to the incongruous notion of a chair behaving like a toad or (less likely, since the remaining instances of animism in this book were accepted without questioning or laughter) to the incongruity of a chair moving on its own. Accordingly we thought it best to classify all separate elements responsible for amusement (incongruity; cue word; exclamatory form and voice tone; personal relevance; slapstick) and assign all elements potentially present in a single response to appropri-ate categories. This procedure yielded the following results: the element of incongruity was present in twenty-three of the examples; cue words or actions in nine; exclamatory form in twelve; personal relevance in three. Incongruity remains the single most important factor, and the way it manifested itself is well exemplified if we look at Anna's responses to Alice in Wonderland, heard for the first time in its entirety during this period.

Her previous acquaintance with the characters and events of Alice had been varied, beginning with Walt Disney's Alice in Wonderland Finds the Garden of Live Flowers (3.9) and another Disney adaptation, "Alice in Wonderland Meets the White Rabbit," as preparation for a rather feeble local stage production (3.10), after which Anna looked through our Tenniel-illustrated volume to compare events and character with those

seen "live." Anna took all of these versions completely seriously, and it was not till we gave her the original text in a
version illustrated by Arthur Rackham at 4.6 that she began to
respond to its manifest absurdities. Her brief laugh at the
Caterpillar's "Who are YOU?" was probably inspired by the
deep, fruity voice Hugh was using for the Caterpillar, as well
as by the abruptness of the exclamation, but the remaining
examples almost all stem from perceived incongruity of some
kind. In the chapter "Pig and Pepper," she laughed at the
description of the baby's nose as it begins to transform itself into a pig: "more like a <u>snout</u> than a real nose"; in
"The Mad Tea-Party," she did not show any amusement at the
first couplet of the Dormouse's version of "Twinkle, Twinkle
Little Star" (which she knows well) but smiled by the time we
reached "like a teatray in the sky." She also smiled at the
concept of a "treacle well." Croquet necessitated a lengthy
explanation as did the special problems involved in cutting
off the head of a vanishing Cheshire Cat, and it was these
explanations rather than the actual text which provoked Anna
to laugh, and to say at the end of the chapter "That was a
funny chapter, wasn't it!" When asked why it was funny she
replied: <u>Because</u> <u>of</u> <u>the</u> <u>end</u> <u>bit</u>, and requested a rereading
of this section. However, the episode of the Cat's execution
failed to hold her interest or to amuse her the second time.
Much of the text must have been obscure to her, and when she
smiled at Alice's correction of her intended derogatory remark
about the Queen we suspect that she was not responding to the
joke Carroll intended (p. 106):

"'How do you like the Queen?' said the Cat in a low voice.

'Not at all,' said Alice: 'she's so extremely--' Just then
she noticed that the Queen was close behind her listening:
so she went on, '---likely to win, that it's hardly worth
while finishing the game.'

The Queen smiled and passed on."

It could, in fact, have been this last sentence that gave Anna
her cue to smile. Similarly, her smile at the King's judgment
on the Cheshire Cat "I don't like the look of it at all" was a
cued response; exclamations featuring the phrase "I don't like
. . ." had long since had this status for her.

In the Trial Scene came the most interesting of all Anna's
instances of amusement. She laughed heartily at the account of
the Hatter biting his teacup instead of his slice of bread and

butter. A few moments later, Hugh reentered the room and Anna interrupted the reading:

A: <u>Next</u> <u>time</u> <u>you</u> <u>read</u> <u>Alice</u> <u>to</u> <u>me</u>, <u>don't</u> <u>read</u> <u>where</u> <u>he</u> <u>dropped</u> <u>his</u> <u>cup</u> <u>'n</u> <u>his</u> <u>bread</u> <u>and</u> <u>butter</u>, <u>'cause</u> <u>I</u> <u>think</u> <u>it's</u> <u>sad</u> . . .

H: <u>I think</u> it's sad too.

A: <u>He</u> <u>bit</u> <u>a</u> <u>big</u> <u>hole</u> <u>out</u> <u>of</u> <u>his</u> <u>cup</u>, <u>Hugh</u>! <u>He's</u> <u>a</u> <u>funny</u> <u>Hatter</u>, <u>isn't</u> <u>he</u>! <u>Isn't</u> <u>he</u> <u>a</u> <u>funny</u> <u>thing</u>!

She subsequently requested a picture of the incident, which is unillustrated in Rackham's version.

Looking back at the sequence of Anna's comments, it seems as though the pathos of the dropped cup superceded the earlier amusement at the incongruous bite; but then Anna seemed to need to reiterate the amusement—perhaps as a defense against the pathos? Greater differentiation of emotions is typical in this period. The <u>Alice</u> record itself contains several examples of a reaction we termed "surprise"—usually expressed by "huh!"—and which seems to have been employed in contexts where, earlier, Anna would simply have laughed. Thus on p. 78 we read Alice's exclamation "That's the most curious thing I ever saw in all my life!" In wording, this closely parallels Anna's own utterances of the period, and the intonation given it by the reader's voice is a clear laugh cue, yet instead of giggling, Anna responded: <u>Huh</u>! <u>same</u> <u>as</u> <u>me</u>! Alongside this differentiation of surprise from amusement, we find an increase in evaluative comments that explicitly identify something as funny. Here again, <u>Alice</u> is typical of its period. Anna was now capable of indicating at the end of a story that the <u>whole</u> <u>book</u> was funny, as well as so describing a particular incident. The number of such comments, as with all evaluative remarks, is still small.

In this period there is a dramatic decrease in the proportion of responses occasioned solely by pictures—only four, as against some ten in the previous year's sample. And in line with this increased focus on the text there is much more responsiveness to distorted words. In <u>An</u> <u>Anteater</u> <u>Named</u> <u>Arthur</u>, read again at 4.9, Anna again laughed at "blion," "brabbit," etc. In <u>Fox</u> <u>in</u> <u>Sox</u>, Anna responded for the first time to the humorous sound of the tongue-twister verses (4.2, 4.9). In <u>Bottersnikes</u> <u>and</u> <u>Gumbles</u>, heard and enjoyed earlier, it was at 4.3 that she realized and remarked upon the funny sound of the name "Bottersnike."

While the familiar categories account for the great bulk of amused responses, there remain, as always, some where the source of laughter is unclear or difficult to pinpoint. In the case of two instances recorded for Russell Hoban's Bread and Jam for Frances it seems that we may be witnessing further examples of predictive or cumulative humor, where laughter signals the listener's recognition that a certain pattern of action, several times repeated, is now coming to its climax or growing increasingly exaggerated: Frances, having refused to eat anything but bread and jam, is eventually given only bread and jam to eat. At each of the several meals described, she has sung a small song of her own composition, originally praising jam. By the time we reach p. 26,

"Frances looked down at her plate and saw that there was no spaghetti and meatballs on it.

There was a slice of bread and a jar of jam.

Frances began to cry. [Anna laughed here.]

'My goodness!' said Mother. 'Frances is crying!'

'What is the matter?' asked Father.

Frances looked down at her plate and sang a little sad song.

She sang so softly that Mother and Father could scarcely hear her: [Anna laughed]

'What I am
Is tired of jam.'"

Anna has chosen to laugh at two points of pathos, which would suggest that her amusement serves the function of denial. But they are also points at which the sequence of events reaches an extreme: this is the fourth time Frances has been offered only bread and jam at a meal, and the seventh time she has sung about food. If we are correct in this analysis, then the Frances examples contrast markedly with most of Anna's humor responses, which depend on the impact of the immediate stimulus only rather than on any cumulative tension set up over time.

CONCLUSIONS

We need not dwell on the extent to which Anna's patterns of response to humor were conditioned by us, both through the

kind of teaching implied in Maureen's behavior in the very
earliest examples at 2.0 and more pervasively and consistently
through our custom of emphasizing exclamations by volume and
intonation so that they stood out from surrounding narrative
and hence drew Anna's attention almost automatically. Her
usual failure to respond with amusement to slapstick comedy
involving falling, hitting, and being hurt doubtless reflects
the fact that we ourselves find it unfunny or even cruel, and
so never led her to see it otherwise. The commonplace "nothing
is as individual as a person's sense of humor" takes on new
meaning when we see its foundations in early childhood in the
unconsciously transmitted values of the home.

At the same time, though, as we have observed throughout this
book, a process of selection is operating: by no means is
Anna simply reproducing learned reactions. What, then, can we
say about the things she found funny, about the abstract basis
for her amusement?

Anna's laughter (if we can trust our sample) has to do with
knowledge. We've already seen how a child may laugh out of
triumph or pleasure at successfully completing a task, guessing an answer, identifying a part of a picture. It shouldn't
surprise us, then, that laughter is one way, and a fundamental
way, of signifying that Anna knows something, is in command of
a situation. A smile, or a laugh, may be the external sign of
an internalized statement of fact. But only certain types of
internal statement are represented externally by humor behavior. We propose to set out three types of stimulus which seem
consistently to produce a laughter response. Though at least
two of the types correspond to commonly recognized categories
of humor (incongruity and identification), we have used our
own labels to state the unifying principle of the category as
a child might state it, given sufficient verbal tools to do
so.

Type One: "Something Is Wrong"

This type covers all the varied forms of incongruity and inconsistency we have examined on our way through this chapter. The
underlying rule for an amused response to this type of stimulus is as follows: Information inside the fictional frame is
inconsistent with the child's existing information outside the
frame (such "outside" information being taken to include previously acquired rules for "what happens in fictional frames").
Whether the thing that is wrong is an absurdity or incongruity
intended by the creator of the picture book, or whether it
is some feature of text or picture that makes sense to an

adult but not to this child, does not matter. From Anna's
point of view, what is inside the picture or the story suddenly contradicts what she in her life so far knows to be
true. So she smiles or laughs, sometimes accompanying this
with an explicit statement of the kind that on other occasions
remains inside her head: The trees have tree fingers! (My Very
Own Sister, Op. 9). Within this category we place what's commonly called "slapstick," because when a character suddenly
against expectation falls over, is hit by an umbrella, or
bangs his head repeatedly against a wall, it is still a case
of something being wrong. Similarly, we would place all humor
that arises from distorted forms of familiar words in this
category.

Type Two: "Like Me"

"Like me" is relatively simple to explain. It can, of course,
be an element present alongside other types of humor response
as well as provoking laughter on its own.

At a very early stage of a child's acquaintance with picture
books, we would guess that every object which a child can
recognize as familiar from her own environment would potentially provoke "like me" laughter, though in Anna's case this
did not happen. As skill with words and familiarity with
pictures increase, the number of occasions on which "like me"
will produce amusement becomes limited to those where there is
a very close parallel indeed with some particular situation,
attribute, or behavior which the child feels to be peculiarly
hers and is thus startled to see in the unfamiliar setting of
a book. Whereas "something is wrong" operated on a basic structure of "this is not me," i.e., "not my established world
picture," "like me" operates on the reverse. It is the laughing recognition of unexpected congruity, not unexpected
incongruity. In Anna's case, we have seen that "like me"
responses declined into insignificance as she grew older.

Type Three: "Different from the Rest"

This category is the one we feel least sure about. Yet in an
important way, it underlies all the others. We speculate that
it has its origins in the child's perception of a sudden
higher level of stimulus during the reading. Such a change
in level could come about through the reader's sudden increase
in volume (e.g., when a character shouts or exclaims) or
through dramatic repetition of a single word or phrase. Likewise, a child could be indirectly taught to laugh if the adult,
by intonation or by posture (e.g., abrupt turning of head
towards the child), indicates that he/she thinks something is

amusing. Anna's learning to giggle when the word "laugh"
occurred in the text was a late transformation of this cueing.
So far we have mentioned mainly reader-transmitted information
that something is special or different; but it can also be the
case that once the child has formed an idea of how words ought
to sound, she herself may perceive a certain word (e.g., "hup-
si-daisy!" in Finn Family Moomintroll, p. 23) as unusual and
worthy of laughter. But here we are coming so close to type
one, "something is wrong," that the dividing line becomes
blurred.

Perhaps the key distinction between type three and the other
two types is that in type three there is something in the
reading experience itself which transmits the message "this
deserves special attention." In the other two types, the child
unaided perceives congruities or incongruities. Clearly, no
individual humor response need be explicable in terms of only
one of these three bases for amusement. But, as we have seen,
each type is observable in our records from the earliest
period, and types one and three continue to be the most prominent elements in responses throughout the time our survey
covers. (For a detailed formulation of the questions of
stimulus discrepancy and incongruity humor, see Paul McGhee,
"On the Cognitive Origins of Incongruity Humor," in Goldstein
and McGhee, The Psychology of Humor [1972].) While the basis
for Anna's laughter thus does not change greatly over time, we
can see some developments: illustration-cued amusement gives
way to text-cued; the number of instances of amusement increases; and in the final year of the period covered, she
becomes more capable of explaining the cause of her mirth, of
differentiating amusement from other feelings, and of describing something as funny (in contradistinction to simply smiling
or laughing at it). There are minor indications that she may
be growing in awareness of humor that depends on predictable
behavior or cumulative repetition of events, and solid evidence for a developing sensitivity to the humor of wordplay.
We can say with conviction that no unambiguous example of a
response to irony exists, though some of her books provided
instances of ironic humor. Similarly, parody (as in "Twinkle,
twinkle little bat") was probably perceived at the level of
individual incongruities in a familiar framework than as a
whole.

The analysis of humor is a serious business and apt to destroy
one's own appreciation for the jokes concerned; if this chapter has a message for us, it must be that the question of
responses to humor can only be seen in the context of Anna's

knowledge of what is and what is not--the realm of fantasy and
reality. So it seems appropriate to explore that question
further in our next chapter.

13

The Limits of Reality:
Perception of the Fantastic

As adults we forget that a picture drawn by an artist, however
"realistic" it may be, does not closely resemble the real
thing it claims to represent. Even a photograph taken by the
speciously objective camera is never more than a symbol of the
reality: the conversion of three dimensions into two results
in inevitable distortions, and it is hardly surprising if a
young child takes some time, and perhaps requires some parental guidance, in the process of matching pictures and things
in the real world, as we saw in chap. 10, "Order from Chaos."
By the very act of teaching Anna to find correspondences between the world pictured in books and the world outside them,
we were also teaching her to see the differences, to accept
that what is within the covers of a book will be of another
order of reality from what is not. While she thus for three
years acted on the expectation that her not-book reality would
hold good for the book reality also--seeking mothers for characters for whom no mother is depicted--[1]she also attempted
to generalize in the other direction, expecting at 2.9 after
hearing The Flying Shoes that she could be taught to fly in
the same way as we had promised her she could be taught to
swim. Our guess is that in the operation of these two simulta-
neous, complementary processes, Anna was by implication
seeking to answer the question: "What are the limits of a
fictional experience; is it coexistent, coterminous with my
own? do the same rules operate in both, do the same values and
structures hold good for both?"

We have said that her initial move to explore the boundary
between book and world was influenced by our example in

identifying objects and encouraging her to do the same; we
also provided another influence of major significance. Only
very rarely, and then for specialized reasons which are irrelevant here, did we ever treat any of the fictional experiences
we shared with Anna as "untrue" or "unreal." Specifically, we
did not frame supernatural or magical elements with such statements as "this isn't real . . . it's just made up," which some
adults employ when threatened by the coexistence of reality
and fantasy which occurs in so many books for the very young.
Indeed, such is the prevalence of animism in publishing for
the preschool market that it would be hard work, as well as
deeply insensitive to the human imagination, to identify every
unreal or fantastic device in any representative selection of
such books.

Surrounded from the time of her earliest book experience with
talking animals, clothed animals, and (let's not forget), with
a language full of animistic images which are known as nonani-
mistic only by convention ("here's the bus coming up the
road"--in what sense is the bus then not "alive"?), Anna
accepted what adults would class as fantastic elements along
with those we would class as reality-based, subjecting them
equally to the testing-out process we mentioned above, expecting that whatever was in a book could be found outside it.
Where such expectations ran counter to everyday reality, adult
intervention was necessary. If Anna asked where ogres lived,
for example, our standard answer was "only in books." This
phrasing, which we can now see to have been an attempt to
preserve the possibility of a separate fictional reality,
could well have helped Anna to treat the world of books as
such a reality. In fact, she rarely asked questions like this;
far more problems arose for her when she attempted to generalize within the world of books, assuming that what had been
true in several stories should also be true in a new one. It
was thus the inner consistency of the book world, rather than
the consistency between book world and everyday world, that
functioned as the precursor of her first grappling with the
fantasy/reality distinction.

The operation of all the factors we have been discussing might
best be demonstrated by a brief survey of Anna's developing
approach to the very common picture-book convention by which
animals are shown to be clothed.

Clothing had from early in her life been of major concern to
Anna, and in her early years she (a winter baby) took strenu-
ous exception to being undressed for a bath. She acquired the

phrases "clothes off" and "clothes on" at a time when her
stock of such two-word phrases was limited. We have seen
already how at 2.1 Anna pointed to the Wild Thing rising from
the sea and said "clothes off," processing the book in terms
of "outside-book" reality. The fact that the creature in question is an imaginary one is of course completely irrelevant.
At 2.3, Anna who had owned Marjorie Flack's The Story about
Ping since 1.4, for the first time remarked Ping not got
clothes and (turning back) not got clothes on cover; here
we can observe the beginning of a wish for uniformity within
the book universe.

When Anna was 2.5, we first regarded her grappling with the
prevalence of clothed animals in picture books as compared
with unclothed ones in life. She was reading something in
which an animal had no clothes and was told that animals wear
clothes only in books and not always then. Very confidently
Anna said:
> Elephants wear clothes.
M: Only in books.
A: Meet Babar and his Family [i.e., the elephant characters
> in this story] wear clothes.
Anna is at this juncture unwilling to accept the distinction,
and since elephants are so far known to her only in books,
this is not surprising. A seemingly increased willingness to
accept unclothed animal protagonists is noted soon after (2.6,
with reference to Lord Rex and The Lion and the Rat) however, and it was at 2.6 that Anna produced a fluent explanation for Mickey's "taking off" his clothes on pp. 30-31 of
In the Night Kitchen ("because they get wet"). We include
this latter reference for two reasons; first, to illustrate
the fact that for Anna the problem of unclothed animals is
still only one aspect of a wider problem of unclothed characters, so that we cannot tell whether or not the fantastic
element is an issue for her. Second, because it exemplifies
how Anna's linguistic development now permits her to enter
verbally into the reality of the fictional world by adding
what is in effect an extra detail to the story—in the process
smoothly rationalizing what would earlier have been more
directly expressed as primitive puzzlement or shock at the
sudden loss of garments.

At 2.8 it seemed to strike Anna for the first time that Foreman's Horatio (Horatio) was naked, and she announced: He
hasn't got clothes. Hippos don't wear clothes (no specific
page reference recorded). Maureen's earlier input had been
effective. But it seems to us that Anna has used the new rule
("hippos don't wear clothes") in much the same way as she

employed her own explanation of Mickey's loss of clothes, to
cope with the immediate reaction of surprise. She still
expects to see the clothes but has learned to explain their
nonappearance. With time and growing experience, Anna's words
will more truly represent understanding and acceptance rather
than defense against a challenge to the rules as she knows
them. We pinpoint 2.11 as the age at which the "clothed animal" convention has ceased to be confusing and become funny,
so well was the rule internalized; pointing to the prancing
rabbit in the long gown in A Very Special House, Anna laughed:
Look, he's wearing clothes! Animals don't usually wear clothes,
do they! Now the rule that operates outside fiction--"animals
don't wear clothes"--has taken precedence over the older knowledge that animals inside fictions are often clothed.

As we said earlier, it is only from our adult viewpoint that
Anna's concern with clothed animals can be considered a
response to the fantastic. For her, it is a response to specific inconsistencies within bodies of knowledge, operating
sometimes outside and sometimes inside books. Under adult
influence, she is in the process of building new rules: real
animals don't wear clothes; animals in books sometimes wear
clothes and sometimes don't. Because the clothed/unclothed
distinction was important to Anna personally, she noticed it
in books. She less frequently questioned the attribution of
speech to animals in fiction, and we may assume that the
seemingly contradictory nature of the evidence when she did
points to an unsureness in her as to whether rules derived
from life (where creatures do not talk) would hold good in
books or not. Thus in the two earliest examples (2.10, 3.0)
Anna described fictional talking animals as "clever," perhaps
because she knew real animals did not speak. Also at 3.0, however, she registered surprise when birds in Noggin the King
failed to answer a question put to them by Noggin. After all,
birds had been able to talk in Babar's Birthday Surprise a
short time before. At 3.1 she stated categorically of Ferdinand that the pacific bull's mother "doesn't talk--because
cows don't talk."[2] This is a crucial example because it
shows two of Anna's previously formulated rules in conflict:
(1) real creatures do not talk; (2) fictional creatures talk.
She resolves the conflict on this occasion by establishing the
precedence of (1) over (2). But from 3.3 onward, a series of
questions showed that she had formulated a new rule to resolve
the conflict differently: (3) fictional creatures may talk,
but this must be established in the case of each individual
story. Thus all of the 3.3 questions were cast in the form
"Can X talk in this book?" Anna had defined her own limits
to fictional reality.

Again in the case of animated machines, the initial phase seems to have been one of unquestioning acceptance, as we saw with The Little Red Lighthouse at 2.7 when she insisted that the lighthouse could switch on his light unaided. And on the title page of Mike Mulligan and his Steam Shovel (owned for months at 2.10, though read infrequently), Anna identified Mary Anne's tracks as her "feet." But in the same reading, in Op. 1, the phase of resistance seemed to begin. Sturdily, Anna insisted: Where is Mary Anne? Is she accepting an animated steam shovel but not willing to accept that it could have a girl's name? The likelihood that she is explicitly rejecting the notion of an animated machine is strengthened by Anna's behavior six months later (at 3.4) while listening to Binette Schroeder's Florian and Tractor Max. Anna unquestioningly accepted Florian (a talking horse) but asked on the fifth reading:

    Where is Tractor Max?
He was pointed out.
A: No, that's not Tractor Max--tractors don't go by them-
    selves.
M: Maybe he's a magic tractor.
A: No, he's not.
In the next reading Anna made her objection even more precise:
I want him to be a person.

Interesting though this evidence is, it is still in the final analysis not evidence about acceptance or rejection of the fantastic from Anna's point of view, though from ours it can be seen as indicating the boundaries of Anna's mental map of what is allowable within a fictional world. Her experience had included very few animated machines apart from the Little Red Lighthouse (if he is to be so classified), and this in itself may account for her rejection of both Mary Anne and Tractor Max, whereas clothed, talking animals had been present in her very earliest books.[3] So far, with the exception of the case of A Very Special House, Anna's responses to what adults would see as intentional fantasy conventions have entirely lacked that element of delighted superiority which we saw operating in her response to incongruity humor in the last chapter: there can be no clearer indication that her reactions to clothed animals or animated machines are as far as she is concerned explorations of fact.

But now we come to the earliest phase at which it would be justifiable to say that Anna began to register the concept of the "fantastic." Two books in particular provide most of our evidence, and it seems worth reproducing the material quite extensively.

HAROLD AND THE PURPLE CRAYON

Having decided to go for a moonlight walk, Harold realizes
there is no moon. So Harold draws one with his magic purple
crayon and goes on his way, using the crayon to create (and
extricate himself from) new adventures. Crockett Johnson's
witty fantasy with its economical use of purple line on a
plain white ground is a minor picture-book classic. Our copy
was read to Anna once or twice as a special treat during her
periods of vast thirst for "a book from the lounge room that
I've never heard before" but she made no comment on those
early readings, and Harold first enters the record when Anna
was 3.2. Ten subsequent readings cover a period of approximately eight months, taking Anna to 3.10.

In the first two readings, Anna seemed to accept unquestioningly Harold's ability to "draw real" with his magic crayon.
Instead, her attention was caught by another mystery, Harold's
inability to find his way back to his bedroom. He couldn't find
his room, could he--but he found it [in the end] (12 September '75). Why couldn't he find his own house?--Didn't he want
his own house? Wasn't it to be seen any more? (13 September
'75, 3.2). Looking through the book on her own, Anna subsequently sought to locate the house, presumably amidst the vast
"city of windows" Harold draws in an effort to find the
windows of his own bedroom. This was the emotional center of
the book for her and provoked extensive, anguished comment
much later, at 3.9.

In the third reading (3.3) Anna seems to have begun tenta-
tively to explore the magic on which the book is based (Ops. 2
and 3, where Harold draws a moon and a straight path): He is
clever!--he is clever! Anna's use of "clever" need not imply
any realization of the extraordinary power of the crayon. At
the time she habitually used the word to denote any skill
possessed by others but beyond her own capacity, but it was
also the word she used to indicate the special abilities of
the talking wolf in Little Red Riding Hood. "He is clever"
is paralleled one reading later by the comment "that's sensible"; Anna uses this word as an unspecific term of approbation.
She realizes that some special power is involved.

In the same reading she showed herself capable of predicting
on the basis of her knowledge of this power: at Op. 18 (text:
"he hoped he would see his bedroom"), she asked: Does he draw
his mother? So it is not surprising that her next question in
this session directly addressed the basis of the fantasy for
the first time. At Op. 22, her mind still digesting the events

of the previous page, she asked: How can he make a balloon, and a basket, and people in it? Hugh explained that Harold had drawn the things with his crayon. What can he draw them on? Hesitantly, Hugh said "air"; but Anna did not consider the question solved, asking a little later on: How can he do that? Why was it the balloon that provoked Anna's wish to explore the nature of Harold's magic power rather than one of his other creations? One clue is perhaps provided by her question: What can he draw them on? Everything else that Harold draws is a prolongation of, or building upon, a "base line" which roughly corresponds to the ground on which Harold walks. The balloon however is drawn on nothing, and since Anna's idea of the nature of air was of the haziest, the challenge to her ideas of what is possible was strongest at this point. We notice too, that none of Anna's comments or questions to date has flatly denied the possibility of any of the book's happenings; they simply register inability to understand a process—exactly as in response to Richard Scarry's What do People do all Day? she might be puzzled at an account of some perfectly ordinary (but to her incomprehensible) piece of machinery.

In the next reading of Harold (8 February '76) Anna was four months older (3.7); her only comment, while containing an element of interest in Harold's drawing, embodies also a concern that was to supercede it: He's a good drawer isn't he, because he can draw windows. It might be claimed that Anna is here attempting to account for Harold's magical powers within the framework of an ordinary human ability. If this was so, a set of references and actions outside the shared reading sessions were shortly to show that her self-devised explanation was insufficient. Ten days after the last-mentioned reading Anna asked Hugh while out on a walk: How can I get up in the sky so I can draw on it with my purple crayon? Hugh told her that it was because Harold's crayon was a magic one that he had been able to get up in the sky. He did not attempt to define "magic," feeling that the concept functions as a sort of algebraic "x," its meaning expanding or contracting to fill whatever plausibility gap exists in an otherwise credible statement. We notice now that Hugh did not come to grips with Anna's use of the first person, treating her words simply as an oblique way of stating something about Harold in the book.

Harold was next read to her almost three weeks later at 3.8 (7 March '76). This time her question: How can he draw things in the air? came at the second opening. There is now definite evidence that she sees all of Harold's drawing as requiring explanation, not merely those parts which are, like the balloon, off the ground. She may, of course, have seen this much earlier. Hugh repeated what he had said about the magic crayon, but she was concerned with the fact that the picture merely shows purple line on empty white background; harking back to her earlier question, but this time hazarding a specific guess, she asked: Um, is he [these words obscure] just drawing it on the cement? Our answer is not recorded, but Anna evidently continued along the same train of thought. On 26 April '76 (3.9) she claimed to have found a "magic pebble" (the phrase comes from William Steig's Sylvester and the Magic Pebble, but is sufficiently close in sound to "magic pencil" to make it an explicable usage, especially since the "pebble," when we came to look at it, proved to be a tiny pencil left by builders). With it she drew on our brick wall a house and swirls of smoke coming from the chimney. And four days later, during the next reading of Harold there came at Op. 3 the comment: One day I will take a blue crayon out of mine [i.e., my pencil container] and draw on our path. What are we to make of all this? We can perhaps see in Anna's persistent behavior an attempt to make the magic drawing explicable in terms of her own range of accomplishments; to translate it into a real, concrete operation such as she herself can perform and hence to escape the insoluble difficulties posed by its occurrence in the book--a parallel, in fact, to her repeated re-creations of the poisoning scene from Snow White which we analyzed in surveying Anna's book-based play.

In one sense, the evidence of Harold differs not at all from the earlier examples quoted in this chapter; it is still evidence of Anna's exploration of discrepancies between known facts and new ones. But now she is not merely exploring scattered inconsistencies but coming to grips with the notion of an efficacious but inexplicable magic, a process that can have multiple, predictable effects, and which strongly contravenes the laws of nature as she knows them. In our earlier examples, Anna ended up with an answer, a rule. For Harold, she fails to force its events into the framework of her existing knowledge, and no rule is forthcoming. She speaks truly when she exclaims at 3.9 about the countless windows in towering city buildings in Op. 28, that it is "more than I can believe"; she might well have said the same thing about the whole book.

JENNIFER'S RABBIT

First published in 1967, Jennifer's Rabbit is a gentle verse story by folk singer Tom Paxton, illustrated with concern for detail both romantic and humorous by Wallace Tripp. It was

first borrowed for Anna in January 1976 (Anna 3.6) and read to
her several times during a visit to her grandparents. We kept
only a general record of this period, but neither then nor
during the two readings after her return did she comment in
any obvious way on the book's fantastic elements. The story is
set within a dream framework; Jennifer dreams that her toys
come alive and that she dances off with them to a magical
shore, where they build castles and sailing ships of "Milky
Way streams," dance with the sailors, and then return to bed.
For the two weeks of her initial acquaintance with the book,
Anna worked through a number of her normal preoccupations: the
location of Jennifer's mother (not shown), the location of a
kangaroo in one opening, and the clothing of the same kangaroo. When she asked of the sailor doll in the final opening,
Didn't he fall asleep? she was hinting at something that
does touch the fantastic base of the tale, but the hint will
only be made explicit later.

On 23 January '76, during the third reading after the holiday,
Anna commented (Op. 2): Oh look! that's a vase with a face
on--what's that? An ornament--And what's that face for? These
are faces produced by Jennifer's night fears; in whatever way
we explained this to Anna, she wanted to search for more, in
the final opening, and to repeat the question: You see faces
here?--Why? As if triggered by this sudden realization of the
book's potential for revealing odd secrets, Anna on coming to
Op. 5, exploded into speculative fantasy of her own.
Text: "They came to the ocean with the cookie crumb sands.
        They called it the sea of the very best dreams, and
        they all built a castle of the best moonbeams, and
        Milky Way streams."

A: That's what I--that's what I promised you that we were
    going to make tomorrow too--and we're going to make a
    castle that a--that a food giant lives in, and we're going
    to make a Play-Doh witch--and we'll make that castle for
    them--and we'll make the house for us, and we'll live
    next--next to the witch.
What makes this so exciting is that Anna has responded to
fantasy with fantasy--thereby indicating that in some way she
has grasped whatever it is that distinguishes the original as
fantastic. Her response resembles the acting behavior prompted
by Harold and the Purple Crayon, but with important differences. This speculation about "food giants" and "Play-Doh
witches" is not an attempt to cope with the inexplicable by
translating it into familiar motor skills--it is playful, un-
committed. Anna only talks about action; she does not seek to

perform it. (Despite her apparently purposeful That's what I promised you we were going to make tomorrow, Anna did not remember her intention the next day.) In choosing a giant and a witch, Anna need not be implying that she sees such creatures as fantastic; the more probable explanation is that she perceives them as appropriate inhabitants of a castle. But her decision to describe them as manufactured from food and Play-Doh again suggests that she has grasped a concept of playful incongruity as being involved in the original creation of ships and castles from "moonbeams and Milky Way streams." And, by asserting that her own family will live "next to the witch," Anna reproduces the theme of familiar-alongside-unfamiliar which characterizes Jennifer's Rabbit. Moreover, by responding differentially to the castle episode and to the earlier transformation of Jennifer's bedroom, Anna shows us that the former is to her a clearer example of the fantastic than the latter. As she was to do again later with the quirk-filled illustrations to Astrid Lindgren's My Very Own Sister, Anna treated the faces on the furniture as an incongruity to be exclaimed over, but not as an indication of a magical transformation at work. (Anna never commented on the transformation of Max's bedroom in Where the Wild Things Are even in readings much later than those reproduced in part 1; that she must have had some conception of the magical basis of the story is however shown by her comment during a reading at 3.9 [Op. 7]: "Did he have a dream?" When asked if she thought so, she said "yes.")

Later in the same reading, Anna for the first time began to tackle the question of Jennifer's being accompanied on her adventure by toys who have for the duration of the dream come to life; she pointed to the same toy sailor lying on the floor on whom she had commented several readings before:
M: What sort of sailor is he?
A: I don't know.
M: Is he a real sailor?
A: Yes.
Maureen then asked the same question of each of the animals, receiving the answer: They're all real, Mother. They then turned back to the title page, where the toys are shown from different angles, and repeated the question. This time Anna identified each as: A toy one--but they're all real.

And so, of course, they are! But Anna had for months been making a toy/real or doll/real distinction herself,[4] so that it cannot be argued that her use of "real" was a valid semantic alternate. It was then explained how the dolls became real, i.e., came alive, during Jennifer's dream.

A: I might dream of Mrs. Sneeze [her own toy rabbit] and then
   Mrs. Sneeze might turn into a real one? I might see how
   quiet rabbits are. All right. I'll say "What a quiet rabbit
   you are," and I'll go back to sleep.

Here again, Anna seems to need to identify with the magical
concept in order to comprehend it. Notice how even in the
midst of her speculation, a doubt rears its head about the
validity of the transformation--perhaps best interpreted by
reference to Anna's curious statement about "how quiet rabbits
are." She is probably dubious about how Mrs. Sneeze would
behave herself if she were a real rabbit and expressing her
concern first by questioning the process of transformation and
then by assuring herself that Mrs. Sneeze would indeed be anything but obstreperous. The problem did not arise. At the
breakfast table the next morning, Anna said she had wanted to
dream of Mrs. Sneeze but had not succeeded.

Significantly, virtually all these references to fantastic
material in Jennifer's Rabbit were confined to this one reading. Subsequent readings showed a decreasing flow of comment
as Anna returned to some of her earlier preoccupations, and
the book lost its pulling power for her.

When Anna was 5.8 we reborrowed Jennifer's Rabbit. Having
heard us mention it,
A: Hugh, did we ever get that book of Jennifer and all her
   toys that came alive in the night? Did we get it again?
We gave her the book to look at. Of Op. 2:
A: I wish I had a rabbit.
M: You have Mrs. Sneeze.
A: Yeah, but she doesn't come alive in the night.
Of the prone sailor in the final opening:
A: I think--he is all of--these men [turning back to show
   sailors in earlier illustrations]. He--formed into lots of
   them, all the different--
In other words, she has suddenly understood that the doll is
the "raw material" out of which part of the dream image has
been constructed--a very sophisticated conception which we
would not have thought her capable of at this age.

JIM BUTTON AND LUKE THE ENGINE DRIVER (ANNA 4.10-4.11)

Michael Ende's lengthy, extravagant fantasy in the Continental
manner made a massive impact on Anna toward the end of our
period of study, and her responses to it provide us with ample
opportunity to observe her interaction with fantastic material

a year later than our last two samples. Her response to the
introductory description of Morrowland (the imaginary island
on which Anna had based the game we analyzed in chap. 8, "Fiction Re-created," made it clear that Anna was likely to treat
everything in the book as potentially located within reality
unless she was provided with compelling evidence to the contrary.

Text: "The country in which the engine-driver, Luke, lived was
     called Morrowland. It was rather a small country."
A: (Indicating about 4 cm. with her fingers) That big? Is it
   that small?
H: A country, it'd have to be much bigger than something we
   could hold with our hands . . .
A: That big?
H (impatiently): Bigger than Wagga [the Australian city where
   we live].
A (excited): Enormous! As big as Sydney?

It simply does not occur to her that Morrowland might not be
in our world at all, and her main concern is to establish its
size relative to places she knows. In the course of the next
reading she asked: Can I go to Morrowland? to which we replied,
as we had done many times previously in similar contexts
"there's no such place; it's only a place in a book, pet."
This explanation influenced her next question in the same
reading: after the text had mentioned "Heaven," Anna asked:
Is Heaven a real country? And when China was mentioned, she
asked: Can I go to China?--a complicated question to answer,
because Ende's China shares little more than its name with the
People's Republic! And it was fantasy China that Anna wanted,
as is clear from the following:

Text (p. 66): "'We might perhaps let you have a temporary
           identity card,' the Chief Boss suggested conde-
           scendingly. 'That's about all we can do for
           you.'

           'Fine,' said Luke. 'Shall we be able to go to
           the Emperor with it?'"

A: Identity card! I've got one of them, so I could go to
   China! [excited]
M: Yes, yes.
A: And see the Emperor!
M: There isn't an Emperor any more, pet.
A: Has he--is he dead?
M: They don't have Emperors in China any more. They have
   someone called a Chairman.
A: Is the Emperor dead?

M: Mmm. A long time ago now, dear. That's a bit sad, isn't it.
A: Mmm. [Wistfully] Then I won't--what are Chairmans like?
M (disparagingly): Pretty ordinary.
A: Like us?
It is worth noting that Anna's question "Is he dead?" is an
example of a common habit of thought in her at this time: she
had taken our explanation that certain historical characters
are now dead and generalized it as a way of coping with other
fictional characters: if she asked to visit them and was told
that it wasn't possible, her immediate recourse was to suggest
that they must be dead or have lived "long ago."[5] As with
Morrowland, she seemed to assume that fictional people are (or
have been) real, until told otherwise.

So far we have seen Anna tackling fantasy simply as new fact,
in a way familiar to us from earlier explorations in this chapter. Similarly when we come to an episode involving dragons,
Anna is able to demonstrate her existing knowledge and in so
doing assert her superiority over the book's heroes: on p. 83
Jim asks the Chief Geographer what dragons look like, and the
learned man is unable to give a definite answer:
A [ba] [exclamation of surprise/derision]: The professor and
   Jim Button don't know what dragons look like! Huh! And I--I
   know what dragons look like! Very unusual.
And she knew what to expect of the giant pictured on pp. 118-
19 (at which she was looking ahead of our actual progress
through the text).
H: It's a giant.
A: Is he a giant?
H: Yeah.
A: Oh. Then I'd better not look at him. 'Cause he might eat
   me up.
Anna's expectations of both dragons and giants are serious
(because threatful); but she was also capable of responding
with amusement to elements that seemed absurd.
Text (p. 107): "mountains . . . were hanging down from the
sky."
A (laughing): This is a strange book!
Though she laughs, she is not merely responding to an obvious
absurdity, as she does later when commenting "it's not real"
about floating islands on p. 213: rather, by using the word
"strange," she is at last able to delimit a response that is
specifically evoked by the fantastic. By this stage, it seems
that she is far enough into the novel to have grasped its nature, as a book in which "strange" things must be expected to
happen. The question of a child's response to the "fantastic"
is partly a question of the child's possession of a vocabulary

which will enable her to differentiate that response. In her fifth year, Anna made increasing use of the word "magic," rarely employed previously, and her references made it obvious that she was developing a range of applications for it that corresponded closely with ours.

4.1: Playing with her toy broom, Anna said: <u>Magic</u> <u>broom</u>, <u>sweep</u> <u>me</u> <u>up</u> <u>in</u> <u>the</u> <u>sky!</u>

4.1: During the Walt Disney film <u>Robin</u> <u>Hood</u>, Anna said of a night scene with pale blue sky, black tracery of leaves, moon and fireflies: <u>Is</u> <u>this</u> <u>magic?</u> thus indicating that she has built up a mental image of a "magic landscape" quite unbeknown to us.

4.4: <u>Hey</u>, <u>the</u> <u>bouncinette's</u> <u>magic</u>--<u>it's</u> <u>bouncing</u> <u>all</u> <u>by</u> <u>itself!</u>

4.5: <u>Will</u> <u>Jonas</u> <u>and</u> <u>Jesse</u> [children she knows] <u>stay</u> <u>the</u> <u>same</u> <u>size</u> <u>and</u> <u>never</u> <u>grow?</u> <u>I</u> <u>won't</u> [i.e., grow]--<u>I'm</u> <u>magical.</u>

4.6 (to her swimming teacher, whom she hadn't seen for a few weeks): <u>Cars</u> <u>always</u> <u>talk</u> <u>to</u> <u>me</u>--<u>they're</u> <u>magic</u> <u>cars</u> (playful tone).

4.7 (at grandparents'): <u>You're</u> <u>magic</u>--<u>you</u> <u>can</u> <u>fly</u> <u>then.</u>
Grandmother: It's good to be magic, isn't it!
A: <u>It's</u> <u>not</u> <u>in</u> <u>me</u>--<u>I'm</u> <u>not</u> <u>magic.</u>

It seems reasonable to say that by Anna's fifth birthday she had established a notion of the fantastic corresponding to that of most adults--with the proviso that <u>novel</u> fantastic concepts will still for some time be explored as potential fact.

CONCLUSIONS

Anna's conception of the limits of reality underwent constant evolution during the period in which we studied her response to fiction. She never ceased working on problems of how far the world of books corresponded to the world she lived in, or of how far different book worlds could be taken to be consistent. Because Anna tackled the problems on the level of individual cases, her overall progress was not always easy to follow: she could, for example, learn that monkeys do not really talk and apply this rule to fictional talking monkeys, but then have to face the same question in relation to rabbits a few months later. Despite this factor, it is clear from the evidence we have presented, and from much other material not printed here, that an initial phase of apparent acceptance of everything within a fictional framework (we say "apparent" because Anna did not have the vocabulary to make such a notion explicit at this stage) gave way to a period in which Anna began to question certain fantasy conventions (approx. 2.6-3.6) but only on a purely factual level in exactly the same way as she engaged with a multitude of other notions. In this period we can see an interaction between Anna's own private rules, built on the basis of her limited experience, and those which we as adults were attempting to teach her. It was also at this time, and as a result of this process (we may guess), that Anna confirmed her notion of potential difference between book world and real world, a distinction which underlay her later ability to ask "is x real?" Age 3.6 seemed to be crucial for the beginnings of Anna's notion of the fantastic as such: the detailed evidence of Harold and Jennifer's Rabbit is supported by other instances both of playful awareness of magic and of the questioning of fantasy frameworks (e.g., the dream in Sarah's Room) in the same period. Nevertheless, we must remember that throughout the period 3.6-5.0, Anna continued to treat established fantasy characters (like ogres, giants, dragons) as fundamentally real--on the few occasions when she asked, she was of course told of their fictional nature. It is clear from our evidence that characters or events in books long familiar to Anna through many readings were much less likely to be questioned than new characters or actions in relatively novel stories, and this probably accounts for Anna's calm acceptance of the witches and dragons she had never seen in reality. At the same time, we can deduce that she queried the various aspects of anthropomorphism (talking, clothed, or otherwise humanized animal heroes) far more frequently than any other fantastic element (animated machines, e.g., or physical impossibilities like flying)--yet another demonstration of Anna's consistent focus on the human or quasi-human figure to the exclusion of much other detail in pictures and stories.

14
Heroes and Villains:
Emotional Impact

It is widely accepted that young children can become intensely
involved in stories, that they can openly demonstrate a range
of emotional responses to events and characters, and that they
readily align themselves with a fictional protagonist to the
point of sharing many of his/her feelings. This chapter will
not contradict any of these obvious truths. Instead, we shall
be trying, as always, to supply the detail which lends solid-
ity and significance to the commonplace, enabling us to ask
more specific questions on the nature of a child's emotional
response to fiction and to advance some tentative answers.
After a brief discussion of Anna's early affective responses,
we shall examine her attitudes to evil or threatening characters, the largest and most clearly defined body of material
on which we have evidence; we then look at the question of her
response to heroes, preferences for certain types of hero, and
evidence for identification.

Anna's earliest emotional reactions to books are difficult to
distinguish from her generalized excitement at seeing anything
new or brightly colored. She was greedy for experience of any
kind, whether it was objects visible from her perch in the
supermarket trolley or new books hidden in Grandmother's suitcase. It is similarly difficult to be sure which responses can
be counted as truly her own, when we are aware of having deliberately <u>taught</u> her some of them.

Her excitement at reunions between fictional characters had a
clear model: when Anna was 1.6, Hugh was away from home for
some eight weeks, and Maureen explained the reunion of Joseph

215

and Jacob in a simplified retelling of the biblical story
(Joseph, p. 21) in terms of her future welcome for Hugh and
demonstrated a joyful hug. Anna needed no such coaching at
1.11, when she was given Natasha's New Doll, and took particular pleasure in Op. 14, in which Natasha is depicted fleeing
from the witch, straight into her father's arms. In her private
time with the book in the days that followed its purchase, she
lingered over this opening. It is impossible to judge how much
she perceived the danger in which Natasha stood, nor did we
inquire at the time. Our attitude was always to take our cue
from Anna; if she said nothing about the hero's predicament,
then we assumed that she did not fully grasp what was happening
because it was not available to her at that stage of her
development. Probably, Anna was just sufficiently aware of the
menace to feel an additional relief when Natasha found her
father again.

Frank Francis's witch, from whom Natasha escapes, has the black
pointed hat that was familiar to Anna from her witch puppet,
and her eyes in two of the four openings in which she appears
show her to be "bad." (More on this later in the chapter.) To
link the puppet with the witch in the story, we followed a
"reading" (i.e., an edited version tailored to Anna's vocabulary and attention span) by some playacting with the puppet;
Anna kept saying: Nice witch, although for the previous
months since the puppet's arrival we had made her exaggeratedly nasty. We guess that the evil witch of the story had
affected Anna's perception of her puppet to the point of
causing her to deny that the latter's frightening behavior
was anything but "nice."

It was at 1.8 that she first expressed discomfort at a character's tears. Her face would pucker in worry when we came to
a picture of a girl crying.[1] In The Story about Ping she used
to look distressed when Ping was pointed out captive beneath
the basket, and on hearing that the family on the houseboat
intended to kill him and eat him, she was very upset (pp. 24-
25). The reader should note that Marjorie Flack's words did
not produce this effect. We had told Anna the story in our own
words, and so in a real sense Anna was not responding to the
book per se but to the story as filtered through our preoccupations.

A month later (1.9) she first displayed concern at physical
pain, in one session with The Pirates' Tale. She pointed to
the crown falling from the head of the king dwarf whom the
pirates have hurled into the sea (Op. 5): Crown she said,

her first use of the word, then, <u>Crown off</u>, <u>hurt</u>, which we then
took to mean that she knew that the pirates intended the dwarf
harm; probably however, she thought that the crown was part of
his head, and that the loss implied physical suffering. She
subsequently transferred her attention to the pirate who wears
a black patch over his eye, and repeated: <u>Hurt</u>. We (not exud-
ing sympathy for the pirate) then repeated earlier explanations
about the black patch; Anna tipped her book, cover upward,
pointed to this pirate again, patted him and cradled her book,
replicating in this way the comfort given to her when she had
done herself some injury. While we have not recorded any instance of Maureen's modeling this behavior for Anna, it could
well be that she did, as she thus cradled and rocked a crum-
pled book to show Morwenna at eighteen months how sorry she
felt for the harm Morwenna had just done it. Once these responses had been learned, Anna was able to repeat the same
type of behavior when faced with similar stimuli later.

These are some of the ways in which Anna before 2.0 showed an
emotional engagement with her books. She could make reference
to a character's sorrow or physical hurt; she could join in
his reunion with someone close; she could be apparently
touched by some of the predicaments in which he found himself.

At 2.0, Anna became aware of villains. For approximately ten
days, at 2.0-2.1, she was fixated on "bad men"; she saw them
everywhere, in the street as well as in her books. At the end
of that period she entered a phase where she sorted the world
into two categories, happy and unhappy, but we notice that she
never went through a need to identify the "good" that would
balance the bad. (Presumably the dualism of happy/unhappy
represents the same thought pattern we have already noted in
chaps. 8, "Fiction Re-created," and 9, "The Singer of Tales."

THE EVOLUTION OF THE "BAD-MAN" STEREOTYPE

When Anna was 2.0 and had for several weeks owned an easy-
reader retelling of the story of the Prodigal Son, <u>The Boy
Who Ran Away</u>, she identified as "bad man" the pig farmer confronting the son (Op. 7). "No," we said, "he's not a bad man."
Anna retorted: <u>Bad eyes</u>, pointing to the man's eyes, which
have heavily frowning brows and pupils low in the whites. At
some earlier point she must have learned that this convention
signified anger or hostile intentions: certainly we had never
identified the man as "bad" nor drawn her attention to this
conventionalized expression in any book.

In an entry under the same date, we noted that Anna identified as "bad man" two figures (the Devil and a witch) from Sendak's <u>Juniper Tree</u> illustrations, which she had never previously seen (pp. 163, 225). Both are in profile (whereas the pig farmer in the previous example was $\frac{3}{4}$ turned to the viewer); both are extraordinarily ugly, with hooked noses and gapped teeth. Because of their position, the eyebrows of both figures are obscured. The iris of the witch is low in the white, as in the previously described figure; so is the Devil's, but this is far less obvious.

When Anna was 2.10, and looking through a small-format volume inspired by Verne's <u>Journey to the Centre of the Earth</u>, she found an illustration on p. 102 showing a humanoid creature (a "Reerg") and said: <u>That is a bad man--frightening man face--frightening man face--that is a mask</u>. She also identified "bad men" drawn on the same pattern on p. 107.[2] The Reerg has no eyebrows, but his eyes are almond-shaped and slant at the now-standard angle. His pupils are high, rather than low, in the whites. It begins to look as if the bad-man gestalt is in which either eyes <u>or</u> brows are slanted. ☺

We conclude, then, that Anna's mental stereotype of a "bad" character was a <u>visual</u> one, based on quite specific cues. She must have made some links between this stereotype and certain kinds of behavior, though we have no direct evidence of it. By the time she encountered <u>Rapunzel</u>, she was sure enough about her witch stereotype to complain that Hoffmann's witch did not conform to it, and the same record, as we saw, shows her reacting with denial to the Witch's more threatening actions and words. Had she met <u>Rapunzel</u> six months later, we might have expected a reaction similar to the massive response to the wicked queen in <u>Snow White</u> (3.7), by which stage Anna was experiencing the full dimensions of the threat in a way she was only beginning to do at 3.0.

To observe the beginnings of this greater awareness of harm and loss that might result from an evil character's actions, we can look at the case of <u>Zeralda's Ogre</u>, owned by Anna since 1.11. Not until 3.0 did an outburst occur, and then it was directed not against the Ogre, but against Ungerer's cheerful heroine Zeralda, who is portrayed preparing a lavish picnic to restore the "hungry giant": <u>She is nasty to him</u>. <u>She is giving him animals to eat--I do think that he is going to eat those fish</u>. The same day she commanded us to <u>Look at that poor rabbit</u>, which is hanging upside down in the castle kitchen, awaiting its turn in the pot. Both of these comments reflect the

fact that we don't eat meat. By contrast, Anna's one comment
about the Ogre's cannibalistic longings on the first page was
comforting: Some men do that. But at 3.3, the indignation[3]
was switched from the Ogre who eats animals to the Ogre who
eats children, although she subsided after discussion:
    He can't eat little children and mothers!--He can't eat
    that baby!--it comes from that pram!
H: Why can't the Ogre eat children?
A: He has his own food.
H: What is his own food?
A: Little children.
Intellectually, she knows the answer, but emotionally she cannot at first accept it. Zeralda's Ogre was next read when Anna
was 3.5, and then for the whole year it was cast aside and refused on the occasions it was offered to her. She observed at
3.8: I don't like Zeralda, because it has an ogre in it. And a
fortnight later: I don't like Zeralda. I don't like ogres.
They eat boys and girls. To neutralize the effects of Anna's
statement, we denied that ogres exist outside of books, but
she made no reply to this and continued to regard Zeralda's
Ogre with disfavor until 4.6, when on two occasions, a week
apart, she requested it, saying the second time: That's a
funny book, isn't it! Our evidence is more extensive than we
have space for here, but the Zeralda record makes plain Anna's
changing awareness of what was implied in the ogre's behavior,
and how her emotional response went hand in hand with this.

In contrast to Zeralda, where because she owned it so early,
the period of avoidance came late in Anna's acquaintance with
the story, the bulk of her verbalized emotional involvement
with Snow White followed an initial phase of avoidance. We
have already discussed her reenactments of parts of Snow White
in chap. 9, "The Singer of Tales." We now return to the record
for the reading sessions with Bernadette Watts's version to
extract from it those comments relating to the Wicked Queen.
Anna's behavior when we sat reading the book was of a piece
with her behavior in play and conversation afterward, except
that the immediate stimulus of text and illustration caused
her to remark on a slightly wider range of elements than sur-
vived when the book was closed. Six days (and two readings)
after the book was borrowed, Anna announced (at 3.7):
    And I will return this one, because I am tired of it.
M: What don't you like about it, Anna? The story or the
    pictures?
A: I don't like the stepmother.
We saw Anna looking at the book by herself, and putting her
hand over the stepmother, she explained: I'm turning over the

page quickly because I don't want to see that one. The pages
she singled out for this treatment were pp. 29-31 where the
stepmother is disguised: we have no way of knowing whether her
disguise heightened her awfulness for Anna.

We at that point decided to intervene, and the same night
offered to read the book to Anna, who accepted. In the fourth
reading a day later, she interrupted: Ah, that stepmother
queen is a bad--is very lucky, isn't she! She has a mirror.
Three days later as we read we came to p. 31 where the disguised stepmother's teeth can be faintly seen, white and even.
Has she got only white teeth, that old woman? The reason for
this question was soon revealed. Have I got any gold in any
of my teeth? When told no, she said to Maureen: But I want
teeth like yours. [Maureen has gold fillings.]

She gave herself away with her slip "bad . . . lucky." Now she
could talk about the queen, but there was no deviation from
her original perception that the queen was bad. Did she want
teeth like Maureen's only because she identified with her (the
way the girl next door once expressed deep disappointment on
discovering that she would not have "fur on her chest like
Daddy's" when she grew up?) More probably, she wanted teeth
like Maureen's precisely because they were not like the daz-
zling pearls in the mouth of the wicked queen. The story was
read twice more, once at Anna's and once at our suggestion.
When the book was returned, we recorded our satisfaction that
Anna seemed to have faced and overcome her earlier fears about
the queen, to the extent that she was able to act out and talk
about the story.

In establishing 3.6-4.6 as a period in which Anna would retreat
from a book she found too emotionally involving, Snow White has
taken us as far as 3.7. She was 3.9 when she borrowed The Tale
of Samuel Whiskers which she wanted read to her twice only. It
evoked several comments during the second reading, and resulted
in a role play that lasted at least half an hour--in which she
took three roles, commanding Maureen to take the appropriate
complementary roles each time. More than a month later, while
eating pumpkin soup, she exclaimed enthusiastically:
    Oh, oh, oh! I just remembered we had Samuel Whiskers!
M (rather sourly): But you told me you didn't like that book!
    [She did, after we returned it.]
A: I didn't like it, 'cause it had a spider in it--a big, big
    spider as big as my book.
Anna's statement implied that for her the real villain of the
piece was not Samuel Whiskers, who wanted to eat Tom in a

roly-poly pudding, but the spider (which was insignificant in
the illustration and plays only a minor role in the plot). In
fact, during the role-playing session in our garden, while
Maureen picked up fragments of bricks and mortar, Anna allotted the part of Samuel Whiskers to Maureen and that of Samuel's
accomplice Anna Maria, to herself. Perhaps she felt too much
affinity for another Anna to be able to cast her in the role
of a villain. She also suggested renaming her toy giraffe
"Anna Maria."

Had Anna not made this statement of disapproval, we would
simply have thought that The Tale of Samuel Whiskers did not
fire her fancy, and would not seriously have imagined that it
had aroused anxiety. And even if we had, we would have assumed
that the villain was really Samuel Whiskers, as indeed he may
still have been, if we posit that he was so threatening that
it was easier for Anna to talk about the spider.

Bernard Waber's Torchy fared even worse with Anna than did
Samuel Whiskers. Her first reaction on finding it had been
chosen for her, at 4.2, was to call it "hateful"; and after
the sole reading that she would accept, she said: Those fireflies and that--chipmunk and that--woodchuck were silly to
tell Torchy to put out his light because he wanted to twinkle
and they should let him twinkle. While this is a fair response
to the early part of the book, it seemed that Anna had felt
Torchy's pain and not his triumph, which Waber recounts at the
book's end. We found her response to the book a sobering gloss
on parent-child relations. It seemed that she found most dis-
tressing the way the other creatures (the adults) refused to
accept the best Torchy (the child) could do. She did not want
repetitions of a book in which the hero was as systematically
rejected as poor Torchy. The villains of the piece did nothing
worse than uphold conventionality and attempt to socialize
him.

Once we reach 4.6, we are at the end of the phase during which
Anna seemed to have a heightened awareness of menace and
seemed best able to cope by withdrawing from contact. In the
six months that take us to the end of our study we see her
exhibiting a greater readiness to deal with evil characters
and, as she gathers confidence, developing more ways of expressing her aversion from them. We look first then at her at
4.6, leafing through a pile of books. We found her scratching
an anteater and a boar on Op. 8 of Scarry's Please and Thank
You Book. She said: Bad people like this and this one I
scratch in this book. These two animals, colored gray and

greeny-gray, glare and push each other. Their color reminded us of an incident which had puzzled us fifty-five weeks earlier (Anna 3.6) at the local airport; she saw a gray-green camouflaged air force plane and observed: <u>That</u> <u>is</u> <u>a</u> <u>nasty</u> <u>one</u>. We wondered if she was referring to the somewhat ugly profile of the plane (as compared with the domestic Fokker we travel in) or to its color. It does appear that Anna had somehow built up a negative association with gray-green. And since she had had the <u>Please</u> <u>and</u> <u>Thank</u> <u>You</u> <u>Book</u> from 1.9, it is probable that her early exposure to this particularly objectionable pair, anteater and boar, had formed a link for her between their color and their behavior, and this may well be relevant to the dislike for gray and kindred colors noted in chap. 11, "The Genesis of Taste."

In scratching the anteater and boar, Anna was deliberately but lightheartedly confronting two villains, albeit malefactors of a minor stature. This sort of behavior seemed primitive, and we expected to see it die out early. But there were two instances at 4.9 and one at 4.11. One of the examples at 4.9 concerned a new alphabet placemat—"J" is represented by the yellow, slyly grinning head of a jackal. Anna was observed scratching him on two occasions, and she described him with loathing as "revolting." His color is one for which she has a known dislike, and his mere appearance was enough to determine her attitude to him—she needed no story <u>casting</u> him as a villain. The jackal's yellow was compounded by the bared-teeth grin; bared teeth were part of the behavior she expected to see in the <u>Rapunzel</u> witch, when she said at 3.0, <u>The</u> <u>witch</u> <u>should</u> <u>be</u> <u>like</u> <u>this</u> [demonstrating stereotyped witchy behavior, baring her teeth and looking fierce], and also a feature of the threat on p. 31 in Watts's <u>Snow</u> <u>White</u>. She spoke at 3.7 (without reference to a particular book) of disliking <u>nasty</u> <u>witches</u> <u>who</u> <u>make</u> <u>faces</u> <u>at</u> <u>us</u> <u>and</u> <u>say</u> <u>they</u> <u>are</u> <u>going</u> <u>to</u> <u>eat</u> <u>us</u> <u>up</u>, so that we need to keep in mind that there are facial distortions other than the frowning brows of the "bad men" which came to signal a villain for Anna.

Did she always perceive the villains as such? The answer to this is implicit in what we have said so far, that after 2.0, Anna could pick out a "bad man" if he were drawn with the slanting, frowning brows of her bad-man stereotype. Before 3.6 she need not be aware of a villain if he did not conform to her visual stereotype, as realistically drawn animals did not (e.g., Old Brown in <u>Squirrel</u> <u>Nutkin</u>). The <u>Zeralda</u> example shows Anna growing into an understanding of just what the Ogre was up to. During her 3.6-4.6 period of silence, unless we

were alert, we ran the risk of failing to notice her dislike
for a villain.

We have already seen something of the range of ways in which
Anna indicated and coped with fictional threats. We now give a
more formalized summary of these in developmental sequence.

Earliest Instance

1.8: She shows concern in her face for a hero's plight (see
n. 1).[4] This behavior continues after age 5.0.

1.11: She denies that there is any trouble (see above, in
reference to Natasha's New Doll and the witch puppet).[5]

2.1: She cuddles close where the reading of a dramatic incident is loud and fierce. (The "terrible roars" passage
of Where the Wild Things Are.) Last exhibited at 3.5,
in reference to "snarled" and "shouted" speeches in A
Birthday for the Princess.[6]

2.6: She puts her hands over her ears (Little Red Light-
house--see chap. 3); only three further instances of
this behavior; two at 3.5, one at 4.6.

2.6: She states her dislike of character or incident (The
Lion and the Rat: "I don't like that page . . . I don't
like that lion in the trap. I don't like that blue,"
Op.7). This persists beyond 5.0.

2.10: She describes a story as "sad". (Watts's Little Red
Riding Hood; on the day she was given this, she summed
it up:
   This is a sad story.
M: Why is it sad, Anna?
A: Because of the wolf.)
This persists beyond 5.0.

2.10: She enjoins misbehaving character(s) to behave otherwise.
(Baba Yaga Op. 6: She must not hurt that little girl.)
This survives to 4.7 as a way of registering threat,[7]
though the injunction form was established before 2.10
and, of course, persists after 5.0.[8]

3.0: She describes a story as "frightening". (The Nanny Goat
and the Fierce Dog, Ops. 13, 14). This survives after
5.0.

3.4: She covers with her hand a picture she finds distasteful
(The Man Who Was Going to Mind the House, picture of
haymakers). Again at 3.4, once at 3.5, and once at 3.7,
the Snow White example quoted earlier in this chapter.

3.5: She requests the omission of a threatening incident
(Bunny in the Honeysuckle Patch: "Don't read that with
the cat--read the bunny pages"). Three occurrences in
all, to 4.6.[9]

4.0:   She expresses pity for a fictional character explicitly.
       She said she was sorry for the Steadfast Tin Soldier,
       seen in a film a month earlier, and then in Monika
       Laimgruber's picture-book version two weeks after that.
       Why was she sorry? "Because he burnt."

4.3:   She scratches a pictured villain with an expressed wish
       to prevent evil. Scratching the man-in-boots in Pleasant
       Fieldmouse (p. 43): "There, I scratched, the man-in-
       boots, so he wouldn't take the mother squirrel. 'Cause
       I like squirrels."[10]

It is apparent as we look back at this chart that Anna's first
manifestation of concern was always nonverbal. Showing distress
in her face came before any of the verbal expressions of denial, speculation, or evaluation. So also she put her hands
over her ears and covered a picture with her hands before she
was able to ask not to have the emotionally charged section of
the story read to her. Similarly we can trace the body language
itself, from the concern shown in her face at 1.8 through to
the scratching of villains at 4.3, which seems to indicate a
more confident posture toward the threat.

Although it appears that in both verbal and nonverbal responses
Anna moves in the direction of specificity, there are exceptions to this particularly, so far as we observed, in the year
between 3.8 and 4.9, roughly approximating to the 3.6-4.6 period of heightened sensibility we have referred to elsewhere.
We shall take one incident from this period, during a reading
of chap. 3 of The Travels of Oggy. The hedgehog hero meets a
fox, for the first time, on his exodus from London in hopeful
search of the family who used to show him kindness. Oggy rolls
up to avoid trouble and the fox unrolls him. A few sentences
after Maureen had begun reading the fox's words in her softly
menacing fox voice: "it's hardly polite to roll up when you're
being spoken to," Anna interrupted to draw attention to the
cover lettering: That says "ANNLA"--that could easily say
"Anna"!

There is in fact very little gap between the "Ann" and the
"Lawrence" on the wrappers of our Penguin copy. Maureen explained that the letters were part of Ann Lawrence's name, and
went back to p. 27. The fox goes on teasing and patronizing
and menacing. Anna endured another quarter of a page, and at
Fox's exclamation, "A bold hedgehog!" she interrupted again,
spelling out the lettering on a gay carton (CRUNCHOLA BARS)
which lay in Morwenna's basket on the floor beside us. It
would be insensitive simply to regard Anna's behavior as

spelling practice or as boredom with the book; she chose to
interrupt only when Fox was speaking. We did not observe much
of this type of avoidance behavior, partly because we were
more cued to the content of Anna's remarks than to their context. In earlier years, too, we would have interpreted her
interruptions as reflecting her short attention span. Once
again the lesson is clear: we need to see Anna's behavior as
a whole, the seemingly trivial and irrelevant along with the
obviously significant.

So far we have said little about heroes; we now begin to explore Anna's ways of responding to the central character of a
story. The evidence available to us through role taking is ambiguous; some incidents lend themselves readily to dramatizing,
and some are less suitable. The personality of the character
whose role she played seemed to be beside the point, providing
his behavior was not seen to be threatening, and the action
lay within her reach. We need to look beyond role taking to
the evidence afforded by responses during reading sessions. In
tracing in detail Anna's responses to Rapunzel, Snow White,
and Zeralda we have by implication shown her to be focused
on the antagonist rather than the protagonist, and this is
accurate: but in the absence of a powerful villain, Anna con-
centrates upon the hero to a much greater extent. We examine
first that type of hero who is plagued by vicissitudes without
being the victim of any dominating evil figure.

We referred to Anna's distress at 1.8 when she saw Ping (in
The Story about Ping) caught under the basket, as an example
of the way in which her sympathies were engaged: her later
responses to Ping's predicament show us something of her attitude to a hero alone in the world. The little duck wearies of
being home last time after time and hides one night, getting
himself into greater danger thereby, but the perils are not
seen as springing from any malevolent figure; instead the
adult reader's energies are devoted to Ping himself, and
whether he can reach home again. We restrict our record of
Anna's comments to those which concern Ping and his fate
directly.

At 2.5, she looked bothered when hearing about Ping under the
basket, but she brightened up and said confidently: He happy.
Ping was doubtless anything but content in his prison, but it
comforted Anna to assert that he was. She asked, Where is the
boat? on pp. 10-11, apparently looking for the wise-eyed boat
that was Ping's home. And mistakenly seizing on the junk on
p. 15, she spoke excitedly: There's the wise-eyed boat!

Confused she may have been, yet she knew it was important that Ping found his home again.

At 3.0 when we read the story she asked: <u>Why</u> <u>is</u> <u>that</u> <u>boat</u> <u>going</u> <u>away</u>? A neutral statement on the surface, and yet if only the wise-eyed boat had sailed away just one night later, Ping would have had no adventure. As the boat sailed off, she asked at 3.2: <u>Is</u> <u>that</u> <u>his</u> <u>home</u>? At 3.3 she said as we read p. 9: <u>I</u> <u>do</u> <u>not</u> <u>like</u> <u>that</u> <u>picture</u>, <u>because</u> <u>the</u> <u>wise-eyed</u> <u>boat</u> <u>has</u> <u>sailed</u> <u>away</u>. And she followed us to the bathroom after we read the book at 3.4, saying: <u>I</u> <u>don't</u> <u>like</u> <u>Ping</u>. <u>He</u> <u>is</u> <u>alone</u> <u>and</u> <u>he</u> <u>is</u> <u>sad</u>. <u>That's</u> <u>why</u> <u>I</u> <u>don't</u> <u>like</u> <u>him</u>. Since then she has heard the story four times, but she has made no relevant comment.

From this volume of response it may seem that Anna asked for <u>Ping</u> very often; in fact, she chose it less often than most of her other books. It occurred to us that her comparative lack of interest in <u>Ping</u> was perhaps due in part to the limited color scheme. But once we take note of the manner in which she received the brilliantly colored <u>The</u> <u>Jay</u> <u>in</u> <u>Peacock's</u> <u>Feathers</u>, owned since 2.9, we suspect that the hero's predicament in both books lay at the heart of Anna's response to them. John wearies of being a plain jay, and decides to be Percival Peacock instead. The other birds scent deceit, set upon him, and strip him of his borrowed peacock feathers, whereupon John exits, weeping, with head bowed. Anna remarked at 3.1: <u>He</u> <u>is</u> <u>crying</u>. <u>He</u> <u>is</u> <u>looking</u> <u>like</u> <u>this</u>. [Demonstrates] <u>Birds</u> <u>shouldn't</u> <u>cry</u>, <u>should</u> <u>they</u>!

At 3.5 she listened in interested silence until the statement that John had "lost" all his friends. Not comprehending "lose" in this sense, she asked: <u>Where</u> <u>are</u> <u>his</u> <u>friends</u>? To the reply that they didn't like him any more, because John had pretended to be a peacock, Anna pointed out anxiously that she pretended to be things too, and we diverted attention to toothbrushing, after assuring her that <u>her</u> pretending games were different.

At 3.7 Anna commented: <u>He</u> <u>should</u> <u>have</u> <u>smacked</u> <u>his</u> <u>friends</u>-- <u>that's</u> <u>because</u> <u>they</u> <u>took</u> <u>all</u> <u>his</u> <u>feathers</u>. When she was 3.11, we were busy and didn't check to see which page she was studying, so that our answer to her query was not the most appropriate:
A: <u>Why</u> <u>are</u> <u>all</u> <u>those</u> <u>blue</u> <u>feathers</u> <u>on</u> <u>the</u> <u>ground</u>--<u>those</u> <u>green</u> <u>and</u> <u>blue</u> <u>feathers</u>?
We told her that peacocks molted, lost their feathers and grew new ones. Anna was worried until she heard the final detail about the new feathers.

A: Those ducklings are being unkind. This is such a sad story.
This was uttered with deep feeling. We tried to explain that
John was trying to trick the other birds, and they had a right
to be annoyed. (The ducklings are laughing at John as the
adult birds pull "his disguise from him feather by feather.")

Anna was never enamored of The Jay in Peacock's Feathers, and
what she chose to talk about in the book was John's humilia-
tion and his desertion by his friends. Far from being an edify-
ing warning, or even a mildly funny tale about a vain bird,
this book was for Anna a tragedy. It ends sadly, unlike The
Story about Ping, and there is little to choose between the
two records, when we assess which seemed to her to be the
sadder book. For Anna it was no more uncomfortable if the book
ended unhappily than if some sort of happy resolution was
reached after the danger had passed.[11]

Some writers show concern with the damage that violence can do
in books for preschoolers, but the anxiety she felt about
Ping's lonely search for his home, and John the Jay's unmask-
ing and rejection by his friends was greater than the distress
she felt at the loss of Squirrel Nutkin's tail; the alarm
caused by the spider's silent observation of the helpless Tom
Kitten may perhaps have been greater than the threat that
Samuel Whiskers and Anna Maria would cook and eat Tom. Equally
important for us to realize was that an ostensibly safe book
for preschoolers like Ping bothered her as much as an ostensibly unsuitable book like Zeralda's Ogre. Ungerer's apparatus
of bloodstained knives, overturned prams, little hands clutch-
ing cage bars, does not appeal to the squeamish. One would
expect it to be rejected by a child fearful for the heroine's
safety, but for Anna, this was not true. Her susceptibility to
fictional threat depended, as we have seen, both on age (which
governed her ability to perceive a threat) and on her personal
psychological vulnerabilities, which need not necessarily correspond with another child's.

From the beginning it was evident that Anna preferred females
to males both in books and everyday life. From the time when
Anna first encountered a book with a heroine, at 1.2, she
showed much pleasure in that little girl (My Teddy Bear). We
used to give her the many catalogues left in our mailbox, and
as she looked through them, she gave her attention only to
those pages showing male and female models, concentrating on
the pages where the models were female. Such was her delight
in color that we could have anticipated that she would study
indiscriminately pages showing people and pages full of
sheets, towels, and carpets, but this was not the case—

another instance of her consistent preference for people over objects.

She was introduced at 1.6 to two books in which men wear robes. She picked out the robes on men and women alike and called them "dresses" in the high-pitched, excited tone she reserved for that word alone. (Maureen had regularly exclaimed over the merits of each item of Anna's clothing.) In one of the books it was only the robes that caught her eye when she was perusing it by herself (The Child in the Bamboo Grove). Despite the length of Hugh's hair, she generalized from the length of hair on many men around her, and in books, and used hair length as a second criterion for discriminating between men and women. When she was 1.8 we noted that on outings she would point to a young man with long hair and say "girl" and when told "no, it's a man," her retort was "hair."

At 1.11, it appeared that Anna was adding function to appearance as a criterion, so that she identified as a "lady robber" the man who brings an abandoned baby from the doorstep in The Three Robbers. By 2.10 she had added pantyhose to the list of clothing or attributes which distinguish women and girls. Notice again, as in the discussion of her gestalt formation, the way she identified categories by selected cues rather than by attention to all details. Interestingly, in these early records, we can see that Anna was able to make an exception for her own father in formulating her rules for distinguishing men and women: men don't have long hair; men don't look after children. Hugh contravened both rules although it is true that Maureen's hair was longer--and so was the amount of time she spent looking after Anna. While our aim was to counterbalance her expressed interest in girls by emphasizing boys, and girls in roles traditionally masculine, the evidence of a preference for females, and females who fit the role stereotypes in both appearance and behavior, is clear[12] and underlies the later massive interest in princesses which we shall now discuss.

We noted that when Anna was 4.6 much of her fantasy play centered on the sleeping/dead princess theme (Snow White or Thorn Rose). In Anna's play a princess (Samantha Doll) lay waiting to be woken by a prince (Hugh) and was then killed, before or after their marriage, by a wicked queen. The game persisted, although as dolls' fortunes ebbed and flowed, others took the central role in the drama. Apart from this, Anna's dressing up, which began at 3.8 with nurses (who remained long in favor), from about 4.6 moved gradually in the direction of princesses. Princesses in Anna's mind always wear long dresses, and splendid ones at that. Perhaps that is why Carol Barker's real princess in The Little Bear and the Princess never rated a mention from Anna--her short dress is disappointingly similar to what any ordinary little girl might wear. One of her expressed intentions was to be a princess when she was a big girl and marry a prince--until she was 5.6, adult explanations made no dent in her certainty any more than did our vexed feminist insistence that girls can be doctors as well as nurses. And whereas Anna had seen nurses in real life, and knew one, her only encounter with princesses to our knowledge was through her books.

Princesses are not only gorgeously attired but beautiful to boot, which is why Jan Pienkowski's silhouette princess on the jacket of A Necklace of Raindrops dismayed Anna at 4.1: Is this the princess?--This princess isn't beautiful enough. Anna had no time for princesses who weren't the best in every way; for her a princess was a model of perfection rather than a king's daughter. A princess, when the fancy takes her, smothers herself in jewels, and Anna learned in consequence a wistful longing for precious stones. When we reborrowed The Three Robbers (Anna was 4.7) we heard Anna sigh at the text of Op. 9 ". . . and precious stones"--the same sigh that she breathes for "gold" and "princesses." In three out of the six readings she said at the appropriate place, "Loot" is treasure, isn't it? omitting the enclitic question after the first time. Once she said, "Loot" is treasure, with loving emphasis on the last word. Added to these statements was one simple repetition of "loot" just after it was mentioned in the text, followed by: "Wedding rings and precious stones" are the nicest jewellry that I'd like to have. I'd like to have some in my hair--all over.

In Jim Button and Luke the Engine Driver at 4.9-4.10 it was Li Si the lost princess who caught her attention. We reborrowed the book when Anna was 5.7, and she looked through the pictures without wanting to hear the story again. Some of the details she had forgotten, but her memory of the princess was accurate and minute.

While we are justified in talking of a preference for princesses over princes, who didn't seem to have much pulling power, Anna was ready to accept male heroes at every stage of her development. We have only to return to part 1 for verification of this--A Lion in the Meadow, The Little Red Lighthouse and the Great Gray Bridge (an all-male cast), Where the Wild Things Are, and The Story of Doctor Dolittle. One book stood

out in our minds because we thought Anna understood that it
was about girls, but we were proved wrong. She chose to borrow
A Bargain for Frances at 3.1 and after eleven readings in ten
days, commented out of the blue: "Farmer" is like "Thelma."
Anna was noticing a sound resemblance, but at the time Maureen
said that the two were not really alike because, to start
with, "Thelma" is a girl's name. At that disclosure Anna
nearly cried (she had clearly believed Thelma to be a male),
but Hugh arrived, and the situation did not develop. Two days
later, the book went back to the library, to be reborrowed
after three weeks, when Anna was 3.2.

"Thelma gave the shopkeeper her money," wrote Russell Hoban,
and Anna at 3.2 said "his money," indicating that she was
still convinced that Thelma was a boy. Four days later she
confirmed this: You shouldn't say "her." That is a boy. And a
further three days later: I wanted Frances to play at a boy
Thelma's house. That's why I wanted Thelma to be a boy. Maybe
a boy Thelma lives next door to Grandma--[and with a new light
in her eyes] Grandma has a library!

We can speculate that Anna, who at that stage of her existence
had not had boys of her own age to play with, was expressing a
strong need for boy playmates. This seems to be upheld by an
incident which occurred when Anna was 2.6, and her grandparents took her for a drive to nearby Lake Albert. Anna's
previous experience of the name Albert was limited to Albert
the badger in another Hoban title, Best Friends for Frances,
borrowed three weeks before. We all worked hard on explaining
the name "Lake Albert," to no avail. Anna concluded: I think
Albert will come out of the water and kiss me.

The cases of Thelma and Albert however, are exceptional in
indicating an occasional strong attachment to male characters.
There is as well the instance of the Snork (quoted in part 1)
where Anna also showed that she was convinced that the sex of
the character was different. (Thelma, Albert, and the Snorks
are all unclothed with little visible mark of gender difference most of the time.) Generally speaking, however, Anna accepted the sex of fictional characters as given.

Anna had one chance to experience really close identification
with a book heroine. For Christmas 1975 (when Anna was 3.5),
Hugh had the idea of making a book especially for her and,
accordingly, wrote and illustrated a domestic tale with her as
the protagonist, calling it "Anna and the Dark." She didn't
quite know what to make of it on the first reading, seeming to

be distressed at the text's suggestion that Mother was cross
with her; apparently it's bad enough in real life but worse in
a book about herself. She showed initial uncertainty about
identifying the girl but within a day was pointing out herself
and her girl bear Winnie. However, Hugh was most disappointed
with the reception his book had; it never really won Anna. We
concluded that it had been unnerving for her at this age to
have a book about herself as a younger child: because she was
herself the heroine, she was not free to criticize that heroine's behavior. But we have not enough comments of hers to be
able to validate our assumptions.

CONCLUSIONS

Anna's first emotional responses to books were of a generalized nature, and following through her progress until 5.0, we
have seen her developing greater awareness of suffering and
threat and also learning to express her own involvement with
the characters. Threat and danger usually stirred her more
powerfully than gratifying stories about unexceptionable
people. So Uncle Timothy's Traviata, with its pleasant car
rides and picnics, affected her less than The Tale of Samuel
Whiskers or Natasha's New Doll. And Anna was still in love
with romanticized princesses; ordinary heroines of everyday
adventures like the little girl of Grandmother Lucy and Her
Hats did not win her attention for long. But put such a run-
of-the-mill hero or heroine into a story which departs from a
realistic setting, and Anna would be swept away by the narrative, as in say, My Very Own Sister or Jim Button and Luke the
Engine Driver. Even so, neither Jim Button nor Barbara, the
heroine of My Very Own Sister, caught Anna's imagination as
much as the princess Jim seeks and Lalla-lee, who is Barbara's
fantasy companion and queen of an underground realm.

Anna could be deeply moved (though not to tears) by the hero's
sufferings, and books in which the hero is oppressed, either
through the machinations of an evil antagonist or through an
unfortunate concatenation of circumstances, were avoided by
her particularly during the 3.6-4.6 period. By the end of that
time, Anna was listening to story books rather than picture
books; consequently, although she still met evil characters
and distressed heroes, each chapter could end with a change
in the hero's fortunes. This is a very different affair from
reading and rereading a picture book, where the repetition
emphasizes the difficulties of the hero's position. Thus the
dangers in, say, Jim Button and Luke the Engine Driver and

The King of the Copper Mountains are encountered, lived
through, and then left behind more readily than Snow White's
or Zeralda's perils.

By her own observations Anna deduced the way in which menacing
people are depicted. She found her own methods of evading them
or expressing her hatred of them when too much tension built
up in a story. These methods were effective. Anna slept with a
light on as a baby and as a toddler, to facilitate caring for
her when she woke, but after her night-light was surrepti-
tiously removed at about 2.6, she has had no problems about
sleeping in the dark. There were no night fears, and her few
nightmares had no relationship to her books.

Some, when faced with the question of what to do when the
child has been distressed by a story, banish the offending
object forthwith. We on the other hand preferred to help Anna
to return to the story to see whether the fear would recede.
It seemed unwise to return Snow White to the library at a
stage when it had been read twice and found distasteful. Any
discomfort Anna felt about it was best openly acknowledged and
discussed, and the real breakthrough came at the moment when
Anna admitted that it was because of the stepmother that she
disliked the book.

It could be argued that to continue with a book that a child
has expressed aversion to is a dangerous proceeding because
that child may then be exposed to more of what has already
distressed her and may find the overload hard to cope with.
Our evidence does not support this hypothesis. While we have
withheld some potentially frightening stories, we have not
always been able to predict which books would threaten Anna.
Hugh (mistakenly) scoffed at the idea that The Tale of
Samuel Whiskers could distress Anna at 3.9; The Tinderbox,
which has always sent shivers up Maureen's spine, did not seem
to bother Anna. She emerged from the time of increased vulnerability to book-borne threat with a greater sensitivity than
she had evinced prior to 3.6, but with an increased capacity
to acknowledge emotions and handle them.

Looking back, we can now see that there is some evidence that
stories in which a girl is menaced by an evil woman (normally
a witch or a witch-queen) seemed crucial to Anna: a villain
alone was not sufficient to involve her to the extent she
became involved in Snow White, Rapunzel, Thorn Rose, or Baba
Yaga. It seems that the girl victim functioned as a character
with whom Anna could readily identify herself, whereas a

soldier (in The Tinderbox) or a boy and girl pair (in
"Hansel and Gretel" or "Jorinda and Jorindel") did not. Early
in her acquaintance with Snow White it almost appeared that
Anna experienced herself as the potential victim of the
Queen, expressing her sense of threat directly rather than
through statements about the fictional heroine, Snow White.
In psychological terms, the pull that the witch-girl theme
exerted on Anna is explained by her having to cope with the
good mother/bad mother dichotomy: i.e., the child's attempt to
deal with the fact that the mother at times fails to gratify
the child's needs and at other times is immediately nurturing.
The child, it is postulated, very early responds to this apparent inconsistency as if there are two mothers, good and bad.
Fairy-tale witches and stepmothers can be seen as symbolizing
the "bad mother." In Anna's case, we can guess that this was
so--and perhaps, that the princesses with whom she was so preoccupied represented the "good mother," an idealized female to
be admired and emulated.

15
What Makes a Story?
Perception of Narrative Conventions

In chap. 9, "The Singer of Tales," we suggested that Anna learned quite early to distinguish between an explanatory adult voice "outside" the fiction, and the same voice "inside" the fiction, flowing freely and rhythmically with the author's narrative. We surmise that it was partly from this initial distinction that Anna built up a concurrent concept of what a "story" ought to sound like. At all events, as early as 2.7 we find her registering a strong expectation that a new picture book would be associated with reading in the "inside" mode: Maureen had borrowed for her a wordless counting book, Yutaka Sugita's One to Eleven, and talked about the pictures, since there was no text. Read it, Mother, don't say it,[1] she said emphatically. Maureen stopped explaining and "read" e.g., "six hippopotami." They went through the book four times. Is this a story book? Anna asked.

It may be that this question is simply a variant way of attacking the same problem as "read it . . . don't say it." Even so, she is demonstrating to us that she is aware of the category "story." Does this mean that she has a concept of a story as a sequence of related actions rather than a series of unrelated individual frames? Though we have later evidence that Anna expected books to lend themselves to "reading" rather than "saying" (Paddy's Evening Out, which is wordless, 2.9; Teddybears 1-10, 3.5) she makes no explicit references in these entries to "stories." She had known counting and alphabet books like Teddybears 1-10 for a long time and for this reason may not have questioned them in the normal course of

234

events. We must remember that <u>One to Eleven</u> was <u>new</u> to Anna
when she made the comment, and our record shows that on the
occasion when <u>Teddybears</u> <u>1-10</u> was questioned, we had in fact
varied the "official" text, simply saying a number and listing
the objects meant for counting. Moreover it is difficult to
know exactly when it was that Anna first grasped the principle
that a series of static pictures could depict stages of an
action or (on a larger scale) that a series of incidents contained in a succession of pictures could add up to a story.

One way in which we could test Anna's understanding of this
principle would be to examine her first verbal responses to
wordless texts in those cases where we did not immediately
offer to interpret the story to her but instead suggested that
she "tell the story" herself. We have already met one case of
this in Anna's first exposure to <u>Where the Wild Things Are</u>,
when without any prompting in those specific terms Anna described the subject of each picture. Her linguistic apparatus
being considerably different from an adult's at that time,
however, it is difficult for us to make any sure deductions
from her performance. Certainly (as we said when examining
the episode) there seems to be some awareness of narrative
suggested by the sequence "then he gets in bed . . . then
he goes outside . . ."

When Anna was 3.10, we had another chance to see whether she
would spontaneously produce storylike discourse in relation to
a previously unseen narrative picture book. We had borrowed
Jeroo Roy's <u>The Shadow</u>, and Anna had examined it once, during her daytime rest, before being asked to "tell us what
happened" in it. In this wordless book, the inhabitants of an
Indian village wake from their sleep to be terrified by an
immense, looming shadow that stretches over their walls and
floors. They sound the alarm and make a mass exodus, but one
boy, bold enough to climb the hill whence the shadow comes,
discovers that the threatening monster is in fact only a
mouse, its shadow magnified by the rising sun.

Op. 4: <u>Look</u>--<u>he's</u> <u>asleep</u>, and <u>they're</u> <u>asleep</u>.
Op. 5: <u>And</u> <u>he's</u> <u>sitting</u> <u>up</u>. <u>And</u> <u>there's</u> a shadow.
Op. 6: <u>Look</u>, <u>he</u> <u>hangs</u> <u>onto</u> the <u>bell</u>. <u>And</u> <u>what</u> <u>else</u>?
Perplexed by this incident, which she doesn't understand, Anna
falls back into a conversational questioning of us, her audi-
ence.
Op. 7: <u>They</u> <u>get</u> <u>up</u> <u>and</u> <u>cry</u>. <u>Why're</u> <u>they</u> <u>crying</u> <u>like</u> <u>that</u>?
M: Something must have frightened them.

A: The shadow must have frightened them.
Anna has not initially grasped the fact that the shadow is the
cause of people's fear. But once the possibility of a causal
link is suggested, she is quick to identify the cause with the
"significant" shadow introduced previously.

Op. 8: And they run away still crying . . . look, he falls
down . . . He falled down too. . . . Who else did,
you know?

Two things point to Anna's perception that she was dealing
with a narrative sequence: "still crying" presupposes a link
between the characters' behavior in previous openings and this
one; and the use of the past tense in "he falled down too" is
conventionally appropriate to a narrative style--this is the
first time Anna has moved out of the "spectator's present."
But immediately, she reverts to pointing out discrete features
of this particular picture, in a manner strongly reminiscent
of the adult's "outside" voice. In this mode it is easy to ask
the listener, as she has done several times before, to supply
additional information: "Who else did, you know?"

Op. 9: Look--he tries to pull 'em [the donkeys] and she runs
away still screaming.
Note her repetition of the syntax established in Op. 8.
Op. 10: They run away.
Op. 11: That's a little girl. [In fact, it is a boy, but the
clothing confuses Anna.] She's not very big is she.
She looks like a girl 'cause she has more hair [Showing
that she has been aware of the potential ambiguity in
the pictorial evidence].
Op. 12: And look, that's a shadow.
Op. 13: That and that [portions of shadow] are the shadow of
that sort of thing [i.e., the mouse].
M: What sort of thing is it?
A: A rat--'cause it's gray.

Had Anna fully comprehended the plot, we might have expected
her to stress the climactic impact of these scenes in some
way, rather than flatly stating "That's a shadow." But her use
of "a" rather than "the," as much as anything else, shows that
she does not fully perceive the link between this shadow and
the one seen earlier in the book, though she is able to connect the giant shadow with its ridiculously small source.

Op. 13 (cont'd): . . . and she went from a castle [Anna's
interpretation of the town in the background

> of this opening] . . . what's that bit?
> [part of the boy's trousers].

"And she went from a castle" seems an attempt to generate a
storylike element, akin to those of which the monologues are
built. But the initiative is dropped in favor of a final
identification question.

In all, we can see Anna's approach to The Shadow as exemplifying some consciousness of its pictorial sequence as a narrative, though Anna was only able to make explicit links between
contiguous openings. On the other hand, consider some of the
other implications of Anna's seemingly rudimentary narrative:
she knows that the story is going to be about the human characters; almost every detail she identifies verbally is a human
figure, usually performing an action of some sort. Though in
their background details and coloring, the pictures present a
number of stimuli exotic and interesting to Anna, she ignores
these at this point. On the contrary, the second time we asked
her to tell the story, she produced almost no narrative, but a
series of evaluative, self-conscious statements covering some
of those very stimuli that she had earlier ignored, e.g.:

Op. 4: I won't tell you about that, because I don't read parts
with the moon in it.

Op. 5: I like that purple [a purple door] I don't read parts
that have black in them.

Op. 7: And I don't know why they're crying. But she has a pink
dress . . .

In other words, by 3.10 Anna did expect that a picture book
would contain a story and could (within the limits of her own
unassisted comprehension) verbalize such a story by identifying characters and describing those characters' actions. It is
reasonable to guess that the same expectation underlay her 2.0
response to Where the Wild Things Are, though the evidence of
her actual words is insufficient to prove it as clearly as in
the case of The Shadow.

The "I" that occurs so often in Anna's second response to The
Shadow (where, incidentally, her negativity reflects her response to being asked again to tell what happened in the
story) is clearly perceived by her to be out of place in the
first; does this point to a conception of narrative as essentially a third-person affair? One aspect of the experience of
a fictional narrative which we tend to forget most of the time
is the question of who is "telling" the story. A literate
adult knows—though he may have some difficulty spelling it
out—that while an author is responsible for creating a

fiction, he need not speak in his own voice within it: he may
assume a detached stance which we have learned to call the
"omniscient third person narrator"; he can speak through an
"I" which may be himself, or attributed to a character inside
the fiction. In either guise he may address the reader direct.
How would a child listener become aware of these possibilities?

In the case of authorship, we did make a concerted attempt to
teach Anna that books were the creation of individual human
beings. We would customarily point to photographs of author or
artist on the jacket of a volume and explain that this was the
person "who made this book." We made a practice of reading the
text of all title pages, with their ascription of authorship;
Anna's attention was drawn to the name of author or illustrator whenever she borrowed a new book by an artist she knew.
She soon learned to chime in with, e.g., "by Maurice Sendak"
at appropriate moments, and in monologues she invented her own
authors, based on names already familiar to her:
> Now, The Great Big Ear Book. In fact, Great Big Ear Book by
> Ezra Gates . . . Ezra Jack Loll Gates . . . One morning, Cat
> was rolling around, but he could not find the end of his
> nails (from monologue spoken over Richard Scarry's Great Big
> Air Book; Anna 3.10).

It seems reasonable to assume that Anna knew that books are
written and drawn by people like those around her--an understanding which must surely have been confirmed by Anna and
the Dark, the story Hugh wrote especially for her. We made
no comparable effort to teach her the convention of authorial
voices, however, and we can safely assume that when she first
commented on the matter, it was not in response to any conscious input of ours. Rather, it would seem that Anna's "training" was the direct result of the great majority of the books
she heard being conventional third-person narratives; first-
person narration or third-person narration with occasional
authorial address to the reader was rare in Anna's experience.
Patsy Scarry's Little Golden Book My Teddy Bear, an example
of the former, was one of her earliest books, but its "I" left
no trace in Anna's recorded responses--not surprisingly, since
her traffic with the volume at that stage (1.2-1.6) was at the
level of picture identification rather than text comprehension.
Beatrix Potter's tales provided a number of instances of direct
authorial address in an otherwise third-person style, but
again Anna's first acquaintance with several of these texts
came long before she was equipped to comment on such a topic,
even had her engagement with the books been on the level of

textual understanding. When Anna (3.1) did respond to authorial voice for the first time, it was to a Potter text:

Text: "She sent them upstairs; and I am sorry to say she told her friends that they were in bed with the measles; which was not true.

Quite the contrary; they were not in bed: not in the least.

Somehow there were very extraordinary noises overhead, which disturbed the dignity and repose of the tea-party.

And I think that some day I shall have to make another, larger book, to tell you more about Tom Kitten!" (The Tale of Tom Kitten pp. 50-54).

A: Who said that?[2]

We notice that Anna's question comes after the second instance of the use of "I"; perhaps the first, being embedded in a brief ritual phrase ("I am sorry to say") drew less attention to itself. In asking "who said that?" she has apparently eliminated two obvious speakers: Mrs. Tabitha Twitchett, the "she" of the text, and Maureen, the reader. But she has not connected her knowledge of authorship with the text's "I."

Later, at 3.7, Anna questioned a first-person narrative proper for the first time. She had heard Joyce Wood's Grandmother Lucy and Her Hats through twice, responding in a way which suggested that she wished to align herself closely with the unnamed heroine (thus she echoed the little girl's statement that the grandfather clock was frightening, and claimed to dislike exactly those of Grandmother Lucy's hats which the girl herself disliked). The day after the third reading, Anna observed spontaneously on a walk to the corner store: I do not like to call the little girl "I" all the time!

We responded to this statement as if it were a request that the girl be named, which indeed it may have been in part; but it seems also to represent a degree of discomfort with the book's first-person narrative. Could it have been that Anna's earlier professions of empathy with the heroine were also a way of trying to cope with this insistent, unfamiliar "I"?

Neither Edith Unnerstad's The Picnic (borrowed when Anna was 3.1) nor Astrid Lindgren's My Very Own Sister (borrowed at

3.6) had provoked any explicit comment on first-person narra-
tive, but when the latter was reborrowed at 3.9, Anna inter-
rupted after the very first sentence on the second reading:
Text: "Shall I tell you a secret? <u>I've got a twin sister</u>!"
A: <u>Who is she telling--that she's got a twin sister</u>?
M: I think she's written it down in the book--or do you think
   I should say: "She's telling <u>you</u>"?
A: <u>No</u>.
M: She's just written it down in a book for anybody to read.

If we trust Anna's "no," then we must assume that she did not
understand the text's "you" as an address to her, but as
directed to some unidentified character within the story. As
with the <u>Tom Kitten</u> example, she seemed to expect that a story
should be <u>self-contained</u>, that there could be no traffic between the people in a fiction and those of the world outside--
not, at any rate, any direct communication.

At 3.11, Anna heard another Astrid Lindgren first-person narrative, <u>The Six Bullerby Children</u>, and accepted it without direct
comment. She did, however, compose an extempore story--in the
first person--which seemed to echo both the style and content
of <u>Bullerby's</u> first paragraph. It was also at 3.11 that Anna
again commented "who said that?" of a parenthetical first-
person intrusion into a third-person narrative (Lydia Pender's
<u>Barnaby and the Horses</u>), indicating that even if she had
grasped the explanations given on previous occasions, she was
not able to generalize her understanding.[3]

Our next instance does not occur until Anna was 4.8, and this
time she copes successfully with quite a complex example. In
one of the verses in Michael Dugan's <u>Stuff and Nonsense</u>
there are two speakers: the main narrator, who is recalling
his childhood, and the narrator's grandfather:
Text: "'When eating figs or coconuts,
     To show you are refined,
     Genteely gnaw the centres out
     And throw away the rind.'"

A: <u>Is that what the Grandfather's saying</u>?

Text: "'Don't butter ice cream when it's warm,
     Or drink soup through a straw.'
     Thus spoke my wise old grandpa
     When I was only four."

A: <u>I'm four</u>. <u>And--he's four and I'm four</u>.

Though Anna apparently fails to realize that the narrator is
not now four years of age, she does manage to sort out the
two speakers accurately; notice too how as in Grandmother
Lucy and Her Hats Anna comes to grips with the narrator's
identity by measuring herself against him/her. If Anna seems,
in Stuff and Nonsense, to have conquered the first-person
narrator, then our final example shows her still unsure of
where statements made within a book should be understood as
governing her. Though not a case of direct address to the
reader, this is still within the same province, since Anna's
ultimate concern seems not so much with simply identifying who
is speaking as with determining what in chap. 13, "The Limits
of Reality," we called the limits of fictional experience
(Anna 4.9):

Text: "'Everyone has to make up a rhyme about the rice
      porridge,' Daddy said. 'You have to do that on
      Christmas Eve'" (Christmas at Bullerby p. 20).

A: Why do we have to do that?
Though a "you" is in question, it seems more likely that
Anna's reaction on this occasion is governed by the clause
"Everyone has to make up a rhyme about the rice porridge."

Here too, if we examine the remainder of the record for this
particular reading, we find hints of the same sort of identi-
ficatory behavior that marked the record for Grandmother Lucy
and Stuff and Nonsense.[4] It begins to look as though Anna
often tackled the puzzle of authorial voice--as she tackled
other puzzles--in two ways simultaneously. On one level, she
might ask directly in an attempt to gain an adult-given explanation of what was baffling her. On the other, she attempts to
assimilate the strange behavior by reproducing it to some
degree.

So far in this chapter we have looked at Anna's concept of
story in terms of her assumption that story would be associated with reading in the "inside" mode; in terms of her expectation that a sequence of illustrations in a new picture book
would constitute a series of linked, causally related actions
by characters; and in terms of her understanding of story as
the creation of a real person, who may address the book's
readers directly as well as in fictional guises. All of these
areas bear on the question of what a story was to Anna, but in
each case we have had only limited and often ambiguous evidence for her concepts. When we turn to Anna's notion of narrative structure we can draw on richer material. The monologues,
obviously, provide evidence of those structures which Anna

generated spontaneously; as we have seen (chap. 9, "The Singer of Tales"), the monologue can be subdivided into a number of brief episodes or sections, each constituting a tiny incident. To these monologue building-blocks there correspond a number of examples of independent "narrations of incidents" which came about when Anna was inspired to retell to one of us or some other audience a portion of a story we had previously told her, or a story or film she had witnessed elsewhere, in our absence. More clearly tied to memories of specific sources than the monologue incidents, these short narratives nevertheless embody similar structural principles.

What are these principles? Briefly, we found that Anna's fundamental structural device in her monologues was the binary composite of statement plus opposite. Apparently present only in a sporadic and rudimentary form in the very early monologues, it emerges fully fledged from 3.6 onward. Though stretches of individual monologues may be based on phonetically or semantically related chains of associations, the binary structure becomes prominent whenever Anna attempts to sustain protagonist-centered narrative. Mature narrative monologue, as we saw in "Another Girl Called Anna," thus becomes an endless chain of such binary oppositions. This need not imply that emotional energy remains constant throughout the chain: we observed that in some senses "Lars and the Robber" built up greater energy toward its end, whereas in "Another Girl Called Anna," intensity appeared to be dissipated as the composition lengthened. But there is little doubt that the short binary episode, not the entire composition, is Anna's basic structural unit.

This, as we hinted above, is confirmed by the structure of the episodes Anna narrated to us when her intention was to recapitulate a portion of a known story or film. Usually, though not invariably, the portions she selected had strong dramatic or emotional appeal. Thus after seeing the Walt Disney film Robin Hood, Anna on several occasions recounted two episodes: one in which the snake Hiss, an evil counselor to Prince John, turns himself into a propeller and flies off in pursuit of his intended victims, and a second in which a poor little rabbit has his birthday gift stolen but is given a bow and arrow instead by kind Robin Hood. The binary loss/restitution pattern in the latter example is immediately clear; a negative is countered by a positive. In the former example, the pattern is less obvious, but we do notice that the incident as Anna narrated it falls into two parts: the transformation (snake into animated propeller) and the pursuit. Thus even though the

material provided by the film does not lend itself to a
positive/negative framework, Anna so orders the material as to
make it bipartite. If we turn now to longer examples of this
kind, where Anna's actual words are recorded, we find the same
sort of thing happening (Anna 3.11; report of a film seen on a
neighbor's television): [A few words missed by transcriber]
and a tiny little monkey which--climbed up a tree and saw some
bananas. He picked one and jumped down. A girl pulled down the
tree and so the bananas [?] fly into the air, and all the bananas fell down onto the nasty sand so they couldn't eat them.

Here the first two sentences form one unit--broadly positive
in content, since the monkey sees and acquires the desired
fruit; the second sentence forms the negative component, in
which the bananas are lost. Now it would appear that it is not
the monkey who loses the bananas but "they"; whether Anna
has arbitrarily shifted protagonists as she does in monologue,
or whether the change reflects a real (though not fully explained) transition in the film itself, which we didn't see,
the key issue is that the second unit presents "loss" to balance the earlier "gain." In general terms, the binary structure
is preserved. Moreover, we can discern a smaller-scale binary
pattern within each unit. Thus in unit one, the monkey "climbs
up" and then "jumps down"; in the second, the bananas "fly up"
and then "fall down."

But what about the narrations which seemingly fail to fall into
the neat structure we have been examining? Consider the following, a recollection at 4.2 of Stein, the Great Retriever,
borrowed when Anna was 3.10: You know that dog that brang
presents to a lady, and he went to her house and his dog friend
was sleeping in a corner of the garden? And a report of a film
seen on a neighbor's television, at 4.1: On Peg's television
there was a story about a storm. And the teddy bear was in the
storm. And the poor teddy was in the wrecked cubbyhouse.

In each case we can see the initial clause as standing apart
from the remainder and constituting a kind of introduction. In
this first example, this is necessary because Anna cannot remember Stein's name and needs another way of communicating his
identity to us; in the second case, she seems genuinely aware
that we have not seen the film and hence need a summarizing
statement of its content. Both these examples are of course
relatively late in the record, and they show less of the
egocentric assumption that the listener shares the speaker's
knowledge than the earlier ones, where Anna simply plunges
in. Our point here, however, is that once we discount the

introductory clause, each narration <u>is</u> bipartite. The structure of the second example is a particularly interesting case
of this, since it presents a bald statement ("the teddy bear
was in the storm") followed by an affectively and factually
amplified version of the same statement ("the <u>poor</u> teddy was
in the <u>wrecked cubbyhouse</u>"). We can still see traces of a
shift from <u>neutral</u> to negative (if not from positive to
negative), just as in the <u>Stein</u> example there is a hint of
search/find. Clearly, the role-playing games described in
Chap. 8, "Fiction Re-created," belong with such retold incidents, and there too we noted the presence of a tendency to
binary construction.

The binary structure, then, seems fundamental, even if it be
present only in an attenuated form in some cases. But the very
fact of its pervading presence points to the likelihood of its
representing something wider than merely an element in Anna's
concept of narrative—some basic characteristic of young children's thought, perhaps, as the work of Wallon (1945) suggests?
Binary patterning only contributes to our knowledge of Anna's
notion of story when we observe it interacting with more specific conventions of narrative structure.

Since Aristotle, theorists of narrative form have talked in
terms of beginning, middle, and end, in terms of "introduction," "climax," and "denouement." In the prototypical
narrative, as most of us understand it, an initial situation
suffers some change; the protagonist moves so as to counter
the change; his move climaxes in a combat (physical or
symbolic) with an antagonist (external or within himself),
and on his victory, stability is restored, though the initial
situation may be altered for the better. Not only is this
pattern typical of traditional folktale, as Propp (1928) was
able to demonstrate so convincingly, it is also broadly true
for the vast majority of the stories to which Anna listened,
even though in some of the recent texts the archetype is less
obvious, since psychological movement, struggle, and alteration may be substituted for the literal journeys, combats,
and transformations that characterize the folktale.

Now it is not hard to see how this structure can be understood
or assimilated in terms of Anna's binary pattern. The initial
situation becomes a "+"; the changing of that situation, a
"–"; the climax, a juxtaposing of positive and negative
elements; and the restitution or return at the end, a final
"+." Very roughly, the sequence would thus be +/-/+/-/+. But,
as we have already seen, this is not quite how Anna seems to

assimilate the sequence. In summarizing our findings at the
end of part 1 we suggested that Anna's explicit responses
clustered noticeably around those sections of the stories
which dealt on the one hand with familiar subject matter
(usually at the beginning of a story) and on the other hand
with unfamiliar subject matter (usually in the geographical or
chronological center of a story). This seems to suggest a simple, two-part polarization. Does it also imply that in Anna's
estimation the beginning of a story was more important structurally than the end? The evidence of the monologues, where
the introductions to each "episode" are of the slightest and
most perfunctory nature, suggests otherwise. There, each
episode is focused on a climactic interaction, with any
introductory material being provided purely in order to get a
protagonist into that interaction as speedily as possible. The
monologue is thus made up of a series of dramatic climaxes;
though each member of the series can be seen to "begin," it
can be hardly said to "end," since in this structure, the end
of one "incident" is the beginning of the next.

The monologue as a whole seems often to have had a conventional opening phrase, but such openings generally bore little
or no relation to the matter of the monologue proper, just as
the arbitrary "the end" with which Anna closed her composition
could have come after almost any climax. These phenomena
indicate that though Anna knew that stories began and ended in
certain ritual ways, she did not conceive of the verbal tags
as having much organic connection with the matter contained
between them. "Once there was . . ." and "the end" might most
accurately be described as signals meaning "switch on" and
"switch off," activating or deactivating Anna's monologue-
generating computer.

Did Anna then have no real conception of what the beginning
and the end of the story implied? Our evidence for her understanding of beginnings is indecisive and weakened by our
failure to catch the openings of most monologues and many
of the "retold incidents" as well. In the case of endings,
however, we have more to offer. First, some examples which
seem to support the theory that Anna lost interest after the
climax of a story had been reached and resolved. At 3.9 Anna
obsessively requested stories from David McKee's Mr. Benn
Annual each of which involved a framing device whereby Mr.
Benn dons a new costume in a magic costume shop and so enters
another world appropriate to the costume. At the conclusion of
each adventure, he steps back into the shop, doffs the costume, and chats briefly with the shopkeeper before returning

to the world outside. Anna consistently withdrew concentration
and began fidgeting or asking about the next story to be read
immediately after Mr. Benn returned from the fantasy world to
the costume shop, even though several paragraphs of text remained at this point and the reader's voice had made no break.
For her, it seemed that the tale had finished, and that the
concluding section was irrelevant. My Very Own Sister (borrowed at 3.6, 3.9, 4.7) also presents a fantasy adventure
within a realistic frame. When Anna, during the course of the
second borrowing period, recited a lengthy paraphrase of the
story while reading in bed one morning, she omitted virtually
the whole of the concluding section that framed the narrative.
Now it could be argued that in both these cases what is in
question is a double ending, as far as Anna is concerned--
having accepted one ending, she rejected the second as redun-
dant. The other examples where no frame story or double ending
was in question indicate otherwise. The first is the case of
Rapunzel, at 3.0-3.6 (see, e.g., readings 3, 10). On reborrowing both Who Will Comfort Toffle? at 4.7 and The Little Red
Lighthouse at 4.8, Anna's attention in at least one reading
dropped away immediately after the climax; indeed in Who Will
Comfort Toffle? she actually instructed the reader to stop
after the Groke's house (for her, the focus of emotional
involvement) had been reached.[5] Note that in these, as in
the earlier examples, the story was already familiar to Anna
when she indicated lack of involvement in the conclusion.

We have at least one instance where at first hearing, Anna
seemed unwilling to accept that a story had actually finished,
and was clearly expecting more to happen. This was "The Fisherman and his Wife," which Hugh told to Anna at 4.6 when she
had woken in some distress. It is easy to see how the simple
binary structure of this particular tale--wish requested/wish
granted--could have created in Anna the expectation that the
sequence would continue indefinitely, especially since in one
hearing, her understanding of the wife's hubris seemed far
from complete, and her fall and punishment by the fish no
necessary fate. This storytelling session was not taped but
recalled by Hugh the next morning. Anna seemed surprised by
the end of the story and asked why that was the end. After
Hugh's reply that the man didn't ever see the fish again, she
speculated that the fish stayed underwater so that the man
couldn't see him; without this additional explanation, she was
not prepared to acknowledge that the tale had finished.

There seem to be three narrative situations in which Anna was
unprepared to accept a story as complete. One (as in "The

Fisherman") where she had not fully understood that a resolution <u>had</u> occurred and saw no reason for the story to end;
one where the story provided such gratifying images that she
wished to prolong the gratification; and one where she considered loose ends to be left untied--perhaps because her own
conceptions of concluding formulas had not been fully realized
by the text.

<u>Thorn</u> <u>Rose</u> (Anna 4.4)--
Text: ". . . lived happily ever after."
A: <u>in</u> <u>the</u> <u>palace</u>.

<u>Who</u> <u>Will</u> <u>Comfort</u> <u>Toffle</u>? (Anna 4.7)--
Text: ". . . and so they lived happily ever after."
A (pointing): <u>in</u> <u>the</u> <u>big</u> <u>shell</u>.

<u>The</u> <u>Pirates'</u> <u>Tale</u> (Anna 4.1)--
Text: "The pirates died. The cat died."
A: <u>And</u> <u>never</u> <u>anything</u> <u>was</u> <u>sawn</u> <u>again</u> <u>of</u> <u>those</u> <u>naughty</u> <u>pirates</u>.
To the last of these Anna added "But it doesn't say that,"
indicating that her supplement could not really become part of
the text. In two of the three she seems to feel that <u>place</u>
should be mentioned (cf. her concern with the location of the
witch's house in the second last opening of <u>Rapunzel</u>), in
the third, the addition has a kind of overkill effect which
she has encountered in a number of tales in which villains
must be emphatically and repetitiously disposed of. All these
instances are late ones; we presume that earlier the same concern would have more likely been voiced as "read it again" or
"is there another book about . . .?"

What does all this add up to? That Anna did have a concept of
how a conclusion should be worded, but that more frequently,
she considered that a <u>known</u> story had concluded <u>when</u> <u>its</u> <u>emo-</u>
<u>tional</u> <u>crux</u> <u>had</u> <u>been</u> <u>resolved</u>, a tendency which parallels her
practice in the monologues and her selection of "climactic
moments" for independent retelling or for re-creation of
fiction in play. Though the evidence is not totally consistent, it does look as though dramatic incident is central to
Anna's concept of narrative[6] and as though she may conceive
of longer stories in terms of a succession of such incidents
rather than a progress to a single principal climax.

In this we can see an interesting resemblance to Propp's con-
tention that while the structure of an individual folktale
may be linear and finite, the end of each tale may lead into
another, so that ultimately the structure is cyclic and
endless. And indeed, why not? Life is continuous, and it is

only by a considerable effort that we maintain the convention
that stories, unlike life, have clear-cut beginnings and endings. It is no accident that radio, print, and TV serials command mass audiences more consistently than individual novels,
plays, or films: it is a question not merely of people wanting
to maintain their involvement with a gratifying fictional
world but of an unwillingness to concede that that world,
unlike ours, can be arbitrarily caused to end its existence
except in the memories of its audience.

If Anna's approach to narrative was as episodic, as incident-
centered as we have suggested, then it may be asked how she
was able to comprehend any novel-length narrative in the
linear way its plot is intended to work. The short answer is
that she may not have understood such plots in that way at
all. Many of her "chapter books" deliberately adopted an
episodic format, so that the problem did not arise; the popularity of Paul Biegel's The King of the Copper Mountains with
Anna between 3.9 and 5.4 may have been due partly to the
extremely close matching between its structure and what we
have deduced to be Anna's own structural expectations: not
only does it combine short, semi-independent tales within a
continuously developing but easily comprehensible frame story,
it even ends inconclusively, in such a manner as to suggest
that only part of an endless cycle of stories has been told.

Other novel-length narratives may have easily been understood
by Anna at the level of a string of independent incidents
also, but the crucial factor for Anna seems to have been the
presence of characters who functioned as linking devices, and
of predictions involving those characters, which she could
grasp early in the novel and cling to until they reach the
point of resolution.[7] This was certainly the case with Jim
Button and Luke the Engine Driver, in which Luke and Jim's
lengthy quest for the Chinese Princess Li Si is the unifying
device, to which Anna alluded spontaneously on more than one
occasion. It was highly unusual for Anna to want to interrupt
the parent reading to bring up to date the other parent who
had just entered the room, but Anna (4.9) did this twice in
Jim Button and both the interruptions concerned the Princess:
I can see the Princess, Maureen! We've come to--see the
Princess! She was pointing to the illustration pp. 162-63.
Three days later: Hugh, the Princess and the other children
are nearly back to Ping. (See also chap. 12, "Funny Ha-Ha
and Funny Peculiar," for her similar interruption to bring
Hugh up to date in a reading of Alice in Wonderland.)

As we have demonstrated in our chapter "Heroes and Villains,"
a princess was an emotionally charged figure for Anna, and a
lost princess who must be sought became doubly significant.
Here again, then, we see the power of the small stock of
dramatic situations which Anna early acquired and continued to
invest with meaning throughout the period of our study. Content enables structure to work for Anna in this, as in many
other places. Without a princess as its goal, a quest would be
less effective--though not unexciting, as is shown by the
Wonder Doctor's quest for the flower in The King of the Copper
Mountains. Moreover we can surmise that the quest plot, which
is virtually inherent in the familiar/unfamiliar dichotomy to
which Anna seemed so frequently to respond, could not help but
be learned as Anna heard story after story in which loss,
search, and restitution were highlighted. But we must remember
that it was the vividness of the loss, the struggle, the restitution in themselves, which conditioned her concept of
narrative. Only gradually and tenuously did a sense of overall story shape make its appearance, and we would be dubious
about the claim that even by her fifth birthday this sense had
established itself to the exclusion of earlier, more fundamental patterns of binary opposition. As we left her at the time
of writing, Anna was still wandering with Don Quixote: she had
yet to enter Bleak House.

Epilogue
Notes
Selected Bibliography

Epilogue

As this book goes to press, Anna is ten years old. She has been a fluent reader since six, and not surprisingly has often tackled books that are longer and more sophisticated than would be normal for a child of her age (she read all of C. S. Lewis's Narnia series at six, Caddie Woodlawn at eight). Since she learned to read, however, she has ceased to be a spontaneous witness to her own experience of fiction. Beyond the occasional evaluative comment ("good"; "boring"), there is little evidence of the rich processing to which Anna subjected her books prior to becoming literate. Doubtless it continues, but silently, as for adults.

In the Prologue we mentioned our original intention of maintaining the record of Anna's responses after age 5.0. But the flow of comment had already begun to diminish by 4.7 when she entered school (which simultaneously meant that we no longer had complete access to her daily conversation and play); as soon as she had mastered the skill of reading, it shrank still further, until the recording of spontaneous responses became almost pointless. Since this development coincided with our own exhaustion after years of nightly transcribing, we decided, with relief, to make no more recordings after Anna's sixth birthday.

For some time after she became literate, Anna was very reluctant to hear books read aloud, preferring to practice her new accomplishment at her own pace. At the time of writing, though, we are again reading aloud each evening to Anna and her six-year-old sister Morwenna. The latter listens to books chosen primarily for Anna's comprehension level (<u>Treasure</u> <u>Island</u>, <u>The</u> <u>Princess</u> <u>and</u> <u>the</u> <u>Goblin</u>) with the same excited verbal commentary that Anna produced at an earlier age. But Anna herself is mostly silent.

The period of Anna's life covered by this study thus forms a natural whole, and our purpose in this concluding chapter is to state more generally those developments and continuities that characterize it. We begin by indicating the main chrono-logical landmarks in Anna's evolving pattern of response, land-marks which, though present by implication in the material cited in part 1, may be more clearly discerned in the light of part 3. Then, having examined the ways her response changed over time, we return to a consideration of those features which remained essentially the same throughout most of the period covered by our records.

Developmentally, the evidence of part 3 enables us to see Anna's fourth year as crucial in several respects. It was at 3.6 that Anna began evaluating illustrations not in terms of their consistency within a particular book, or from one book to another, but in terms of their match with <u>reality</u> (see chap. 10); 3.7 marks her first questioning of continuous first-person narrative (chap. 15). Chap. 13 shows that she began to demonstrate awareness of fantastic conventions as such at 3.6. Most significant of all, 3.6 was the beginning of the phase of heightened susceptibility to fictional threat noted in chap. 14, in the sense that familiar books like <u>Zeralda's</u> <u>Ogre</u> and <u>Snow</u> <u>White</u> were now suddenly perceived in fully articulated emotional terms.

The major shift that occurred around the middle of the fourth year seems to us most usefully described in terms of a change in the relationship Anna perceived between reality, the world she lived in, and fictional reality, the world offered her by her books. For each of the developments above to have oc-curred, Anna needed to have experienced and understood the fictional world as <u>completely</u> <u>separate</u> <u>from</u> <u>her</u> <u>own</u>. Comparing illustrations with the real world is so obvious an example of this that it requires no further explanation. "Fantasy" cannot be appreciated at all unless one possesses a firm grasp on a nonfantastic "reality"--otherwise, as in Anna's earlier grap-plings with fantastic conventions, it will be approached only as unfamiliar or potential fact. By 3.6 Anna knew for sure that things could happen in books that had no parallel in life. The use of first-person narrative voice was questioned at the same period precisely because it <u>breaches</u> the clear

boundary between fiction and reality by putting into the mouth
of a book character the mode of address that properly (as far
as Anna was concerned) belongs to oneself. The development at
3.6 of heightened vulnerability to book-based threat may seem
less easy to explain in terms of a book/world boundary. However, we surmise that as long as a story was experienced as
incompletely separated from Anna herself, it could not evoke
fear or hurt in the same way that it could once the separation
was achieved. Paradoxically, by knowing a fiction to be
"unreal," Anna was more able to be emotionally manipulated
by it.

Margaret Mahler, the psychoanalytic developmental theorist,
describes a gradual process, both physiological and psychological, by which a child evolves the ability to be physically
separated and emotionally individuated from its mother, with
whom it was once--for the months following birth--fused in a
symbiotic relationship. Symbiosis, Mahler hypothesizes, is
marked by the infant's having no consciousness of its mother
as a being external to itself: infant and mother are essentially one being. To a progressively decreasing extent, the
child retains until the beginning of its fourth year some of
this sense of fusion. In gradually evolving a grasp of "self"
and "mother" as distinct, the child also evolves a knowledge
that self and world are distinct (Mahler et al. 1967; Kaplan,
1978).[1] And (we would add) a knowledge that self and book are
distinct.

We postulate that in the period prior to 3.0, Anna's books
were not firmly or fully felt as existing apart from herself.
As her own psychic separation from Maureen was achieved, Anna
was simultaneously freer to experience a powerful, fascinating,
but external, fictional world that was clearly distinct from
herself.

We have already noted Anna's habit of asking the whereabouts
of fictional characters' home or mother where these were not
pictured. In the majority of cases, these requests are directly related to the presence of some threatening material in
the story in question (though this often became apparent to us
only long after the event). It is surely significant that
these questions, too, ceased during Anna's fourth year (at 3.2
she last asked "where his home?"; at 3.8 she stopped assigning
parents and siblings to protagonists; at 3.9 she last asked
"where his/her mother?" [for more detail, see Crago, 1978]).
That homes and mothers were assumed, or desired, for fictional characters until this period is a particularly concrete

demonstration of the degree to which self/book separation had not fully been achieved.

Once the distinction had been fully assimilated, the major development in the period 4.0-4.6 is the emergence of explicit language for what had been previously articulated indirectly or (before that) nonverbally. At 4.0 she expresses pity for a character directly (chap. 14); at 4.6 she describes characters and situations as "funny" rather than simply laughing at them (chap. 12). From 4.1 to 4.7 she employs the word "magic" (chap. 13); at 4.7 she first uses the word "real" in an evaluation that evokes the criterion of realism (chap. 11). None of these is a "new" response, insofar as Anna has previously understood the concepts involved; the change is in her ability to articulate them. By about 4.6 she possesses a rudimentary aesthetic vocabulary comparable to that of an older child--or for that matter, a critically unsophisticated adult (see further, below).

For the period prior to 3.0 it is harder to claim precise equations between Anna's book-oriented behavior and developmental theory--our records are less complete, Anna's language less amenable to definitive interpretation. However there is overwhelming evidence in Anna's third year of a need for consistency. The "house and mummy" questions (the phrase is White's, 1954) which we saw ending in the fourth year began around 2.0. At 2.4 consistency of color was demanded, and Anna also began to correct us if our reading deviated by even a single word from the text which she knew and expected to hear. Rote memorizing flourished from 2.4 until 2.11. Consistency between text and picture became an issue at 2.10. Is it in fact, mother that she wants to be "constant," at a time when her own growing individuation is setting up anxieties that mother might not, in fact, always "be there" as Anna once magically believed her to be? It is certainly attractive to see this behind her desire that pictures be whole, not fragmented; texts invariable; fictions governed by a single, not multiple, rules.

Given broadly similar environments and allowing for the inevitable differences in the timing of cognitive and emotional development from child to child, these are, in outline, the stages we might expect other young children also to evince. It is not our intention to make detailed comparisons here, though our footnotes throughout have provided clues to the existence of similar developments in at least a few children. Rather, as befits the conclusion of a case study, we return now to the

features of Anna's experience of fiction that seem both individual and unchanging throughout the period we have covered.
Here, too, there may well be similarities to other preschool
children, but these must await further detailed studies before
they can be demonstrated.

It remains incontrovertible that Anna's response to fiction
was shaped by us, the adults who mediated between her and her
books so much of the time, and that a child surrounded by
other mediating adults would necessarily have responded differently. But it is not as simple as that. Specifically, we
believe that we influenced many of the attitudes Anna brought
to stories and pictures--for example, the respect for the possibility of a separate fictional reality on which we commented
in chap. 13; and our speech provided a range of sentence forms
in which responses might be cast: it is doubtful that Anna
would have questioned, predicted, or exclaimed had she not
heard one of us do the same (not necessarily in relation to
a book, of course). From this range of forms Anna then freely
selected.

Specifically, for example, we taught her to speculate about
fictional gaps (missing parts of objects, events, or characters not depicted) by offering her our own speculations
rather than giving her either flat statements or "I don't
know." It seems possible that we also shaped some of her content preoccupations, such as her consistent concentration on
human and animal forms to the exclusion of inanimates and
landscape (by modeling it in Maureen's early selection of
features to name in illustrations). It may well have been our
own dramatic reading style which influenced her preoccupation
with exclamations, which were always among the earliest pieces
of rote-memorized text for a new book, which formed the basis
of many of her book-based games and which were a resource for
many of her monologues.

But it is important to emphasize that the individual books
helped to form her response too. Our evidence does not support
the conclusion that all or even most of the features of Anna's
earliest books were sought, or preferred, in her later experience, but it does suggest that what Anna selected from those
first books was consistently selected later, and that this
applied both to content (characters like girls, witches) and
to style (the "archetypal picture" we analyzed in chap. 11).
Perhaps it would be better put this way: patterns of response
established very early in Anna's experience of books persisted,
substantially unchanged. This did not mean that Anna's response

was entirely conservative. Each new book offered new key experiences, so that her stock of core responses increased continually. But our examples in part 1 show that newly selected material tended to grow <u>around</u> the areas to which Anna had initially responded because they resonated with associations established in earlier fictional experience: the familiar element drew attention to the unfamiliar element in its new context, and in time the two might become linked.

The often-stated belief that young children like strongly repetitive texts can, we think, be seen now as an instance of the core cue response within a single work. Adults who witness a child with a picture book only once or twice may think their expectations confirmed when the child responds explicitly only to those elements which the text, by repetition, establishes as familiar. But if they were to study responses over a longer period, as we have done with Anna, they might well see those predictable reactions being supplemented, or even replaced, by ones unrelated to the little stock of known phrases and expected events.

Indeed, our evidence suggests that the adult belief that children respond most readily to the familiar can easily become a self-fulfilling prophecy. Given only books judged suitable by their similarity to previous ones, a child may well be initially disconcerted by a book that falls well outside that experience and hence respond with overt negativity. With Anna, on the other hand, it was noticeable that books that stretched her beyond her normal range (like <u>Rapunzel</u> at age 3 or <u>Finn Family Moomintroll</u> at 4) almost always elicited more extensive and diverse commentary than books which were thoroughly within her grasp. Much of that commentary was generated by her grappling with precisely what was new and strange in the experience; had we denied her those books as "too hard," we would probably have lacked our richest evidence of her developing understanding of the rules of fiction.

Moreover, it is clear that had we taken at face value Anna's negative reactions to individual books we would likewise have denied ourselves the chance to comprehend the basis of her dislike, which often revealed itself only in later readings. Freud's theory that lack of interest or boredom may be a cover for hostility or fear is borne out in our experience with Anna--as we saw in the case of <u>Snow White</u> (chap. 8) and of <u>Oggy</u> (chap. 14). Thus an initial negative reaction to a new book might mean far more than that the work was simply too alien or too difficult. And a negative response is by no means

to be equated with a nonresponse: there is no doubt that Anna
got a good deal from some books that she did not _like_, just
as it is verifiable that a book-posed threat was by no means
canceled out, in her eyes, by a happy ending. In this case, at
least, the common adult prescription that reassuring conclusions can correct any potential fearful episode earlier in the
story, does not hold up at all.

Both the mediating adults, and the books themselves, then,
created (and limited) the scope of Anna's response; in one
respect, the very fact that we were concerned with and prepared to record her response allowed it to expand and to take
on meaning for all of us beyond what might otherwise have been
the case while not (we suspect) altering its fundamental characteristics. But whatever we can guess about the extent of
outside influences, it remains true that Anna's pattern of
response was also her own. As we have seen, formative elements
of that pattern were set up very early in Anna's book experience and show little real change over the period covered by
our study. Many _apparent_ alterations can be shown to depend
largely on Anna's constantly maturing linguistic resources,
which enabled her to say far more explicitly at 4.0 what she
would have been able only to imply or to say ambiguously at
2.0. Working _backward_ through the record (from _Little Red
Lighthouse_ at 4.8 to _Little Red Lighthouse_ at 2.7; from _The
Shadow_ at 3.10 to _Where the Wild Things Are_ at 2.0; from _King
Tree_ at 3.11 all the way back to _The Pirates' Tale_ at 1.0) has
helped us to clarify the meanings of those earlier responses
and to see their essential continuity with the responses that
followed them. What were these "core responses," this grid or
pattern that is present throughout, despite the major developmental changes on which we have already commented above?

We have had plenty of opportunity to observe the predictability
of certain of her reactions: the delight in exclamations and
in two-character dialogues; the fascination with incongruities;
the concern with hurt and loss--shipwreck, theft of a baby,
being stripped of one's borrowed finery. It seems to us that
the same basic elements lie behind each of these, elements
which are responsible for Anna's memorizing a passage, or
thinking it amusing, or questioning it, or basing a game on
it, or responding emotionally to it. Stated in its most
abstract terms, that constellation of elements requires a
temporary union of the familiar and the unfamiliar, the known
and the unknown, the predictable and the exotic. Since chap.
7, when we saw how Anna's gross response to entire individual
fictions polarized around these two elements, we have been

able to discern that the same pattern underlies much smaller
units of response. In incongruity humor, amusement occurs
because "something is wrong" with an otherwise familiar thing;
when Anna memorizes or echoes an exclamation she does so
because she is reacting to a suddenly higher level of excitement than in the surrounding text--it is easy to see, then,
how her response can broaden to encompass not just a single
exclamation but a sequence of several dramatic utterances
mouthed in turn by two characters; when she questions or comments on some feature of text or illustration it is because it
presents a challenge to her established picture of the world--
an unfamiliar element in a familiar setting; when a character
denies or negates what has been said or assumed to be so, the
same pattern is present (hence Anna's consistent memorizing of
denials and her tendency to use them heavily in role-taking
games); similarly a loss or a hurt represents a denial of what
has been, of the secure status quo. The element of familiarity
may, we think, consist not only in some perceived resemblance
to Anna's own life or world but in a recognition that what is
going on is similar to a previous _literary_ experience: "I've
been here before."

It is easy to see how this same pattern is consistent with
Anna's notions of narrative structure, which we examined in
chaps. 10 and 15. In responding to a single stimulus while
reading a book, Anna reacts to the familiar/unfamiliar dichotomy without perhaps fully being aware of it and channels her
response into one of a number of different forms--question,
memorized quotation, prediction, injunction--which make it
appear that entirely different types of response are involved;
in monologue she is forced to make explicit her awareness of
complementary opposites as the stuff of which incidents are
fashioned. And we have had abundant evidence of the way in
which her creative imagination is dominated by a binary system: when she replays a fictional narrative, she prefers to
cast two opposing characters and to confine herself to two
separate incidents; in monologue compositions there are nearly
always either two individual characters or two opposing _sets_
of characters who function as a unit much of the time.

In structural terms, then, Anna's pattern of response seems
validly described as dualistic. But, while this may help us to
understand the way a young child's mental processes work, it
is on a level of abstraction which is not immediately useful
in explaining other aspects of her response, for example, the
evidence for emotional and evaluative sensibilities, which are
more readily related to existing views about the aesthetics of

young children. It is to these issues that we now turn our attention.

We already know, from part 1, that the apparent literal, un-emotional quality of Anna's commentary--seemingly a straight-forward cognitive processing of new data--is often deceptive. A clustering of "factual" statements and questions may imply the existence of some underlying emotional concern, long before developmental changes enabled her to voice that concern explic-itly. We had no particular faith in psychoanalytic notions when we first drafted this study, but as we have examined and reexamined our evidence, we have found more and more grounds for agreeing with them. Nothing but the analytic concept of "latent affect," unavailable to consciousness but expressed obliquely or symbolically, can account for the consistent match between otherwise baffling lexical questions or factual statements and the presence of threatening incidents or char-acters. In the earlier period, only the recording of repeated readings over time enabled us to trace this link; the later records, where Anna had evolved sharper linguistic tools and greater psychic separation from fictions, show much more plainly the relationship between unconscious or warded-off affect and cognitively oriented questioning. Thus in the fourth reading of <u>Who Will Comfort Toffle</u>? Anna (3.8) heard the couplet describing "The wild black mountain chain/ . . . Toffle knew the Groke lived there, in cold and dark and rain" and asked: <u>What does "rain" mean</u>? Incredulous (of <u>course</u> Anna knew "rain"), we explained. Anna's reply: <u>Has she got any doors</u>? enabled us to see that she might have understood the line as meaning "lived there in a cold, dark house." A few minutes later, she rephrased more explicitly: <u>Where are the Grokes in our country</u>? <u>Where are the Grokes where we live</u>? making it apparent that she was concerned to establish if Grokes were real. The latent fear of the threatening Groke is obvious: but who would have deduced it from the initial lexi-cal question alone? (which at 2.0 might have been all that Anna was capable of articulating).

Time and time again we have seen Anna employ the defenses that Freudians catalogue: denial of what is threatening; reaction formation ("I could do anything I liked with the Groke!"); splitting (all-good, idealized princesses and all-bad ugly witches). Once we learned that it is part of denial to speak of emotionally charged topics in a matter-of-fact, or even laughing, tone it became even more obvious that a far larger proportion of Anna's reactions to books were fueled by emo-tional concerns than we had realized at the time of recording.

As chap. 14 has shown, Anna was not an emotionally disturbed child, and the defenses she employed to master threat were those we all employ. The degree to which she responded to books in affective terms is not, we believe, likely to be atypical. To those who dismiss the Freudian focus on childhood fears and are skeptical of the notion of latent affect, we can only say that our material does not give us grounds for joining them any longer.

Just as the degree of the emotional component in Anna's response was not at first apparent, so we have shown that she responded evaluatively to a greater extent than has sometimes been stated to be possible for a child so young--though once again it is only in the later records that this response is expressed explicitly. Conventional testing at a single point in time would have probably detected as little of her aesthetic sensibility as it would have of her emotional involvement.

This brings us again to the question of whether Anna's response to fiction differed in any major ways from an adult response. In the past, when children's aesthetics have been compared with the aesthetics of adults, many students of the area have fallen into the trap of assuming that the responses they themselves evince--or those of their academic peers--are typical of adult aesthetics in general. The adults who are asked to articulate their response to a story or painting, or who do so voluntarily at any length, are nearly always highly literate, culturally sophisticated individuals. As such, they are likely to employ a range of aesthetic terms and concepts of which a young child would be ignorant, and to suppress or take for granted a great many immediate processing reactions in favor of more generalized responses. When we compare such an adult with Anna, there appears to be a very large difference--quite enough to support the many critics and educationalists who over the years have given sanction to the idea that young children, being fundamentally underdeveloped aesthetically, are best catered for by deliberate simplification and explicitness. But this difference seems to us to be an illusion. Lacking anything but a rudimentary aesthetic vocabulary, Anna is restricted in the range of comments she can make, but as we have demonstrated, this means that her aesthetic must be _inferred_ by us on the basis of indirect evidence--which there is in plenty if we want to look for it. Moreover, Anna was capable of internalizing adult-given explanations of aesthetic principles as well as building her own rules from direct experience of pictures and stories.

Because she articulated a much larger proportion of her immediate processing than most adults would do, her comments do sometimes appear naïve, especially because of the frequency of lexical questions and of remarks which compare fictional characters and settings with those known to herself. Yet an unsophisticated adult would probably--if encouraged to do so--ask just as many lexical questions of a fiction well beyond his normal scope; and any adult, however culturally literate and intelligent does compare himself with the characters of whom he reads: he does not <u>articulate</u> the fact, because his training in criticism has taught him to suppress such responses as irrelevant or subjective. The difference between Anna's response to a new book and an adult's is largely a matter of the degree to which things are expressed openly, not of the degree to which they are experienced. Similarly, we should remember that Anna's responses, as we have preserved them in part 1 of this book, are, as it were, articulated in slow motion--presented in fragments over numerous readings covering weeks or even months; only by comparing individual bits of response over time do we arrive at a full picture; whereas an adult reaction can be expected to be more immediately coherent. But this again is a difference of degree rather than of kind. Arguably, Anna's response to fictional experience is more <u>honest</u> than ours--more honest because more fully presented, less censored, unpruned of mental revisions, errors of understanding, and shifts of judgement. Apart from the inevitable differences in subject matter occasioned by Anna's limited experience of reality, there is to our mind far less distinction to be made between her dealings with fiction and ours than most adults would suppose. When we study the interaction between Anna's mind and her book experience, we see a reminder of what in our own trafficking with the world of fiction we often lose sight of--the process, for example, by which descriptions of fictional places are given life through mental images of real places known to the reader: here is Anna (5.5), talking after a radio broadcast of <u>Watership</u> Down: <u>That's what I think it was like--where the rabbits lived--trees and bushes, with grass all around</u> . . . <u>because that's what it's like at Kapooka</u> [a local army base which Anna has visited]--<u>and all the rabbits live there. They must like that sort of thing.</u>

It is comments of this kind--fleeting, soon forgotten, or misremembered unless immediately recorded--which provide justification for a study like this one. Irresistibly we are drawn to the analogy of the social anthropologist working to re-create the life and mental functioning of a society seemingly remote from his own and yet highly relevant to it. For us, these pages preserve a record of struggles and triumphs, gods and demons most adults forget too readily even though they underlie their own literate experience of all story, all art.

Notes

PROLOGUE

1. Anna's younger sister Morwenna (born 7 September '76) was at the point of writing this section 18 months old, and we tape recorded entire reading sessions in order to have detailed material available for the period in which we lacked it for Anna. Maureen's input in the following sample is comparable with what she would have supplied for Anna at the same age:

Half title:	Mn:	What's this book? [Natasha's New Doll]
	Ma:	[dɒ] = doll
	Mn:	Doll.
Title page	Ma:	[tʌ dʒːˑ] = ? girl
	Mn:	Girl. See the house. See all the trees.
Op. 1	Ma:	[fa] = father (or mother).
	Mn:	Lady. Chair, doll, milk, tablecloth.
	Ma:	[‑ɪ] (Initial vowel not clear.)
Op. 2	Ma:	[fa]
	Mn:	Mother, lady, little girl.
Op. 3	Ma:	[dɒ]
	Mn:	Doll.
	Ma:	[fa]
	Mn:	No, that's the mother, that's the lady.
Op. 4	Ma:	[tʃɛə hɒ] = chair, hot
	Mn:	Yes, Natasha's near the hot stove.
Op. 5	Ma:	[dɒk] dog?(!)
	Mn:	Yes, there's Natasha. She's going outside, looking for her father.

265

Op. 6   Ma: [faə dɛə] = An attempt to copy "father"?
          Mn: Natasha stands there.
          Ma: [dɛə]   [a: dɛə dɛə]

It will be noted that this is a pointing-out exercise,
rather than a reading session, and the child is allowed
much space.

2. In particular, see Darlene Hoffmann, "Ten Days with Inga
   and In the Night Kitchen" (1976) where the investigator
   apparently assumed that it was impossible to gauge the
   child's comprehension of a picture book without asking
   questions on every page.

3. See, e.g., The Child's Conception of the World (1973),
   pp. 14-21.

4. See the work of Virginia Lowe, reported in part in "Books
   and a Pre-verbal Child" (1975).

5. See Dorothy Butler, Cushla and her Books (1979); Annis
   Duff, Bequest of Wings (1944), which is unspecific in its
   reporting; Margaret Graetz, "Books for the Under-Twos"
   (1971) and "From Picture Books to Illustrated Stories"
   (1976); Virginia Lowe, "Cushla, Carol, and Rebecca" (1977)
   and Adult, Book, Child (1979); Judith Saunders, "Exploring
   Books with a Pre-schooler" (1970); Judith Schmitzer, "The
   Pre-school Child and Books: A Case Study" (1973);
   S. Simsová, "Books Before Two" (1962).

6. See, e.g., D. Elkind, R. Koegler, and E. Go: "Studies in
   Perceptual Development II: Part-Whole Perception" (1964);
   Rosslyn Suchman and Tom Trabasso, "Color and Form Preference in Young Children" (1966); Sarah Friedman and
   Marguerite Stevenson, "Developmental Changes in the Understanding of Implied Motion in Two-Dimensional Pictures"
   (1975).

7. E.g., Howard Gardner and William Lohman, "Children's
   Sensitivity to Literary Styles" (1975); Irvin L. Child,
   "Aesthetic Judgement in Children" (1970).

2 WHERE THE WILD THINGS ARE

1. Cf. Ralph (3.3; Lowe, unpublished diary) having heard
   Where the Wild Things Are approximately thirty times

(commenting on title opening): "Those are more fierce than Max.
Lowe: Are they?
R.: Yes.
Lowe: Aren't they scared of Max?
R: Yes [pause] No! Max is scared of them!"
He insisted on Max's fear despite his mother's broad hint, his long familiarity with the story, and the evidence of respective facial expressions.

8 FICTION RE-CREATED: CONVERSATION AND PLAY

1. Cf. Rebecca who one night at 3.9 chose to take to bed with her two toys she did not usually have together--Rosetree the gingham rabbit and Myrtle the Turtle. When they were tucked in with her she laughed: "I could play The Hare and the Tortoise." This Wildsmith title was thoroughly familiar to Rebecca, who requested it as a bedtime book at least every second night in the period 3.3-3.9 (Lowe, unpublished diary).

9 THE SINGER OF TALES: ANNA AS STORYTELLER

1. The linguistic aspects of the monologues of a two-year old are intensively explored in Ruth Weir, Language in the Crib (1962); James Britton in Language and Learning (1972) and Martin et al., Understanding Children Talking (1976), focus on the broader questions of the type of discourse found in monologue and its relationship to other kinds of discourse. Both books include transcripts with speculative, and far from exhaustive, analysis. So far as we are aware, no study previous to our own has been made of monologues spoken while a child turns the pages of books, though the existence of such monologues has been recognized: examples are quoted in Peggy Napear, Brain Child (1974); in Gwenda Bissex, "Do Nat Dstrb Genys at Wrk" (1976); and in Butler (1979). Material comparable in some respects has been elicited when young children are asked to tell a story (with or without a verbal or pictorial stimulus): see Ruth Griffiths, A Study of Imagination in Early Childhood (1935); Sylvia Anthony, The Discovery of Death in Childhood and After (1973); Evelyn Pitcher and Ernst Prelinger's Children Tell Stories (1963) is a full-length study devoted to such narratives, analyzing them from a predominantly psychoanalytic basis and showing little

interest in their structure. Stories specifically evoked by adult request must differ in some key ways from spontaneous discourse of the type we are concerned with in this chapter. Applebee in The Child's Concept of Story reanalyzes Pitcher and Prelinger's and Weir's material extensively. The most recent analysis of spontaneous monologue is Sutton-Smith (1980).

2. Rupert annuals contain four frames per page: for convenient reference we have titled these left to right, top to bottom, a, b, c, d.

3. See Weir for a full and fascinating treatment of sound play in monologue. Here we have simply noted obvious cases of content links being developed by sound association and have made no attempt at proper psycholinguistic analysis, though the material is obviously present in Anna's monologues too.

4. For a theory of binary oppositions as basic to the thought processes of young children, see Wallon, Les Origines de la Pensée chez l'Enfant (1945), chap. 3 "Les Structures Elementaires: 'les couples.'"

5. See Kornei Chukovsky, From Two to Five, pp. 77-78, on the poetry of young children: "Verbs and not adjectives predominated. This is characteristic of most poems of preschool children."

6. Cf. Albert B. Lord, The Singer of Tales, pp. 30-67, for a full treatment of formulaic composition among Yugoslav oral poets of this century.

10 ORDER FROM CHAOS: LEARNING TO READ PICTURES

1. With Anna we can compare Rebecca: correct orientation of pictures at 14 months (Lowe, 1975, p. 78); Cushla at 11 months (Butler, p. 33) and Ben at 2.5 (Anthony, 1973, p. 70). It seems likely that the age at which a child as a matter of course correctly orients a page depends largely on the amount of book experience she has had. For a review of the research on orientation, see Vurpillot.

2. Arnheim, Art and Visual Perception (1954), p. 184.

3. See Vurpillot, pp. 132-34, for a discussion of Part-Whole Confusion: "An error often made by young children is, on

the one hand to identify an object on the basis of a single detail, and on the other hand, to judge two objects as identical because they have a part in common" (p. 132). See Saunders, p. 7.

4. Vurpillot cites the consensus of researchers that "approximately 70 percent of 4-year-olds are successful in identifying overlapping figures" (p. 37).

5. Arnheim, pp. 155-57: "Perceptual identity depends relatively little on size. The shape and orientation of an object remains unimpaired by a change of size" (p. 155).

   Vurpillot, p. 203, cites her 1969 research involving children from 4½ to 7½ years: "As early as 4½ years, suppressions and changes of form were almost all detected and were also the first to be mentioned; it was only at 7½ years that the differences in size were discovered as often as the suppressions and changes in form, but even then they were detected after the latter."

6. Sarah Hayes reviewing Eric Carle's Animals and their Babies, Times Literary Supplement, 6 December 1974, p. 1378.

7. See Joan Cass Literature and the Young Child, p. 5: "Many two-year-olds, for example, will at first be confused if a picture shows only part of a thing--the bonnet of a car, or the front legs of an animal. Alan aged 2.2 was quite upset as he looked at Marjorie Flack's Angus Lost, which shows just the front wheels of a motor car and the two back legs of a dog vanishing off the page, and kept murmuring to himself sadly, 'Poor thing, all broke.'"

   Cf. White, p. 27: "In the d'Aulaire Too Big the boy is shown holding to mother's apron strings, but the mother stops at the waist. 'Where is that mummy's head?' Ann demanded of her mother. Any explanations were useless. Ann was convinced that the mother was decapitated."

   Dorothy White's own daughter Carol is described (p. 32) as encountering the same difficulty in Angus Lost when she was 2.11; in Angus Lost there is a 'milkman who is cut off at the waist."

8. Jean Chapman's review of Nonny Hogrogian's One Fine Day in Reading Time: New Books for Boys and Girls (The

Children's Book Council of Australia), no. 47 (April 1972) p. 7: "However, the tail did worry me for a different reason. There, on a title page, is the fox chopped in half. . . . Small children are often disconcerted by parts of figures only on view and an illustrator of Nonny Hogrogian's calibre would be aware of this."

9. Cf. White, p. 26: "The second watering-can picture where only Peter's ears protrude worried her. 'Where's the rest of him?'" Butler, p. 50: At 2.9 (?) Cushla, asked where the rest of Peter was: "'In there,' said Cushla firmly, pointing to the can."

10. Cf. Cushla, listening to Kaj Beckman's Susan Cannot Sleep at some point in the period 3.3-3.9: "Susan's pillow has her name embroidered on it in one picture, but it is missing in the next. 'Where's Susan's name gone,' asked Cushla. While her father looked baffled, she fortunately found an explanation herself. 'I know. She turned her pillow over!'" (Butler, p. 79).

11. "One can see from Elkind and Weiss's (1967) experiment that the left-right strategy is already employed by half the 5-year-old children with an unstructured stimulus. Learning to read does not cause it to appear, but encourages its more systematic employment, since it is most frequent at 6 years" (Vurpillot, p. 244). It would seem that in noticing a figure disappearing off the right-hand edge, Anna is employing a left-right strategy.

12. Cf. Rebecca at 3.9, who laughed to see a dog accidentally hosed in Summer (Low). She mistook the water for paint, because it was colored blue (Lowe, unpublished diary).

13. Virginia Lowe's unpublished diaries contain several examples (2.2-4.10) which suggest that Rebecca could interpret multiple images of a character as repeated images of him; that is to say that she knew there was only one character who looked like this, despite the several contiguous representations. But once there were multiple images of an object, or an animal treated in a naturalistic way, she took the repetitions to mean that there really were as many examples of the object as there were representations. This suggests to us that Rebecca, like Anna, was human-focused much of the time.

11 THE GENESIS OF TASTE: ANNA'S PICTURE PREFERENCES

1. Cf. White (1954), p. 11: Carol at 2.4 showed distaste for uncolored openings in an otherwise colorful book. See also Saunders (1970), p. 6. But cf. Cushla and Rebecca, who showed no preference for color over b/w (Lowe, 1977, pp. 143-44).

2. Rebecca Lowe clearly <u>had</u> reached this stage. Lowe (unpublished diary):

   "Rebecca (5.0); seeing Wanda Gag: <u>Three Gay Tales from Grimm</u>: 'I know who this is by. It's the <u>Millions of Cats</u> person.'
   V.L.: 'How do you know?'
   R: 'It's got the same clouds.'

   (4.11) of Burningham's <u>A</u>. <u>B</u>. <u>C</u>.: 'That's by the same person as <u>Trubloff</u>. It's got exactly the same mouse in.'"

   There are also examples at earlier ages expressed in a form similar to those we have cited for Anna. <u>N</u>. <u>B</u>. that Lowe several times questioned Rebecca in the form: "What does this book remind you of?" and this constitutes training in the notion of stylistic signatures.

3. See Joan Cass (1971), chap. 2; Gerald Smerdon (1976); Patrick Groff (1977).

4. See Cass (1971), p. 7; Nicholas Tucker (1974).

5. E.g., Lillian H. Smith (1953), p. 116: "Picture books also appeal to little children through the eye. But it is not, as with an adult, the appeal of aesthetic pleasure in the artist's line, color harmony, composition and style."

13 THE LIMITS OF REALITY: PERCEPTION OF THE FANTASTIC

1. See Maureen Crago, "Missing Home, Missing Mother" (1978).

2. Rebecca at about 3.6 was trying to verbalize: "'animals can't talk'--and quite often that they can't actually perform other tasks assigned to them in stories either. <u>Miffy at the Zoo</u> inspired delighted laughter and 'animals can't talk' (about the zoo animals only, not Miffy and her

father--she feels these two categories are different, obviously) from the first hearing at 3.7, through each subsequent one up to 4.0" (Lowe, unpublished diary).

3. Apart from her remarks apropos of books, we have a little evidence of Anna's spontaneous animistic references. We recorded the first of these statements at 3.9, a speculation that our vacuum cleaner might come and "get us--and take us to hospital!" Since this was uttered amidst much giggling, it is as likely to be evidence for Anna's rejection of animism as for her belief in it. At 3.10 she asked Hugh if our lawnmower would be angry with us for touching it--this time apparently in earnest. However in the same period she is recorded as asking "no tools can live, can they?" This does not negate the possibility of animism in the preceding example, but it does suggest that Anna is clear about the inanimate status of at least some objects. By 4.5, the line was clearly drawn, for Anna gigglingly produced a flood of consciously absurd questions involving animals and objects in anthromorphic behavior: Does a candle remark? Do wolves get up and walk around the kitchen? There is no doubt that she was creating deliberately "wrong" statements. Apart from showing her rejection of animism and anthropomorphism, the episode also casts light on her attitude to fictional anthropomorphism. Among the sequence of statements, two attribute speech to inanimates, but none refers to clothed animals. We assume then, that the former was for her a stronger criterion of human status than the latter.

4. Cf. White (1954), p. 72 (Carol 3.7): "She makes a clear distinction between the animate and the inanimate. A doll or a toy of course comes in the animate class."

5. Cf. Applebee, The Child's Concept of Story, p. 44: "relegating characters to the status of long-dead but once-living," he considers a transitional form between children's acceptance of fictional characters as wholly real and recognition of their imaginary status. The whole of Applebee chap. 5, and especially pp. 41-47, make a useful comparison to this chapter.

14 HEROES AND VILLAINS: EMOTIONAL IMPACT

1. In the 1964 Rupert Annual, p. 31, frames a, b, and c, Margaret is crying. Anna at 1.8 would say "crying" and want

to be reassured that all was well. Cf. Cushla, in the
period 2.0-2.6, looking at Petronella Breinberg's My
Brother Sean (U.S., Shawn Goes to School) in which Sean
is distressed when his mother leaves him at play school:
"Cushla solicitously kissed his howling little face at
every reading and beamed with relief when he finally
'smiled a teeny-weeny smile'" (Butler, 1979, p. 50).

2. When she saw them again at 3.6 she said: Don't like the
look of those two--they look like merchants. The equation
"merchant = bad" is another she has deduced, presumably
from Joseph, p. 6 "Just then some merchants came by."
Opposite is a collage showing two of Joseph's brothers
holding him and beating him. Anna had now owned this book
for two years. It is possible that she associated the
illustration with the merchants even though she had been
told that these were Joseph's brothers.

3. Like Anna, L. B. at 3.8 commented critically on the behavior of heroes: Navarra, p. 87:
   "5PE 1054--January 28, 1952[.] L. N. was looking at the
   illustrations which accompanied a true story about a
   gorilla. He had previously had the story read to him.
   L. B. inquired, 'would he really kill people, Mommy?'
   Mother said that he probably would. L. B. continued to
   flip the pages and then asked with a shake of his head,
   'Why doesn't he be nice?'"

4. Cf. Carol at 4.1, White (1954), p. 118.

5. For similar denials of uncomfortable situations see White
(1954), pp. 70-71, 166; Saunders (1970), p. 10.

6. In the first rereading of A Birthday for the Princess at
4.7, Hugh observed that she began to tense herself some-
where between Ops. 6 and 10, before he had begun to raise
his voice. This seemed to be a memory of her earlier
reaction, although when Hugh reached the crucial lines,
Anna did not flinch. Her newly won capacity for coping with
harsh tones when listening to reading thus passed the test
posed by this reborrowing. Cf. Sally at 2.9 (Schmitzer, p.
41) who accepted a further reading of Stobbs's The Story
of The Three Billy Goats Gruff, providing her mother used
an ordinary speaking voice. But three months later Sally
accepted appropriate voices when listening to a reading of
Stobbs's The Story of the Three Bears (ibid., p. 57:
Sally 3.0).

7. Cf. White, p. 151. Carol at 4.5 regretted Little Tim's shipwreck and said: "The <u>engineer</u> should have <u>seen</u> the rock."

8. Cf. Cushla, who in a monologue five hours after she had first heard Galdone's <u>The Three Billy Goats Gruff</u> at 3.3, spoke of her fear three times: "Troll make me fright . . . Troll gave me terrible fright . . . Oo-oo, gave me terrible fright" (Butler, 1979, p. 64).

   Ralph Lowe evinced dramatic avoidance behavior, beginning at a considerably earlier age even than Anna, accompanying the verbal statement of fear with a quick exit: "At 2.11 he left the room while I was reading <u>Peter and the Wolf</u> to both him and Rebecca: 'I'm scared of the wolf' and returned cautiously a page or so later" (Lowe, unpublished diary).

9. We have cited elsewhere the 4.6 example of Anna's request that part of a story not be read. In <u>Alice in Wonderland</u> she was disturbed by the incident in which the Mad Hatter took a bite out of his cup (see chap. 12). Compare Ben's request at 6.8 that the title of a story that had frightened him not be read aloud from the contents list of a book his mother had just finished reading to him (Graetz, "From Picture Books to Illustrated Stories," p. 86).

   Cf. also Carol's distress at 4.5 (White, p. 152) when discussing a museum larger and richer than the one she knew, and vast distances and suns we cannot see. Carol first wanted to turn away, and later said: "We won't go on talking about this any more."

10. Cf. Cushla (3.3), who in a monologue after hearing <u>The Three Billy Goats Gruff</u> responded ambivalently to the troll, but said: "Me take troll's eye out (picking at page)" (Butler, 1979, p. 64).

   Cf. also Jean-Paul Sartre writing of himself as an older child: "I had to force myself not to spit on the illustration which showed Horace, with helmet and naked sword, chasing after poor Camille" (<u>Words</u>, pp. 35-36).

11. Rosemary Milne (1977) discusses the value of happy endings, and when an anthropomorphized hero's plight acquires power to distress a child. Cf. White (1954) p. 59; Carol

was at 3.4 not "unduly harrowed or disturbed" at a story which Dorothy White describes as an "ordeal" and "purgatory" for the mouse hero.

12. Cf. Carol's tendency to make every possible "he" into a "she" at 3.4 (White, 1954, p. 56) and her refusal at 4.5 to accept robed shepherds as men, p. 154.

Annis Duff also discovered in her daughter a leaning toward things thought appropriate for girls: "That even very tiny children have definite interests became manifest at once; how absurdly and delightfully funny it was to discover that whereas a two-year-old girl baby had loved pictures of other babies, and furry animals, and all soft and pretty things, a two-year-old gentleman loves cars and trains and boats, and has a passion for wheels" (Duff, 1944, p. 24). Mrs. Duff appears insensitive to her own influence on this aspect of the children's behavior.

15 WHAT MAKES A STORY? PERCEPTION OF NARRATIVE CONVENTIONS

1. Packenham, Points for Parents (1954), p. 69: "I first showed Antonia the Babar books when she was ten months only. Very soon 'showing pictures' developed into 'telling a story', too. At about three years old she began to say 'Don't tell the story, read it.'" This sounds very much like the distinction Anna was making. See also Lowe (1977), pp. 145-46, where Rebecca makes the same distinction.

2. Cf. White (1954) pp. 100-101: ". . . Rose Fyleman's 'Mice.' When we came to the concluding line of this, 'But I think mice/Are nice,' 'Who thinks?' Carol asked yesterday" (Carol 4.2).

Rebecca's brother Ralph is reported as asking "Who likes Peter?" in response to the statement "I like Peter" in Murray's Play With Us, a Ladybird reader. This is at 3.1, the same age as Anna when she first questioned the convention (Lowe, unpublished diary.)

3. Lowe reports that Rebecca was puzzled by the use of the first person in John Burningham's The Cupboard at 4.0, though earlier (3.9) she had seemed to grasp that the "I" in Just So Stories could be identified as "the lady [sic] who made the book" (Lowe, unpublished diary).

4. Christmas at Bullerby. When we pointed to the Advent candles on the window ledge, Anna said: We have red ones. When the children get skis for Christmas, Anna asked: Can I have some skis one day?--I know how to ski; you get on the things and then you push things [demonstrates]--and then you go skiing.

   And pointing to the illustration of a cookie: Are those gingerbread [gingersnap] pigs? Why do they have to be those? Forced laughter followed; she had recently eaten a gingerbread rabbit.

5. Cf. Graetz (1976), p. 84: "We borrowed Leila Berg's Fire Engine by Mistake first when Ben was 5½ and it was read a couple of times. Six months later it was borrowed again. My husband read it to them that night and there was much giggling from their room. There wasn't time to finish it the same night and he asked Ben what had happened to the people who had wanted the road sprinkler. Ben told him the whole story to the end of the big fire in detail, but could remember no more" (Ben about 6.0).

6. "Another feature of the reasoning of the preoperational child is a tendency to focus attention on a single, striking detail of an experience, to the neglect of other important aspects. Piaget has called this phenomenon centration . . . when asked to explain why they like stories, children will say 'It's nice' or 'It's good' . . . when elaboration occurs, it is usually linked syncretistically to another memorable incident in the story, rather than integrated into a conceptualisation of the whole" (Applebee, p. 99).
The evidence supplied by Graetz (1976) supports the view that a young child's concept of narrative may be incident-centered: "The whole plot . . . has been of minor importance to Ben and Dan. The last of the Jack the Giant Killer stories was requested many times. The whole story was not important--questions Ben asked two years later showed that he had not understood the plot. He put up with most of those words for the sake of the description of the enchanter, 'Till nothing was left but the scream'" (p. 84; Ben 4.4).

7. Cf. Graetz, p. 84: "I put off reading it [Alice in Wonderland] for six months; . . . he commented at the end 'I'm glad she got out of the rabbit hole.' The part of the story

that interested him most happened to come at each end of the book with a lot of words in between" (Ben about 4.10).

EPILOGUE

1. Louise Kaplan's <u>Oneness</u> <u>and</u> <u>Separateness</u> offers a readable and often vivid introduction to the work of Mahler and other analytic students of early childhood. Mahler's own <u>Psychological</u> <u>Birth</u> <u>of</u> <u>the</u> <u>Human</u> <u>Infant</u> is probably the most accessible of her books and papers, many of which deal rather turgidly with severely disturbed, rather than normal, children.

Selected Bibliography

BOOKS MENTIONED IN THE TEXT

The Adventures of Mole and Troll. By Tony Johnston. Illustrated by Wallace Tripp. Kingswood: World's Work, 1975.

Albert and Henry. By Alison Jezard. Illustrations by Margaret Gordon. London: Gollancz, 1970.

Alfie and the Ferryboat. By Charles Keeping. London: O.U.P., 1968.

Alice in Wonderland Finds the Garden of Live Flowers. Told by Jane Werner. Pictures from the Walt Disney Studio. Adapted from the motion picture Alice in Wonderland by Campbell Grant. Sydney: Golden, 1965.

"Alice in Wonderland Meets the White Rabbit." Adapted from the motion picture based on the story by Lewis Carroll. In Walt Disney's Story Land: 55 Favorite Stories Adapted from Walt Disney Films, illustrated by the Walt Disney Studio, stories selected by Frances Saldinger. New York: Golden, 1974, pp. 122-25.

Alice's Adventures in Wonderland. By Lewis Carroll. Illustrated by Arthur Rackham. Reprint ed. London: Heinemann, 1907.

Alligators All Around: An Alphabet. By Maurice Sendak. London: Collins, 1974.

And So My Garden Grows. By Peter Spier. Kingswood: World's Work, 1969.

The Animals' Lullaby. By Trude Alberti. Illustrated by Chiyoko Nakatani. London: Bodley Head, 1967.

Anna and the Dark. By Hugh Crago. Unique copy for Anna.

An Anteater Named Arthur. By Bernard Waber. Boston: Houghton Mifflin, 1967.

Babar's Birthday Surprise. By Laurent de Brunhoff. London: Methuen, 1971.

Baba Yaga. Illustrated by Céline Leopold. London: Bodley Head, 1973.

A Baby Sister for Frances. By Russell Hoban. Pictures by Lillian Hoban. London: Faber, 1965.

A Bargain for Frances. By Russell Hoban. Pictures by Lillian Hoban. Kingswood: World's Work, 1971.

Barnaby and the Horses. By Lydia Pender. Pictures by Alie Evers. London and N.Y.: Abelard-Schuman, 1961.

The Bears' Picnic. By Stan and Jan Berenstain. London: Collins & Harvill, 1973.

The Bee. By Eleanor Stodart. Photographs by Ederic Slater. Sydney: Angus and Robertson, 1973.

The Berenstain Bears' New Baby. By Stan and Jan Berenstain. London: Collins, 1975.

Best Friends for Frances. By Russell Hoban. Pictures by Lillian Hoban. London: Faber, 1971.

The Bible Story. By Guy Daniel. London: Grosvenor, 1955.

A Birthday for the Princess. By Anita Lobel. Kingswood: World's Work, 1975.

Black Dolly: The Story of a Junk Cart Pony. By Charles Keeping. Leicester: Brockhampton, 1966.

Bob Bodden and the Seagoing Farm. By Elizabeth Coatsworth. Illustrated by Frank Aloise. London: Watts, 1972.

Bottersnikes and Gumbles. By S. A. Wakefield. Drawings by Desmond Digby. London: Collins, 1968.

The Boy and the Magic. By Colette. Translated by Christopher Fry. Illustrated by Gerard Hoffnung. London: Dennis Dobson, 1964.

The Boy Who Ran Away. By Irene Elmer. Illustrated by Sally Mathews. St. Louis: Concordia, Arch Books, 1964.

Bread and Jam for Frances. By Russell Hoban. Pictures by Lillian Hoban. London: Faber, 1966.

A Brother for Momoko. Illustrations by Chihiro Iwasaki. London: Bodley Head, 1970.

Bunny in the Honeysuckle Patch. By Jane Thayer. Pictures by Seymour Fleishman. Kingswood: World's Work, 1966.

The Cabbage Princess. By Errol Le Cain. London: Faber, 1969.

The Carrot Seed. By Ruth Krauss. Illustrated by Crockett Johnson. New York and London: Harper & Brothers, 1945.

Cherry Time at Bullerby. By Astrid Lindgren. Translated by Florence Lamborn. Illustrated by Ilon Wikland. London: Methuen, 1964.

Childbirth. By C. E. V. Nixon. London: Duckworth, 1955.

The Child in the Bamboo Grove. By Rosemary Harris. Illustrated by Errol Le Cain. London: Faber, 1971.

A Child's Garden of Verses. By R. L. Stevenson. Illustrated by Brian Wildsmith. London: O.U.P., 1966.

Christmas at Bullerby. By Astrid Lindgren. Pictures by Ilon Wikland. London: Methuen, 1964.

Clanky the Mechanical Boy. By [Kenneth] Mahood. London: Collins, 1971.

The Cow Who Fell in the Canal. By Phyllis Krasilovsky. Illustrated by Peter Spier. Kingswood: World's Work, 1958.

The Crows of Pearblossom. By Aldous Huxley. Illustrated by Barbara Cooney. New York: Random House, 1967.

Davy's Day. By Lois Lenski. New York and London: O.U.P., 1943.

Dinosaurs and All that Rubbish. By Michael Foreman. London: Hamilton, 1972.

Discovering Northumbria. By H. O. Wade. Aylesbury: Shire, 1973.

Dragons and Other Things. By Gwen Crago. Rushcutters' Bay, N.S.W.: Pergamon, 1975.

Farmer Barnes at the County Show. By John Cunliffe. Pictures by Jill McDonald. London: Deutsch, 1969.

Father Bear Comes Home. By Else Holmelund Minarik. Illustrated by Maurice Sendak. Kingswood: World's Work, 1960.

Fee Fi Fo Fum: A Picture Book of Nursery Rhymes. Illustrated by Raymond Briggs. New York: McCann, 1964.

Finn Family Moomintroll. Written and illustrated by Tove Jansson. Translated by Elizabeth Portch. London: Benn, 1950.

A Firefly Named Torchy. By Bernard Waber. Boston: Houghton Mifflin, 1970.

Florian and Tractor Max. By Binette Schroeder. London: Collins, 1972.

The Flying Mouse. By Ivan Gantschev. English text by Ann Herring. Tokyo: Universe Picture Books/Gakken, 1973.

The Flying Shoes. By Cynthia Jameson. Pictures by Lawrence Di Fiori. New York: Parents' Magazine, 1973.

Fox in Sox: A Tongue Twister for Super Children. By Dr. Seuss. New York: Collins and Harvill, 1965.

Frog and Toad Are Friends. By Arnold Lobel. Kingswood: World's Work, 1971.

Frog and Toad Together. By Arnold Lobel. New York: Harper, 1972.

The Garden Shed. By Charles Keeping. London: O.U.P., 1971.

Goggles by Ezra Jack Keats. London: Bodley Head, 1970.

The Good Robber Willibald. By Rudolf Otto Wiemer. Drawings by Marie Marcks. Translated by Barbara Kowal Gollob. New York: Atheneum, 1968.

Grandmother Lucy and Her Hats. By Joyce Wood. Pictures by Frank Francis. London: Collins, 1968.

Great Big Air Book. Written and illustrated by Richard Scarry. London: Collins, 1971.

Harold and the Purple Crayon. By Crockett Johnson. London: Longmans Young Books, 1957.

Heaven and Hell in Western Art. By Robert Hughes. London: Weidenfeld and Nicolson, 1968.

Hop-o'-my-thumb. By Dick Bruna. London: Methuen, 1968.

Horatio. By Michael Foreman. London: Hamilton, 1970.

Hosie's Alphabet. Pictures by Leonard Baskin. Words by Hosea, Tobias, and Lisa Baskin. New York: Viking, 1972.

How the World Began. By Carol Barker. London: Abelard-Schuman, 1974.

Hurrah, We're Outward Bound! Illustrated by Peter Spier. Kingswood: World's Work, 1968.

I Can Keep a Secret. By Margaret Howell. Pictures by Terence Greer. New York: Scholastic, 1974.

In the Night Kitchen. By Maurice Sendak. London: Bodley Head, 1971.

The Jay in Peacock's Feathers: An Animal Fable. Pictures by Nemo. English version by Hilary Smyth. Leicester: Brockhampton, 1974.

Jennifer's Rabbit. By Tom Paxton. Pictures by Wallace Tripp. Kingswood: World's Work, 1974.

Jim Button and Luke the Engine Driver. by Michael Ende. Illustrated by Maurice S. Dodd. London: Harrap, 1963.

Johnny Lion's Rubber Boots. By Edith Thacher Hurd. Pictures by Clement Hurd. Kingswood: World's Work, 1973.

Joseph. By O. B. Gregory. Illustrated by Toni Woodward.
Exeter: Wheaton, 1968.

Journey to the Center of the Earth: The Fiery Foe. By Paul
S. Newman. Racine, Wis.: Whitman, 1968.

The Juniper Tree and Other Tales from Grimm. Selected by Lore
Segal and Maurice Sendak. Translated by Lore Segal, with four
tales translated by Randall Jarrell. Pictures by Maurice Sendak. New York: Farrar, Straus and Giroux, 1973.

King Grisly-Beard: A Tale from the Brothers Grimm. Translated
by Edgar Taylor. Pictures by Maurice Sendak. New York: Farrar,
Straus and Giroux, 1973.

King Midas and the Golden Touch. By Carol Barker. London and
New York: Watts, 1972.

The King of the Copper Mountains. By Paul Biegel. English
version by Gillian Hume and Paul Biegel. Illustrations by Babs
van Wely. London: Dent, 1969.

King Tree. By Fiona French. London: O.U.P., 1973.

The Lion and the Rat. by LaFontaine. Illustrated and retold
by Brian Wildsmith. London: O.U.P., 1963.

A Lion in the Meadow. By Margaret Mahy. Pictures by Jenny
Williams. London: Dent, 1969.

The Little Bear and the Princess. By Jane Brown Gemmill.
Illustrated by Carol Barker. London and New York: Abelard-
Schuman, 1961.

The Little Farm. By Lois Lenski. London and New York: O.U.P.,
1942.

The Little Hedgehog. By Gina Ruck-Pauquet. Illustrated by
Marianne Richter. London: Constable, 1959.

The Little Red Lighthouse and the Great Gray Bridge. By
Hildegard H. Swift and Lynd Ward. New York: Harcourt Brace
and World, 1942.

Little Red Riding Hood. By Jacob and Wilhelm Grimm. Illustrated by Bernadette Watts. New York: Scholastic, 1971.

Lord Rex: The Lion Who Wished. By David McKee. London and
New York: Abelard-Schuman, 1973.

Lyonel Feininger: City at the Edge of the World. Text by
T. Lux Feininger. Photographs by Andreas Feininger. New York:
Praeger, 1965.

Madeline and the Bad Hat. Written and illustrated by Ludwig
Bemelmans. London: Deutsch, 1958.

The Magic Circle. By Ludovica Lombardi. London: Hamlyn, n.d.

The Man Who Was Going to Mind the House. Retold and illustrated
by David McKee. New York and London: Abelard-Schuman, 1972.

Marvin K. Mooney Will You Please Go Now! By Dr. Seuss. London:
Collins and Harvill, 1973.

Me and My Flying Machine. By Marianna and Mercer Mayer. London:
Collins, 1973.

Meet Babar and His Family. By Laurent de Brunhoff. London:
Collins, 1973.

Mike Mulligan and His Steam Shovel. By Virginia Lee Burton.
London: Faber, 1942.

The Miller, the Boy, and the Donkey. By Brian Wildsmith, based
on a fable by LaFontaine. London: O.U.P., 1969.

Mr. Benn Annual. By David McKee. London: Polystyle, 1971.

Mrs. Beggs and the Wizard. Written and illustrated by Mercer
Mayer. Newton Abbott and London: David and Charles, 1974.

Moose. By Michael Foreman. London: Hamilton, 1971.

Mouse Tales. By Arnold Lobel. Kingswood: World's Work, 1973.

Mulga Bill's Bicycle. Poem by A. B. Paterson. Illustrated by
Kilmeny and Deborah Niland. Sydney, London: Collins, 1972.

My Teddy Bear. By Patsy Scarry. Pictures by Eloise Wilkin.
New York: Simon and Schuster, 1953.

My Very Own Sister. By Astrid Lindgren. Illustrated by Hans
Arnold. London: Methuen, 1974.

The Nanny Goat and the Fierce Dog. By Charles Keeping. London: Abelard-Schuman, 1973.

Natasha's New Doll. Written and illustrated by Frank Francis. London: Collins, 1971.

A Necklace of Raindrops and Other Stories. By Joan Aiken. Illustrated by Jan Pienkowski. London: Cape, 1968.

Noggin and the Moon Mouse. By Oliver Postgate and Peter Firmin. London: Kaye & Ward, 1967.

Noggin and the Whale. By Oliver Postgate and Peter Firmin. London: Ward, 1965.

Noggin the King. By Oliver Postgate and Peter Firmin. London: Ward, in association with Hicks Smith, Sydney and Wellington, 1965.

Old MacDonald Had Some Flats. Written by Judith Barrett. Illustrated by Ron Barrett. London: Pan, 1970.

Old Mother Hubbard and Her Dog. Pictures by Paul Galdone. London: Bodley Head, 1961.

One to Eleven. By Yutaka Sugita. London: Evans, 1971.

On the Day Peter Stuyvesant Sailed into Town. By Arnold Lobel. New York: Harper & Row, 1971.

Over in the Meadow. By Ezra Jack Keats. New York: Four Winds, 1971.

Paddy's Evening Out. By John S. Goodall. London: Macmillan, 1974.

Peg's Fairy Book. Written and illustrated by Peg Maltby. Melbourne: Murfett, 1944.

Péronnique: A Celtic Folk Tale from Brittany. Translated by Roseanna Hoover. Illustrated by Monique Michel-Dansac. Oxford: Basil Blackwell, 1970.

Peter's Chair. By Ezra Jack Keats. London: Bodley Head, 1968.

The Picnic. By Edith Unnerstad. Pictures by Ylva Källström. London: Oliver and Boyd, 1964.

Pig Tale. By Helen Oxenbury. London: Heinemann, 1973.

The Pirates' Tale. By Janet Aitchison and Jill McDonald. Harmondsworth: Penguin, 1970.

Pleasant Fieldmouse. By Jan Wahl. Pictures by Maurice Sendak. Kingswood: World's Work, 1969.

Please and Thank You Book. By Richard Scarry. London: Collins, 1973.

Railway Passage. By Charles Keeping. London: O.U.P., 1974.

Rapunzel: A Story by the Brothers Grimm. Pictures by Felix Hoffmann. Translated by Katya Sheppard. London: O.U.P., 1960.

Rupert Annual. [By A. E. Bestall]. London: Beaverbrook News- papers, 1960. Also 1964 Annual.

Sarah's Room. By Doris Orgel. Pictures by Maurice Sendak. London: Bodley Head, 1972.

The School. By Dick Bruna. London: Methuen, 1966.

The Selfish Giant. By Oscar Wilde. Illustrations from the prizewinning film by Gertraud and Walter Reiner. London: Oliver and Boyd, 1967.

The Shadow. By Jeroo Roy. Glasgow: Blackie, 1973.

Sir Lance-a-Little and the Knights of the Kitchen Table. By Jon Chalon [John Seymour Chaloner]. Indianapolis: Bobbs- Merrill, [1971].

Sir Orfeo. By Anthea Davies. Illustrated by Errol Le Cain. London: Faber, 1970.

The Six Bullerby Children. By Astrid Lindgren. Translated by Evelyn Ramsden. Illustrated by Ilon Wikland. London: Methuen, 1969.

The Six Swans. By the Brothers Grimm. Illustrated by Adrie Hospes. London: Bodley Head, 1973.

Snow White and the Seven Dwarfs. By Bernadette Watts. London and New York: Watts, 1971.

Snow White and the Seven Dwarfs: A Tale from the Brothers Grimm. Translated by Randall Jarrell. Pictures by Nancy Burkert. Harmondsworth: Kestrel, 1975.

The Spider's Web. By Charles Keeping. London: O.U.P., 1972.

Stein, the Great Retriever. By Ruth Shaw Redlauer. Pictures by Susan Perl. Kingswood: World's Work, 1966.

The Story about Ping. By Marjorie Flack and Kurt Wiese. London: Bodley Head, 1935.

The Story of Doctor Dolittle. By Hugh Lofting. London: Cape, 1922.

The Story of Ferdinand. By Munro Leaf. Drawings by Robert Lawson. London: Hamilton, 1970.

Stuff and Nonsense. Compiled by Michael Dugan. Illustrated by Deborah Niland. Sydney: Collins, 1974.

Sylvester and the Magic Pebble. By William Steig. New York: Simon and Schuster, 1969.

The Tale of Mrs. Tiggy-Winkle. By Beatrix Potter. London and New York: Warne, 1905.

The Tale of Mrs. Tittlemouse. By Beatrix Potter. London and New York: Warne, 1910.

The Tale of Peter Rabbit. By Beatrix Potter. London: Warne, 1901.

The Tale of Samuel Whiskers, or The Roly-Poly Pudding. By Beatrix Potter. London: Warne, 1908.

The Tale of Squirrel Nutkin. By Beatrix Potter. London: Warne, 1907.

The Tale of Tom Kitten. By Beatrix Potter. London: Warne, 1907.

The Tale of Two Bad Mice. By Beatrix Potter. London and New York: Warne, 1904.

Teddybears 1-10. By Susanna Gretz. Chicago: Follet, 1967.

Thomas Goes Out. By Gunilla Wolde. English text by Alison Winn. Leicester: Brockhampton, 1971.

Thorn Rose. By the Brothers Grimm. Illustrated by Errol Le Cain. London: Faber, 1975.

The Three Robbers. By Tomi Ungerer. London: Methuen, 1961.

The Tinderbox. From the story by Hans Christian Andersen. Pictures by Eva Johanna Rubin. London: Methuen, 1967 [1968].

To Market, To Market. Illustrated by Peter Spier. Kingswood: World's Work, 1968.

The Travels of Oggy. By Ann Lawrence. Illustrated by Hans Helweg. London: Gollancz, 1973.

Trubloff: The Mouse Who Wanted to Play a Balalaika. By John Burningham. London: Cape, 1964.

Uncle Timothy's Traviata. By Fernando Krahn. Words by Alastair Reid. New York: Delacorte, 1967.

The Upstairs Witch and the Downstairs Witch. By Susan Terris. Illustrated by Olivia H. H. Cole. New York: Doubleday, 1970.

The Very Hungry Cat. By Haakon Bjørklid. London: Methuen, 1974.

A Very Special House. By Ruth Krauss. Pictures by Maurice Sendak. New York: Scholastic, 1953.

What Do People Do All Day? Written and illustrated by Richard Scarry. Glasgow and London: Collins, 1968.

When We Were Very Young. by A. A. Milne. Illustrated by E. H. Shepard. London: Methuen, 1924.

Where the Wild Things Are. Story and pictures by Maurice Sendak. London: Bodley Head, 1967.

Whistle for Willie. By Ezra Jack Keats. London: Bodley Head, 1966.

Who Will Comfort Toffle? By Tove Jansson. Translated by Kingsley Hart. London: Benn, 1969.

Wish Again, Big Bear. By Richard J. Margolis. Illustrated by Robert Lopshire. Kingswood: World's Work, 1973.

The Wonderful Ball. From a story by Karen Gunthorp. Illustrated by Attilio Cassinelli. New York: Doubleday, 1968.

Zeralda's Ogre. By Tomi Ungerer. London: Bodley Head, 1970.

SECONDARY WORKS TO WHICH REFERENCE IS MADE

Anthony, Sylvia. The Discovery of Death in Childhood and After. Harmondsworth: Penguin, 1973.

Applebee, Arthur N. The Child's Concept of Story Ages Two to Seventeen. Chicago and London: University of Chicago Press, 1978.

Arnheim, Rudolf. Art and Visual Perception: A Psychology of the Creative Eye. Berkeley: University of California Press, 1954.

Bettelheim, Bruno. The Uses of Enchantment: The Meaning and Importance of Fairy Tales. New York: Alfred Knopf, 1976.

Bissex, Glenda L. "Do Nat Dstrb Gnys at Wrk: A Case Study of Pre-school Spelling, Reading, and Metalinguistic Development (Paul, age 5-6)." Unpublished qualifying paper, Harvard Graduate School 1976.

Britton, James. Language and Learning. Harmondsworth: Penguin, 1972.

Butler, Christine. "Humour for Children." Children's Literature Association (New Zealand) Yearbook, 1975.

Butler, Dorothy. Cushla and her Books. London: Hodder and Stoughton, 1979.

Cass, Joan E. Literature and the Young Child. London: Longman, 1971.

Child, Irvin L. "Aesthetic Judgment in Children." Transaction 7, no. 7 (1970).

Chukovsky, Kornei. From Two to Five. Translated and edited by Miriam Morton. Rev. ed. Berkeley: University of California Press, 1968.

Crago, Maureen. "Missing Home, Missing Mother: One Child's Preoccupation with their Location in Picture Books: A Case Study," Orana 14, no. 3 (1978).

Duff, Annis. Bequest of Wings: A Family's Pleasure with Books. New York: Viking, 1944.

Elkind, David; Koegler, Ronald; and Go, Elsie. "Studies in Perceptual Development II: Part-Whole Perception," Child Development 35 (1964).

Friedman, Sarah L., and Stevenson, Marguerite B. "Developmental Changes in the Understanding of Implied Motion in Two-Dimensional Pictures," Child Development 46 (1975).

Gardner, Howard. "Style Sensitivity in Children," Human Development 15 (1972).

_____, and Lohman, William. "Children's Sensitivity to Literary Styles," Merrill-Palmer Quarterly (1970).

Goldstein, Jeffrey, and McGhee, Paul, eds. The Psychology of Humor. New York: Academic Press, 1972.

Graetz, Margaret. "Books for the Under-Twos," Children's Libraries Newsletter (Australia) 7, no. 3 (1971).

_____. "From Picture-Books to Illustrated Stories: How Children Understand all those Words," Children's Libraries Newsletter 13, nos. 3, 4 (1976).

Griffiths, Ruth. A Study of Imagination in Early Childhood. London: Routledge and Kegan Paul, 1935.

Groff, Patrick. "Should Picture Books and Young Children be Matched?" Language Arts 54 (April 1977).

Hickman, Janet. "Children's Response to Literature: What Happens in the Classroom," Language Arts 57, no. 5 (May 1980).

Hoffman, Darlene Haffner. "Ten Days with Inga and In the Night Kitchen: An Episode in Language Development," Communication Education 25, no. 1 (January 1976).

Holland, Norman. 5 Readers Reading. New Haven: Yale University Press, 1975.

Jones, Anthony, and Buttrey, June. Children and Stories. Oxford: Basil Blackwell, 1970.

Kaplan, Louise J. Oneness and Separateness: From Infant to Individual. New York: Simon and Schuster, 1978.

Kappas, Katherine H. "A Developmental Analysis of Children's Response to Humor." In Sarah Innis Fenwick, ed., A Critical Approach to Children's Literature. Chicago: University of Chicago Press, 1967.

Lord, Albert B. The Singer of Tales. Cambridge, Mass.: Harvard University Press, 1964.

Lowe, Virginia. "Books and a Pre-verbal Child," Children's Libraries Newletter 11 (1975).

_____. "Cushla, Carol, and Rebecca," Signal 24 (September, 1977).

_____. Adult, Book, Child. Melbourne: Australian Library Promotion Council, 1979.

_____. Unpublished diary. 1972-

Machotka, Pavel. "Aesthetic Criteria in Childhood: Justifications of Preference," Child Development 37 (1966).

Mahler, Margaret, et al. The Psychological Birth of the Human Infant. New York: Basic Books, 1967.

Martin, Nancy; Williams, Paul; Wilding, Joan; Hemmings, Susan; and Medway, Peter. Understanding Children Talking. Harmondsworth: Penguin, 1976.

Milne, Rosemary. "Fantasy in Literature for Early Childhood." In Moira Robinson, ed., Readings in Children's Literature. Frankston State College, Victoria, 1977.

Napear, Peggy. Brain Child: A Mother's Diary. New York: Harper & Row, 1974.

Navarra, John Gabriel. The Development of Scientific Concepts in a Young Child: A Case Study. New York: Bureau of Publications, Teachers' College, Columbia University, 1955.

Newson, John and Elizabeth. Four Years Old in an Urban Community. Harmondsworth: Penguin, 1970.

Packenham, Elizabeth. Points for Parents. London: Weidenfield and Nicolson, 1954.

Piaget, Jean. The Child's Conception of the World. Translated by Joan and Andrew Tomlinson. London: Paladin, 1973.

Pitcher, Evelyn Goodenough, and Prelinger, Ernst. Children Tell Stories: An Analysis of Fantasy. New York: International Universities Press, 1963.

Propp, Vladimir. Morphology of the Folktale. Translated by Laurence Scott. 2d ed., revised and edited by Louis A. Wagner. Austin: University of Texas Press, 1968.

Sartre, Jean-Paul. Words. Translated by Irene Clephane. Harmondsworth: Penguin, 1967.

Saunders, Judith M. "Exploring Books with a Pre-Schooler," Children's Libraries Newsletter 6, no. 1 (1970).

Schmitzer, Judith. "The Pre-School Child and Books: A Case Study." Diploma assignment, Tasmanian College of Advanced Education, Hobart, 1973.

Singer, Jerome L. Daydreaming and Fantasy. London: George Allen & Unwin, 1975.

Samsová, S. "Books Before Two: Some Observations on the Reading of the Very Young," Assistant Librarian 55, no. 9 (1962).

Smerdon, Gerald. "Children's Preferences in Illustration," Children's Literature in Education 20 (Spring 1976).

Smith, Lillian H. The Unreluctant Years. Chicago: A.L.A., 1953.

Suchman, Rosslyn, and Trabasso, Tom. "Color and Form Preference in Young Children," Journal of Experimental Child Psychology 3 (1966).

Sutton-Smith, Brian, et al. The Folkstories of Children. Philadelphia: University of Pennsylvania Press, 1980.

Tucker, Nicholas. "Looking at Pictures," Children's Literature in Education 14 (1974).

Vurpillot, Eliane. The Visual World of the Child. Translated by W. E. C. Gilham. Foreword by Jerome Bruner. Preface by Paul Fraisse. London: George Allen and Unwin, 1976.

Wallon, H. _Les Origines de la Pensée Chez l'Enfant._ 2 vols. Paris, 1945.

Weir, Ruth Hirsch. _Language in the Crib._ The Hague: Mouton, 1962.

Whalen-Levett, Peggy. "Carol, Cushla, Rebecca, Anna, Dan, and Ben." in Whalen-Levett, ed., _Children's Literature Association Quarterly_ (Winter 1980).

White, Dorothy Neal. _Books Before Five._ Christchurch: Whitcombe and Tombs/N.Z. Council for Educational Research, 1954.

Wood, Elizabeth. "Preschool Children and Libraries--I." In _Proceedings, 18th Biennial Conference of the Library Association of Australia._ Melbourne, 1976.

Maureen and Hugh Crago are graduates of the University of New England (Australia), from which Maureen holds a master's degree in comparative philology, and of Antioch University, where both completed master's degrees in counseling psychology. Maureen, who undertook the research for this book while a fulltime mother (1972-78) is now working as a psychotherapist. Hugh held the University of New England's traveling scholarship at Merton College, Oxford, from 1969 to 1972, taught literature and interpersonal communication at Riverina College (Australia) from 1972 to 1979 and now combines writing and research with a private practice as a psychotherapist.